MORMON SISTERS

Women in Early Utah

Edited by

Claudia L. Bushman

Introduction to the New Edition by

Anne Firor Scott

New Edition

Utah State University Press
Logan, Utah
1997

Utah State University Press
Logan, Utah 84322-7800

Cover Design by Michelle Sellers

Mormon sisters : women in early Utah / edited by Claudia L.
  Bushman ; introduction to the new edition by Anne Firor Scott
    p.   cm.
    Originally published: Cambridge, Mass. ; Emmeline Press,
  c 1976. With new introd.
    Includes bibliographical references (p.   ) and index.
    ISBN 0-87421-233-2
    1. Mormon women—Utah—History.   2. Mormon Church—
Utah—History.   I. Bushman, Claudia L.
305.4'09792—dc21   97-13396
                                                            CIP

For *Leonard J. Arrington*
He takes us seriously.

Contents

Illustrations

Preface

Several years ago a group of Mormon women began to meet together to discuss their lives. Looking for models who combined a dedication to the faith with a spirit of individual action, their discussions ranged far and wide. The discovery of a special issue of the *Utah Historical Quarterly* edited by Leonard Arrington and devoted entirely to early Mormon women provided the examples they were looking for. They wanted to know more about their nineteenth century sisters.

The discussion group was invited to present a class for the Cambridge Latter-day Saint Institute headed by Steve Gilliland. Under the direction of Judith Dushku and assisted by Bonnie Horne, the women chose topics and made their plans. The group spent a semester researching their topics and then offered weekly classes on various topics concerning nineteenth century Mormon women. A sizeable and enthusiastic audience attended the seminar.

The hardest part came next as lecture notes and quotations were turned into written papers. The papers were criticized and rewritten, criticized and written again. Some fell by the wayside, victims of the endless trek, but nine essays remain of that original group. In addition to the women represented here, papers were presented by Mimmu Sloan, Patricia Derr, Judy Gilliland, Maryann MacMurray, and Susan Kohler; much of their work has been incorporated into this volume.

Many others have been of assistance in the preparation of this book. The Latter-day Saint Church Historical Department has been very helpful. Though they exercised no final control over the work, historians there were generous with their time and facilities. Maureen Ursenbach Beecher, Jill Mulvay, and Chris Rigby Arrington contributed essays as well as reading manuscripts and checking details. Maureen Ursenbach Beecher's article grew out of the speech she presented as the first Woman's Exponent Day speaker in Cambridge, Massachusetts. Davis Bitton made practical suggestions which shaped the final form of the volume. To Leonard Arrington, the Historian of the LDS Church, goes our special thanks. Without his encouragement this project would never have been completed.

Laurel Ulrich, Nancy Dredge, and Heather Cannon helped with the editing. General appreciation is extended to others for their help and support, including some husbands and children who made suggestions and checked references. Carrel Sheldon, Grethe Peterson, Sharon Miller, Vicky Deutsch, and Fred Holton have been particularly helpful.

The contemporary photographs which add so much to the volume were collected with the help of Jill Mulvay of Salt Lake City, Utah; Eleanor Gehres of the Denver Public Library; Susan Sessions Rugh of Provo, Utah; Janiece L. Pompa and Dennis Rowley of the Harold B. Lee Library at Brigham Young University; and Rell G. Francis of Springville, Utah.

A long time dream of the writers has been that other groups of Mormon women might join together to learn about their sisters of the past. Their stories are illuminating and inspirational in the best way: they help us to see new possibilities for our own lives. The topical essays are of a suitable length and style to be used for single group discussions. Supplementary readings can be chosen from the notes or the reading list at the end.

The Boston women are spiritually and often physically descended from the women who figure in this book. Writing about them has been a trial equivalent to crossing the plains. That an untrained, grass-roots group of sisters should have come this far at all is a modern spiritual experience. The authors feel that they have made history by making history.

Many simple spelling errors have been modernized in the quotations in individual essays. But syntactical and spelling errors have been retained when, in the opinion of the editor, they add some period charm.

Claudia L. Bushman
Belmont, Massachusetts
1 October 1976

Writing these essays and compiling this book was a voyage of discovery for all of us. When we began, we had only the sketchiest idea of our pioneer past but wanted to find our own roots. We were looking for incidents and styles that could direct our own lives, and we were fortunate to find them.

We began rather unsystematically. We did not set out to write a book; we only planned a set of lectures for a class we were offering to Mormon women. No subjects were originally assigned; contributors chose topics that interested them. Carolyn Person was drawn to her notable ancestress Susa Young Gates. I originally set out to write on conversion stories, but could not find enough of what I wanted and ended up discussing spiritual gifts. Some of the research on polygamy overlapped, so eventually some material written by Nancy Dredge was incorporated into Stephanie Goodson's article. Despite all, the lectures evolved into a workable book.

We wrote this book in Boston where we had no

access to materials from the Church of Jesus Christ of Latter-day Saints (LDS) Archives and were not aware of what was available anyway. We mostly used materials from the Widener Library at Harvard University and from the Boston Public Library.

Since the publication of *Mormon Sisters*, much additional work has been done on all the topics in it; if we started again, we would write a different book. Beginning again, we would certainly consider chapters dealing with less visible women and women at a greater distance from Salt Lake City. I think we might explore the worlds of the Native Americans, the Chicanas, and the Gentiles.

Circumstances have led me to look again at some of the materials we used at a time when I am no longer in the stage of thrilled discovery or searching for role models and freedom within the Mormon tradition. Casting an old, cold eye over the sources, I am surprised to find myself demystifying the pioneers. As I read the documents now, I find many feisty and accomplished women, but I would no longer use words like heroism and sacrifice. I find many women doggedly doing their duty, much wishful thinking about home industry, much effort to rise above difficult situations, and much heavy rhetoric about gentility and refinement. I find women who are strong of necessity, who did what they had to do, rising to the opportunities and challenges that beset them, but women who are very much like their great-granddaughters of today. This is not a master race of foremothers set apart by their nobility; these are our own sisters. In their place, we would have done as well.

Claudia L. Bushman
New York City
1 June 1997

Introduction to the New Edition
Anne Firor Scott

Educational theorists from Aristotle to John Dewey
and beyond have suggested that the acquisition of knowledge is highly dependent on motivation. In the 1970s, as
the so-called "new feminism" swept across the country,
young women in many places suddenly became curious
about the past. How *had* their great grandmothers coped
with life? What had been their primary concerns? Would
they have understood the kinds of questions their great
granddaughters were raising in the late twentieth century? "Women's history" began to appear in college cata-
logs and on conference programs. Graduate students
searched for mentors and designed research projects
dealing with women's past. The tendency was to begin
with women most like oneself—women among Quakers,
Jews, southerners, westerners, New Englanders—and
from there to move on to the broader history of American
women in all their complex diversity.

One intriguing example of this phenomenon took
place in Boston when a group of young Mormon women,
feeling the fresh breeze of feminism ruffling their commitment to an intensely patriarchal religious structure,
began to ask questions about the women who were part
of the early history of the Latter-day Saints. In a pattern
familiar to students of American women's voluntary
organizations (one well known to Mormon women), the

group set out to educate themselves. Each assumed responsibility for learning about some part of the Mormon past in order to teach the others. What they discovered surprised them. As one member of the group remembered twenty-five years later: "To find FEMINISM right in the middle of the familiar tale of faith and pioneer courage was pretty amazing. . . . history energized us." Intrigued by what they were finding, anxious to spread the word that "Mormon feminism" was not a new phenomenon, they undertook to teach a seminar for other Mormon women.

Their first venture into publication was the editing of an issue of *Dialogue: A Journal of Mormon Thought*.[1] Next came a more ambitious project. Nine women, along with three historians recruited from Utah, undertook to write essays detailing what they had learned. The subjects ranged widely around life in Utah and the early days of the Mormon settlement.

Few members of the group were yet trained as historians, but with a burning need to know, they began to make themselves into serious scholars searching for answers to many questions. What part had women played in the church since it's founding? How had their foremothers dealt with the pressures and opportunities presented to Mormon women? What had polygamy meant to the women in plural marriages? Why, in the early days of the twentieth century, had the gender ideas of their church moved in a conservative direction just at a time when in the country at large women were beginning to achieve new political and social freedoms? And how did this bear on their present concerns?

Fortunately, material for answering these questions was plentiful. The Mormon Church had always been interested in keeping records. The nine volumes of *Heart Throbs of the West,* the thirteen of *Our Pioneer Heritage,* and the six of *Treasures of Pioneer History,* all publications of the

Daughters of Utah Pioneers, were a treasure trove, as were the accumulated diaries, memoirs, and letters the church and others so carefully preserved.

As it turned out those essays, printed here, represented the first stage of what has now become a massive historiographical achievement—although one known principally to Mormons, especially to members of the Mormon History Association. It is a puzzling fact that while historians of Mormon women are thoroughly acquainted with the work of their colleagues in the dominant culture, few historians outside of Utah realize how much good work has been and is being done by Mormon historians. Admirers of Laurel Ulrich's *Midwife's Tale* or Claudia Bushman's *A Good Poor Man's Wife* may be surprised to find some of these authors' earliest work in this volume.

As one reads, it becomes clear that while Mormon women were in many ways very much like other American women of their race and class, they were also in some ways unique. For example, the Church of Jesus Christ of Latter-day Saints had been formed in the midst of the Second Great Awakening and shared certain characteristics with that revival movement. The charismatic experiences—visions, speaking in tongues, and revelations—Claudia Bushman describes in "Mystics and Healers" though an important part of early Mormon experience were not peculiar to it. Such phenomena had been common among Methodists fifty years earlier and in many other religious groups.

Mormon midwives resembled rural midwives everywhere in the practice of practical obstetrics, but they were also known for their "spiritual gifts." Folk medicine flourished as it did in many parts of the countryside, but Mormons relied more visibly than most on faith healing.

At the same time, some Mormon women, thanks to the freedom provided by plural marriage, were among the earliest American women to take medical degrees. At a point in the late nineteenth century, Utah was said to have the largest number of women studying medicine, in proportion to population, of any state or territory. These women helped to move Mormon medical practice closer to the mainstream.

Similarities and differences also are evident in the frontier experience. Like all pioneers, Mormons faced physical and mental stress, periods of food shortage, hazards of weather, financial stringency, and Native American conflict. But they were unusual among American frontierspeople both in meeting extraordinary antagonism and persecution and in creating a high level of community organization. Especially after the move to Utah, Mormon women were thoroughly integrated into the systems developed by male leaders to insure survival in an inhospitable environment. Women built and managed cooperative stores, raised money for the Perpetual Emigrating Fund, initiated silk culture, organized the Deseret Silk Association, saved grain, developed home industries, organized "retrenchment societies" (to conserve capital), taught children, and helped young women who wanted to go to medical school.

Mormon women were among the earliest and most dedicated supporters of woman suffrage. When Utah Territory enfranchised women in 1870—the second state or territory in the nation to do so—supporters of women's rights elsewhere hailed this fact as a victory and began to establish relationships with Mormon feminists. As Lola Van Wagenen has shown in her recent dissertation, Utah suffrage, because it was so closely related to Mormonism, created some problems for the mainstream suffrage movement.[2] However, in 1879 Emmeline Wells, a leading Mormon suffragist, was invited to speak to the annual convention of the National Woman Suffrage Association. Elizabeth Cady Stanton and Susan B. Anthony visited Salt Lake City and forged lasting ties with Utah women. In

1883 Wells spoke of their influence: "[The] seed was planted in my soul by reading *The Revolution.* . . . I could never have done the work I have done in this territory had it not been for the work Miss Anthony did before me."[3] On the other hand, the more conservative American Woman Suffrage Association was leery of so controversial a group and joined other Americans in castigating polygamy.

Along with their support for suffrage, Mormon women were early political activists. In the 1870s they organized mass meetings to protest proposed legislation outlawing polygamy and had no hesitation in petitioning the Congress to grant Utah statehood.

Much of this political history is documented in the *Woman's Exponent,* which became one of the three major feminist journals in the country.[4] Eliza Snow, who encouraged its creation and watched over its development, also had a hand in almost every Mormon woman's organization, beginning with the reconstituted Relief Society in 1867. It was through these associations that Mormon women developed a far-reaching influence on the way the community developed. Like most of the leading women, Snow was married to leading men, first to Joseph Smith and later to Brigham Young. Along with Emmeline Wells she established a warm relationship with Stanton and Anthony.

The high value placed on education reminds us that many of the earliest Mormons came from New England. As was true everywhere on the frontier, the multiple demands upon the men to build a new society created opportunities for women to become school teachers. Creating schools when there were many competing demands for resources was an uphill job, and for many years the dream exceeded the reality. "Zion's schoolmarms," though, like their sisters in the Relief Society, were essential to the maintenance of the close-knit community to which the church leaders aspired.

xix

With the vital subject of plural marriage, we come to an unequivocally Mormon topic, to which there were few comparable experiences among American women generally. The early nineteenth century had witnessed many small communitarian groups dedicated to experiments in family structure, but for the vast majority of Americans, who were dedicated in principle, if not always in practice, to monogamy, these experiments were viewed as aberrations.

To a nonbeliever the shocked protests of men when Joseph Smith first began to talk about his revelation on this subject and his assertions that polygamy was a requirement for "celestial advancement" have an odd ring. However, there was certainly Biblical precedent for plural marriage, and one must be slow to be skeptical of believers in any group.

Although Mormon women supported the institution in public, sometimes with enthusiasm, their personal documents—letters and journals—indicate that for many of them plural marriage was a very difficult institution. For some, however, polygamy offered an opportunity to share child raising as well as to develop independence. Occasionally sister-wives took over so one of their number could acquire professional training. It is also clear, puzzling as it may be, that women had more power in the Mormon community while polygamy was permitted than they had in the ensuing sixty or seventy years.

Despite the urging of the leadership, only a minority of church members adopted polygamy. Practical considerations overweighed the hope of heaven, since supporting several wives and their children could be a heavy burden for any man. Stephanie Goodson's essay suggests just how complex the practice of plural marriage could be, and how difficult it is to generalize. While some first wives resolutely opposed additional marriages, others took a hand in choosing the next wife. Some men were sensitive to the feelings of their existing wives; others simply made the decision and presented a spouse or spouses with a *fait accompli*. Some attempted to solve the problem of jealousy by maintaining separate households. In other cases, several women lived together harmoniously. One intriguing fact revealed by this partial history of polygamy is that as men aged they continued to marry young women. In this they were not much different from their counterparts outside the church whose "polygamy" was serial rather than simultaneous. The custom helped account for the traditionally large Mormon families.

Carrel Hilton Sheldon's essay on Mormon haters leads one to wonder why people elsewhere cared so much what the Mormons did. Exposés of polygamy were standard subjects in the sensational press. These apparently fed a public appetite for scandal with sexual overtones. Congress was urged by Protestant churches to act against the Mormons. What was their concern? Did they recognize that the real victims of the various anti-polygamy acts were largely women and children—though some men spent time in hiding, which must have played havoc with their business or professional lives.

Taken together these essays present a complex picture of women who were part of a highly structured, thoroughly male-dominated organization but who nonetheless played a vital part in its creation and maintenance. What at first glance seems an anomaly may be partly explained by the fact that Brigham Young's bold effort to establish a tightly knit community in a remote, initially inaccessible part of the West required mobilizing every bit of available energy. When capital had to be conserved, women, who established consumption patterns, had to be part of the effort. Furthermore, as long as the church practiced polygamy, the loyalty and support of the leading women was essential to survival.

My own first acquaintance with this book and its subject came in 1984 when I was invited to bring the perspective of a historian of American women's voluntary associations to the annual meeting of the Mormon History Association. I began the project by reading *Mormon Sisters* and was led on from there to spend countless hours reading the *Woman's Exponent*. Like the authors of these essays, I was startled by what I found. In the process I came to have enormous respect for Mormon women, past and present.

Re-reading today I am struck by the careful documentation and the sensible skepticism of these self-made scholars. There are, inevitably, some errors. For example, no one would now suggest that the Relief Society was the first woman's organization nor that it was the longest lived, but given when this book was written, errors are remarkably few.[5]

Perhaps the most startling thing I learned in the early stages of doing the research for what became "Mormon Women, Other Women: Paradoxes and Challenges"[6] was how little any of us non-Mormons knew about Mormon history in general but especially about the work being done on Mormon women. Most of my colleagues in the field were quite unaware that this work was going on; I spent a lot of time recommending *Mormon Sisters* as well as much of the work that followed it.

Perhaps the reissue of this pioneering volume will serve to lead younger historians in many places to the work of Maureen Beecher, Carol Madsen, Jill Mulvay Derr, and many others of the talented Mormon women who have done so much in the intervening decades to illuminate the ways Mormon women have helped to shape Mormon culture. Although the subjects dealt with here have been extended and expanded in many ways since this book was written, it remains one of the best introductions to the subject and may be the most accessible work for the numerous Mormons who are not historians but who are curious about their own past.

Notes

1. In 1981 Laurel Thatcher Ulrich published a fascinating description of the process by which the group arrived at the special issue. See *Dialogue* 14 (1981): 28–39. Indirectly, the article also illuminates the composition of this book.
2. Lola Van Wagenen, "Sister-Wives and Suffragists: Polygamy and the Politics of Woman Suffrage, 1870–1896" (Ph.D. diss., New York University, 1994).
3. *Woman's Exponent,* September 15, 1883.
4. The contributors to *Mormon Sisters* were also involved in the creation of *Exponent II,* a contemporary journal of Mormon feminism. See Laurel Thatcher Ulrich and Emma Lou Thayne, *All God's Critters Got a Place in the Choir* (Salt Lake City: Aspen Books, 1995) for a marvelous collection of columns from this journal.
5. The earliest women's associations were organized in the eighteenth century, and—as an example—one founded in 1812 in Boston is still active today.
6. *Journal of Mormon History* 13 (1986–87): 3–19.

A pioneer group, probably Mormon, in the 1870s, possibly the Joseph Henry Byington family. #F12921, photo by the Denver Public Library, Western History Collection.

Introduction

When Joseph Smith, a New York State farm boy, saw God in 1820, his actions drastically changed the lives of thousands of people. Those who accepted his story of deity appearing in the woods and his translation of "golden plates" as an actual history of early people on the American continent followed the charismatic leader with total dedication. The Church of Jesus Christ of Latter-day Saints, which he organized in 1830, became the central fact of their lives, replacing loyalties to nations, friends, and families.

Perhaps the followers of Joseph Smith, and later Brigham Young, would have hesitated in their commitment if they had known what lay ahead. They would be scorned by neighbors in Ohio, Missouri, and Illinois; attacked verbally and physically by civil authorities as well as mobs; deprived of their homes, goods, and livelihoods. The long trek west and the establishment of Zion in the mountain deserts cut them off from their former lives forever.

Fortunately, they could not see their future. As they left their treasures by the roadside and bore babies only to bury them, they were sustained by the faith that they would soon find a haven from persecution. Each new town was settled as a permanent home. The vision persisted as some fell away in death and disillusion. When their beautiful city Nauvoo could no longer be peacefully maintained, strong leadership led the group, at terrible personal cost, to complete the largest organized mass migration in the history of the world and to establish an enduring, religiously-based, inland empire. Considered from any angle, the achievement was vast and heroic.

The story is usually told with a masculine focus: Joseph and Hyrum Smith, unjustly jailed and shot by a mob; Brigham Young, the great colonizer surveying his vast domain; the Mormon Battalion marching off for gold and glory. The conquering of the wilderness with shovel and gun, muscle and might is traditionally man's work. But the Utah settlements were unusual in that they included an astonishing percentage of women. Not only did women travel with the advance company, they marched with the Mormon Battalion. By the end of 1847 the ratio of sexes was approximately equal and remained so as settlement continued.

Mormon women were much like other American women of their day, but their allegiance to the faith led them in some new directions. Daughters of New England and the Middle West, emigrants from the British Isles and Scandinavia, they were children of the reformation and enlightenment. Primarily members of the working class, they had lived monotonous lives characterized by hard work, thrift, and strict morality. The message that Joseph and his elders preached promised additional meaning to their lives on earth and in heaven. The gospel of Jesus Christ, newly interpreted by this dynamic sect, brought religious rebirth to many young girls who faced dull futures and to many older women who thought their lives were over. In addition to enriching their lives, the gospel undoubtedly made them more adventurous as a group than their sisters who stayed at home.

Traditionally women are noted for their conservative qualities, for their role as nurturers, guardians, and preservers of the culture. The Mormon women filled this role with great ingenuity as they nested into homes in wagon boxes along the trail and raised families in dug-outs, tents, and caves in their new Zion. Pioneer photographs show attractive, stylishly dressed women in front of tiny, sod huts and leaky board lean-tos. A genteel appearance was a hard-won achievement, but one essential to the self-respect of frontier women. Girls did a lot of field work, but they were not proud of it. They valued their female dignity and did not want to be men.

Frontier women managed the family home, the one important social, cultural, and educational institution in a new settlement. They contributed to the economy in meaningful ways as well as producing new population to swell the scant labor supply. The economic value of a wife was greater in a frontier community than in an eastern town where someone could be hired to do part of the household work.

But while women were valued on the frontier, their life was a difficult one. The hard realities of scratching a living out of virgin land wore settlers out. In some gentile communities women aged very rapidly; travellers commented that some of the toothless hags they encountered in frontier settlements were only thirty years old. If a man wanted land free from the sight of another man's campfire or the sound of another man's gun, the loneliness was hard on his wife.

By contrast, Mormon frontier life was community life. Group settlement with planned townships and neighbor interaction was always the rule. Cooperation and the subordination of individual ambition made it possible to get a new town functioning quickly. Successful colonizing of the arid, alkaline desert would probably have been impossible otherwise.

While Mormon women in the salt valley were coping together with sagebrush and crickets, back in America's eastern cities women occupied an ever more restricted "sphere" in society. Education, for those who could afford it, stressed the polite accomplishments of music, fancy needlework, and French. Fashionable young ladies were prepared to be decorative rather than practical members of society. Education groomed girls to "catch" husbands without giving them practical preparation for housekeeping and motherhood. Until marriage, young girls who could not afford school worked as poorly paid domestics, seamstresses, teachers or as employees in America's emerging textile industries. In any case their role was circumscribed by society's view of what was proper.

To sum up then, women living in groups on the frontier were in a relatively good position in the early nineteenth century. All their native gifts were encouraged for the benefit of the community, and imagination and initiative brought them social recognition. The loneliness of isolation and the false limitations of polite society were both missing. The pervasive Church became the cultural and economic unit as well as the religious one.

The Mormon Church encouraged the participation of women. From the beginning they "voted" to sustain Church officials. They participated in holy ordinances and pronounced blessings to heal the sick. The sacred temple ceremonies assured them that they would hold places of high honor in the next world. In 1842 the Female Relief Society of Nauvoo, one of the first women's organizations in the United States and the longest lived, was founded under the direction and with the blessing of Joseph Smith.

Mormons were most distinctly separated from other Americans by their conspicuous and notorious marital arrangements. Joseph Smith had received divine instruction to follow the pattern of Father Abraham and marry more than one wife. He taught the Principle to other Church leaders who quietly added wives to their households. Nineteenth century Americans who glorified the nuclear family were offended by such deviants and by other religious sects defending practices ranging from celibacy to free love which grew up at the same time. The first years of polygamy were marked by scandal and secrecy, but after 1852, plural marriage was preached from the pulpit, lived openly, and defended as a divine commandment by the Saints.

For the women of Zion the importance of polygamy cannot be overstressed, even though only a small proportion of the populace was directly involved. The Mormon sisters were required to defend the Principle or leave the Church entirely. They had to make plural marriage work to prove they were right. The Principle, more than anything else, set up a competition between the Mormons and the Gentiles, the first intent on proving their righteousness and the second on forcing the miscreant group to recant their evil ways.

More important, the practical requirements of living as plural wives challenged the limiting stereotype of women accepted by civilized America. A plural wife could not be the helpless, fainting, protected female or she would likely faint alone. Plural wives often had to look to themselves rather than their husbands for financial support and physical labor. For practical purposes many were more like widows than traditional wives. The regular absence of their husbands simplified their housekeeping chores, allowing them to participate in a broader range of activities than their eastern sisters. In one of the neatest ironic contradictions of the period, the "enslaved harems" of Utah produced some of America's most efficient early feminists.

Utah's women voted in 1870, the first in the United States. Though the women in Wyoming were the first to be granted the franchise, Utah's women won it quickly afterwards, and an election in Utah came first. Utah women exercised the franchise for seventeen years before the Washington politicians, impatient at their reluctance to

A group of Mormon women, including Emmeline B. Wells, Rachel Ivins Grant, and Bathsheba B. Smith, gather about 1880 for an unknown reason. Charles Roscoe Savage, photographer. #P4124, courtesy of LDS Archives.

vote down polygamy, snatched the privilege away. Even after 1896, when Utah finally became a state with full political equality for her women, it was only the third state in the nation with female suffrage. Though not all local residents supported agitation for women's rights, there was much less friction *against* it than in the east. If, as has been postulated, the opposition to suffrage grew in direct proportion to the fighting for it, Utah women were fortunate in belonging to a community that gave them the vote (with help from Congress) with little effort.

Readers will want to know if Mormon women of the past were more "liberated" than other women of their day. They probably were. The next question will be whether the pioneers were freer to carry out their ambitions than today's Mormon women. They probably were not. Looking back it appears that nineteenth century Mormon women were remarkably free to act in the world and that they were independent of their husbands. Yet it is also clear that they practiced their traditional mothering role and assumed that it was of primary importance.

Today's Mormon leaders stress mothering far more than those in the nineteenth century. But the current emphasis on the importance of family life reflects a concern about the breakdown of traditional family structures. Leaders urge women to give first attention to roles their old-time sisters accepted without question. A consideration of today's proscriptive literature would indicate that fewer activities were possible for current women. Actually, while mothering has been the primary activity for adult women in both eras, and women of the past participated in a broad range of the world's activities, women are freer now than ever before to pursue their other interests.

It is not the purpose of this book to compare closely Mormon women of the past and present. Time and distance distort the evidence. Women of the present share much with their sisters of the past, but it is clear that their lives were different then. The purpose here is to give contemporary women a sense of the richness and variety of their foremothers' lives. Readers should make their own comparisons.

These essays share an interest in subject matter, but they differ in scope, focus, and style. Though they do follow in a loose chronological order, and the later ones presuppose some knowledge from earlier essays, they have little else in common. In some essays the focus broadens from the exclusively female to the Mormon experience. Mormon women were so closely identified with their families and their greater society that sometimes discussing them in a vacuum seems sterile. Though each essay tells interesting things about Mormon women, the experiences were not always unique to them.

Two women have been given their own chapters in this book. In her time each was probably the most powerful woman in Utah. The accomplishments of both are legendary. Eliza R. Snow, as the plural wife of Joseph Smith and later Brigham Young, dominated female activities in the Church from the end of the Nauvoo period until her death in 1887. Susa Young Gates, one of Brigham Young's daughters, began her *Young Woman's Journal* in 1889, and thereafter, with her impressive suffrage, educational, and musical activities, became a powerful figure. Her constant literary outpourings have influenced current Mormon assumptions to a degree still unmeasured.

The question of whether these two women and others mentioned in this book were typical must be raised. Most of these remarkable early women belonged to an elite echelon; they were leaders of their community or noted for their special accomplishments. That they were more productive and energetic than their sisters, or at least better placed, seems likely. But they do not seem to be far in advance of countless other lively women. Before generalizations can be made, a much larger group of famous and unknown women will have to be considered in some depth. Fortunately, existing records provide the raw data for finding out much more about the women in early settlements. In the future, it should be possible to become acquainted with many less notable women.

The story of Mormondom's heroic woman-host is not well known either in the Church or out of it. Hopefully this book will help to bring the past closer.

A CENTURY OF MORMON WOMEN:

A Selective Chronology of Significant Dates

National events	Women in the U.S.
(1817–1825) James Monroe	
1820 Missouri Compromise	1820s Women organize missionary, temperance groups. Aid fallen women
1823 Monroe Doctrine	
(1825–1829) J. Q. Adams	
1825 Erie Canal opens for business	
	1826 Lowell textile mills open with jobs for women
(1829–1837) Andrew Jackson	
1830 First steam locomotive	
1831 Underground railway begun	
1832 Nullification crisis	
	1833 Philadelphia Female Anti-Slavery Society organized
1834 McCormack reaper patented	
1836 Siege of the Alamo	
(1837–1841) Martin Van Buren	
1837 Economic depression	1837 Mt. Holyoke opens
	1839 Margaret Fuller's conversations

A COMPARATIVE CHRONOLOGY

in Mormondom and the United States

LDS Church Events	*Women in the Church*
1820 First Vision	
1827 Joseph gets plates	
1830 Church of Jesus Christ of Latter-day Saints organized Book of Mormon published Kirtland period begins	
(1830–1844) Joseph Smith	
1831 Zion = Jackson County, Mo.	
1833 "Word of Wisdom" recorded	
1835 D. & C. published in Kirtland Quorum of Twelve organized First Quorum of Seventy organized	1835 First book of hymns compiled by Emma Smith published
1836 Kirtland Temple dedicated	
1837 Exodus from Kirtland	
1838 Gov. Boggs orders Saints exterminated or expelled from Missouri	
1840 Nauvoo, the beautiful, chartered	

(1841) W. H. Harrison	1841 Dorothea Dix investigates jails & asylums
(1841–1845) John Tyler	
(1845–1849) J. K. Polk	
1845 Annexation of Texas	1845 Lowell Female Labor Reform Assoc. organized
	1846 Sewing machine patented
1847 California gold rush	
1848 War with Mexico ended	1848 Seneca Falls Convention
(1849–1850) Zachary Taylor	1849 Married women get property rights in N. Y. state. Safety pin patented
(1850–1853) Millard Fillmore	
1850 Slavery compromise of 1850	
	1851 *Uncle Tom's Cabin* published
(1853–1857) Franklin Pierce	
1854 Kansas-Nebraska Act Republican Party organized	
(1857–1861) James Buchanan	
1859 John Brown raids Harper's Ferry	
1860 S. Carolina secedes	

1841	Baptism for the dead introduced	1841	Eliza R. Snow married to Joseph Smith
1842	Temple endowments begun	1842	Female Relief Society of Nauvoo organized
		1843	D & C 132 recorded— Celestial & Plural Marriage
1844	Joseph Smith for President! Martyrdom of Joseph and Hyrum		

(1844–1877) Brigham Young

1846 Nauvoo Temple dedicated

1847 Trek West
This is the place!

1848 Treaty of Guadalupe-Hidalgo
makes valley U.S. territory
First visitation of crickets and
seagulls

1849 First statehood petition sent to
Congress
Perpetual Emigrating Fund
set up

1850 *Deseret News* begins
publication
University of Deseret
(U of U) chartered

		1852	Plural marriage publicly announced
		1853	First Relief Societies in Utah organized

1856 1st handcarts leave Iowa City
Reformation

1857 Mtn. Meadows massacre—
Utah War

xxxvii

(1861–1865) Abraham Lincoln

1861 Civil War begins

1863 Emancipation Proclamation

(1865–1869) Andrew Johnson

1865 Surrender at Appomatox

1867 Alaska purchased from Russia

1868 First practical typewriter

(1869–1877) U. S. Grant

1869 Transcontinental railway
     completed

1872 End of Tweed Ring in NYC

1873 Severe financial panic

1876 Telephone patented
     Custer's Last Stand

(1877–1881) R. B. Hayes

1879 Incandescent lightbulb

(1881) J. A. Garfield

(1881–1885) Chester Arthur

1861 Sanitary Commission of
     Civil War
     Nursing care of soldiers

1862 Co-ed land grant colleges
     begun

1868 New England Women's Club
     founded

1869 Wyoming women get the vote
     National Women's Suffrage
     Assoc. & American Women's
     Suffrage Assoc. founded

1871 Michigan Med. School
     admits women

1874 Women's Christian Temperance
     Union

1875 Mary Baker Eddy founds
     Church of Christ, Scientist

1879 Belva Lockwood admitted to
     practice before Supreme Court

1881 Clara Barton founds Red Cross

1862 Salt Lake Theatre dedicated and opened	1862 Morrill Act—plural marriage prohibited
1865–76 Black Hawk War	
1867 Temple Square Tabernacle completed	1867 Relief Society organized under E. R. Snow
	1868 1st R.S. hall dedicated—15th ward, SLC
1869 Golden Spike driven at Promontory Point completes transcontinental railroad	1869 Retrenchment assoc. organized (precursor of MIA)
	1870 Utah women VOTE!
	1871 Women protest anti-Mormon Cullom Bill at Mass Meeting
	1872 *Woman's Exponent* established Two women admitted to Utah bar
1874 United Order commences	
1875 YMMIA begins	
1876 Brigham Young founds BYU with Karl G. Maeser, director	1876 Womans' Commission Store founded R.S. asked to grow silk, store grain
(1877–1887) John Taylor	
1877 Stakes organized throughout Utah Brigham Young dies	
	1878 Aurelia Rogers founds Primary Ellis Shipp becomes M.D.
1879 Reynolds case—Supreme Court upholds anti-polygamy laws	1879 E. B. Wells, Zina Y. Williams attend National Woman's Suffrage Conv. in Wash.
	1880 Gen'l presidencies & central boards organized for R.S., MIA & Primary

(1885–1889) Grover Cleveland
1886   Labor Unions organized

(1889–1893) Benjamin Harrison

1889   Jane Addams moves into Hull
House
1890   NWSA & AWSA merged.
Becomes NAWSA
Wyoming become state with
women's suffrage

1892   Gasoline automobile
Riots, Homestead Steel
Mills, PA.
(1893–1897) Grover Cleveland

1896   Klondike gold rush
(1897–1901) William McKinley

1897   First U.S. subway—Boston
1898   Spanish-American War

1898   Charlotte Perkins Gilman
publishes *Women & Economics*

(1901–1909) T. Roosevelt

1903   Wright Brothers flight

1903   National Women's Trade Union
League established

1906   Pure Food & Drug Act
(1909–1913) W. H. Taft
1909   Model T Ford
1911   1st Transcontinental plane flight

1911   Triangle Shirtwaist Factory
Fire kills at least 145

1912   Titanic sinks

1882	Edmunds Act—heavy penalties for polygamy and cohabitation	1882	Deseret Hospital founded by Relief Society
1884	Underground		

(1887–1898) Wilford Woodruff

1887	Federal Edmunds-Tucker Act— disfranchised polygamists and all women		
		1889	Susa Young Gates publishes *Young Woman's Journal*
1890	Manifesto—the practice of plural marriage is officially discontinued		
		1891	R.S. joins National Council of Women
		1892	R.S. becomes Nat'l Woman's Relief Society
1893	SL Temple dedicated Amnesty for polygamists, voting restrictions removed		
1894	Genealogical Society organized		
1896	Utah admitted as a state	1896	Women full voters ın new state! Dr. Martha Hughes Cannon elected state senator
1897	*Improvement Era* first published		
		1898	R.S. Nurse School organized 1st single lady missionaries called

(1898–1901) Lorenzo Snow

		1900	A black dress of Utah silk for Susan B. Anthony's birthday

(1901–1918) Joseph F. Smith

		1902	*Children's Friend* born

1904	Joseph F. Smith delivers "Second Manifesto"		

(1913–1921) Woodrow Wilson

1914   Panama Canal completed

1916   National Park Service established

1917   War"Over There"

1920   18th and 19th Amendments—
        National prohibition and women's
        suffrage

Presidents of the Relief Society

Emma Hale Smith 1842–
Eliza Roxcy Snow 1867–1887
Zina D. Huntington Young 1888–1901
Bathsheba W. Bigler Smith 1901–1910
Emmeline B. Woodward Wells 1910–1921
Clarissa Smith Williams 1921–1928
Louise Yates Robison 1928–1940
Amy Brown Lyman 1940–1945
Belle Marion Isabell Smith Spafford 1945–1974
Barbara B. Smith 1974–1984
Barbara Woodhead Winder 1984–1990
Elaine Low Jack 1990–1997
Mary Ellen Wood Smoot 1997–

General Presidents of Young Women

Elmina Shepard Taylor 1880–1904
Martha Horne Tingey 1905–1929
Ruth May Fox 1929–1937
Lucy Grant Cannon 1937–1948
Bertha Stone Reeder 1948–1961
Florence Smith Jacobsen 1961–1972
Ruth Hardy Funk 1972–1978
Elaine Anderson Cannon 1978–1984
Ardeth Greene Kapp 1984–1992
Janette Callister Hales Beckham 1992–

Primary Association Presidents

Aurelia Spencer Rogers, founder 1878
Louie Bouton Felt 1880–1925
May Anderson 1925–1940
May Green Hinckley 1940–1943
Adele Cannon Howells 1943–1951
La Vern Watts Parmley 1951–1974
Naomi M. Shumway 1974–1980
Dwan Jacobsen Young 1980–1988
Michaelene Packer Grassli 1988–1994
Patricia Peterson Pinegar 1994–

Four generations of Mormon women, in a studio portrait of an unidentified family. #P4125, courtesy of LDS Archives.

Mystics and Healers

Claudia Lauper Bushman

It was late at night in May 1859 when the two women and two little girls reached Florence, Nebraska. They were installed in a vacant house and soon slept soundly. The next morning they awoke to the knock of a little girl bringing milk.

"Is there a little woman here with two children?" she asked.

"Yes, come in."

"If you please my ma wants to see you; she has sent this milk to your little girls."

The benefactor's name was unfamiliar, but the newcomer went to visit, thinking to find an old acquaintance. To her surprise she was introduced to a complete stranger.

"No," said the stranger, "and I never saw you before [either]. I am Hyrum Smith's daughter; my father appeared to me three times last night, and told me that you were the child of God, that you was without money, provisions or friends, and that I must help you."[1]

So began a long and mutually beneficial friendship between Elizabeth Drake Davis and Lovina Walker, Hyrum's daughter. They told of the experience as evidence of God's loving care throughout their lives.

The early restored Church was characterized by an outpouring of such miraculous occurrences. The Saints rejoiced in the evidence of their chosen status as signs "followed those that believed." Much more then than now, Mormons not only received communications from the spiritual world, they expected to receive them. The achievement of a personal testimony of the truthfulness of the gospel is still expected of Church members, but fewer seek miracles.

The women of the early Church were as involved in spiritual experiences as men. The spirit did not come through priesthood leaders alone, but was available to everyone. In fact, women seemed to have had a special affinity for mystical incidents. As "better instruments" than men, women tended to be more receptive to the spirit. They were particularly blessed in the "woman's sphere": their children were healed, their husbands blessed, their families provided for.

The spiritual gifts they practiced were of two kinds. The first group included visions, dreams, speaking in tongues, revelations, and miraculous help in extreme need. These gifts indicated direct supernatural intervention, and the sisters' reactions were characterized by religious excitement, an exalted state of mind, and a joyful belief that a miracle had occurred. Over the years, these phenomena gradually decreased in number and intensity.

In the second expression of spiritual powers, women prayed over each other and their families in an effort to heal and bless. The practice of administration by women began in the early days of the Church and continued well into the twentieth century. These prayers were often offered in the business-like way characteristic of contemporary Church work. Although the practice of female administration was officially discontinued in 1914 in favor of priesthood blessings, the spirit in which the work was done is more in keeping with the practical, down-to-earth tone of the Church today.

These two strands of religious experience, seemingly so at odds, mark the boundaries of the spiritual lives of Mormon women. Both practical and mystical, these women called on divine powers under the most humble and exalted of circumstances. The more dramatic and ecstatic experiences seemed to come during crises; the greatest help came in the time of the greatest need.

Early converts to the Church came to expect dramatic miraculous occurrences. Fanny Stenhouse recorded her confirmation blessing in her book *Tell It All*, and along with the familiar blessings new members are still promised today, she was told, "You shall have visions and dreams, and angels shall visit you by day and by night. . . . You shall speak in tongues, and prophesy; and the Lord shall bless you abundantly, both temporally and spiritually."[2] It was assumed that spiritual experiences were the legacy of those who believed in Christ.

This assumption was partly derived from the religious environment. Mormons were not alone in claiming power to communicate with "the other side." Lucy Mack Smith's biography of Joseph indicates that the family had been visionary over several generations, long before Joseph's first vision.[3] Other sects that developed in the nineteenth century—the Shakers, the Rappites, the spiritualists—claimed communication with the world beyond. Converts did not have to be taught to seek spiritual experiences. The desire was in the air. If anything, it was necessary to dampen their eagerness for the miraculous. The Church eventually found it necessary to impose some rationality, channeling the results of spiritual experiences into acceptable forms. The Saints had to learn that private revelations were not instructions for the Church; the prophet alone had that prerogative. False prophets who rose up were cut down to size, and enthusiastic, emotional outpourings in meetings were discouraged.

Although looking back we may think that the Saints constantly experienced miracles, they actually never were commonplace. Marvelous occurrences happened infrequently enough to be anticipated, prayed for, and cherished. They seem so prominent, perhaps, because when they did occur, they were described in loving detail in journals and have been quoted or retold many times since. By comparison, deaths in the family received only a line or two. But spiritual gifts, while immensely valued, were never part of the everyday life nor central to the kingdom. The Saints' extraordinary spiritual experiences tended to be personal, limited in scope, and peripheral to the organized activities of the Church. Joseph was told before the organization of the Church to "require not miracles."[4] In short, nothing in doctrine or practice prevented the general evolution of the Church away from nineteenth century spiritual enthusiasm toward the more matter-of-fact, practical twentieth century faith we know today.

Spiritual experiences are difficult to categorize, but some organizing threads do run through. Personal revelations in time of great trial form a major category. Aurelia Rogers, who founded the Primary organization, had such a revelation. She had lost several children in death, and being in bad health herself, had gone to visit her sister, taking her daughter Lucy with her. Lucy broke out with measles and then scarlet fever. The sister's daughter Ivy caught the diseases and became dangerously ill. Sister Rogers blamed herself for this calamity and experienced horrible feelings. She prayed fervently to the Lord to spare both the children, but asked that if either child must be taken it should be hers as her sister had already buried four children.

While in the midst of this anxiety, lying on my bed, wondering if the Lord had indeed forsaken us, all at once a change came over me; everything seemed so lovely and beautiful, and I was as happy as could be for a few minutes. I saw no person, heard no voice, yet knew the Comforter was there, and accepted it as such, feeling to thank the Lord for even a glimmer of light.[5]

Both children were spared.

A similar story is told of Sister Amanda Smith, whose son and husband were murdered at Haun's Mill. Another son, his hip socket shot away by mob members, was miraculously healed by special treatment revealed to his mother. Sister Smith spent the night of the massacre in prayer and was answered by voices directing her to treat the grievous injury with lye and slippery elm leaves. The boy Alma obediently lay still for five weeks, and his body grew a "flexible gristle" which allowed him to move normally for forty years.[6]

The two incidents are alike. Both sisters suffered, prayed, and in answer were comforted. The miraculous intervention was of limited duration and extent. The murdered son and father were not restored. The Saints were not spirited away to safety. Future prosperity was not guaranteed. Neither woman was protected from further harm or sorrow. But these incidents, complete in themselves, remained as touchstones in times of trial.

Help came to the sisters in other ways when they badly needed it. Hannah Cornaby, who later wrote "Who's on the Lord's Side, Who?," was often without food during the famine in early Utah days. Her children understood the value of prayer and urged her to pray for food to eat. She wrote, "I, feeling most anxious that my darlings should not lose confidence in prayer, would plead with great earnestness, they lisping the words after me. Many times the prayer was answered almost immediately."[7] Again the prayer was not answered with a drastic change of life, or food for the next month. The family was fed for a day.

Miraculous visions also occurred in the early days. Visions dramatized a woman's feeling of closeness to the next world, but otherwise it is difficult to generalize about their meaning and intention. Some served an important and useful purpose, as in the well-publicized instance when the "mantle of the Prophet" fell upon Brigham Young; he seemed to be Joseph and spoke in Joseph's voice. Scores of people witnessed the event and were directed to their new leader.[8] The design of other visions was less clear. What purpose was served when Elizabeth Duncanson, a Church member in Scotland, saw the martyrdom of Joseph and Hyrum at the time it happened and waited six weeks for confirmation?[9] Of what value was the vision of Zina D. Huntington Young, who saw angels walking about on the roof of the temple during a fast meeting? She mentioned no particular spiritual feelings and only identified the angels by their habit of disappearing and returning.[10] What can we learn from the intriguing vision of Hannah Cornaby, aged seven, in which a wingless angel, clothed in a loose robe, traversed the arch of the sky waving a roll of paper in his hand as if showing it to the inhabitants of the earth? This scene, lit up by brilliant red lights, was witnessed by several people.[11] None of these incidents added to revealed knowledge. Instead they served to reenforce the feeling of closeness to the Lord. Supernatural manifestations simply strengthened the commitment of the Saints.

Feeling miracles in the air, the sisters would strive mightily to read the future from their dreams. Although some dreams were so distant from reality that a real effort had to be made to relate them to life, the people still regarded them as spiritual manifestations. Sister Wilcox interpreted a dream for Christopher Merkley, a practical man of action. Merkley dreamed that he was rafting lumber, and altogether the timber, oars, floats, and traverses totalled twenty-seven pieces. Sister Wilcox saw the dream as a sign that he would baptize twenty-seven more people. Merkley was doubtful, as he had come to the end of this mission, one of eight he served. But delays kept him around and, sure enough, he baptized twenty-seven more people before starting for home.[12]

Sister Wilcox had foreseen the dream's meaning, but as has been suggested, dreams of this kind served as confirmation, not direction. A person still had to find his own way. Only afterwards did he receive assurance that he had chosen correctly.

Other dreams and visions forecast events to come and were of practical value. It was common for the sisters to have visions of the elders prior to their arrival or for women to recognize their intended mates when they saw them for the first time. Abigail Leonard prayed to know which church to join in 1829. She was told to join none, that a righteous people would soon be raised up. When the Book of Mormon was presented to her, she accepted it immediately.[13]

A stranger phenomenon, and one widely current in the early Church, was speaking in tongues. A person would go into a trance and speak in what seemed a foreign language; then often another would interpret, telling what the speaker had really said. These people, usually women, spoke the "Adamic tongue" as well as contemporary languages.

Occasionally the gift of tongues served a useful purpose. Tullidge reported the case of a wagonload of pioneers suddenly surrounded by hostile Indians intent on murder. A seventeen year old girl was inspired to speak to them in their own language, urging them to reconsider. The Indians, somewhat taken aback, retreated.[14] But such instances are exceptional.

Presendia Lathrop Kimball related many examples of speaking in tongues, most of which were not to help penetrate a language barrier. In her life story she described the strong spirit that accompanied these events:

Brother Leonard spoke in tongues in an Indian language, and prophesied of the destruction of this nation before the coming of the Savior. The power that rested upon him was so great as to produce such an intense sympathy with those in the room that [we] were all wonderfully affected. Sister Eliza Snow walked the floor to keep her breath. All felt the distress and agony that awaited the nation, more particularly the priests and harlots being destroyed in their wickedness. Sister Eliza Snow spoke afterwards in the pure language of Adam, with great power, and the interpretation was given.[15]

Such occasions could be impressive even to non-believers. Prescindia Huntington related an incident in Kirtland when one of her non-member relatives attended a fast meeting hoping to hear someone sing or speak in tongues because she wanted to have a "hearty laugh." During the meeting one Brother McCarter rose and sang a song in tongues. Prescindia got up and sang with him "ending each verse in perfect unison without varying a word." The cousin observed, after they came out of the meeting, "Instead of laughing, I never felt so solemn in my life."[16]

Many people still living remember hearing tongues spoken in LDS Church meetings. Serge J. Lauper recalls an unusual occasion in Sugarville, Utah, about 1918, when a neighbor lady rose in testimony meeting and spoke in a melodic language which was not the French his family used. A ripple of excited comment passed through the congregation: the sister was speaking in tongues. She spoke for eight or ten minutes. Another lady stood up and more briefly interpreted the first speech. She said the first speaker invoked the blessings of the Lord upon the people and urged them to keep the commandments. Both sisters seemed to speak more easily and fluently than in their daily conversation and seemed unaffected after the incident was over. The seventeen year old boy, though impressed spiritually, was mystified by the event.[17]

The purpose of these phenomena was, in fact, not clear to observers. Some other power seemed to be affecting these women, but the messages as interpreted were generally commonplace. Any benefits seemed to be to the people who spoke rather than to those who listened. Significantly, Joseph warned that the "devil [would] take advantage of the innocent and unwary" who exercised the gift of tongues too often. He said the gift could be used for the women's comfort, but that nothing received by tongues could be considered doctrine.[18]

A possible explanation is that the sisters who were visited by such phenomena, weighed down as they were with the hardships of pioneer life, could escape to a more exalted plane through spiritual experiences such as the speaking of tongues. After achieving a certain mentality, they became mediums for spiritual outpourings. The point was less the message than the exalted frame of mind.

Franklin D. Richards, who had spoken in tongues himself, described his experience:

> You have sometimes been impressed with overwhelming Emotions upon you and attempt to say something and could not, that is just the way the spirit works, you say something even if you do not know anything about it and find out that it was something that ought to be proper and right. . . . If a man goes out to preach and [has] not had a good education he naturally feels backward and diffident as if he could not,—then by faith the Spirit comes upon him, he talks things he never knew of before both edifying and profitable to people. . . . The ways of the spirit are not as mens ways it is wonderful marvellously singular.[19]

Strong emotion enabled him to do things he could not ordinarily do. The sisters' speaking in tongues must have operated in the same way.

Having faith that spiritual experiences would occur, the sisters found them everywhere. Some might argue with the interpretation of the following incident, but it is indicative of the way the sisters saw the world. Eliza R. Snow reported that a woman came a great distance to attend the dedication of the Nauvoo Temple, not hearing that babes in arms were barred. She went to the patriarch in distress as she had no one to leave her infant with. Brother Smith told her to attend the service and promised that the baby would make no disturbance. Eliza R. Snow reported, "But when the congregation shouted hosanna, that babe joined in the shout."[20]

Even the most sympathetic member might question the childless Sister Snow on the reason the child leapt up and shouted out at the sudden noise, but she recorded the incident without apology. One reason spiritual experiences were impressive was because the people to whom they occurred were so sure of their meaning and authenticity. From the outside they could look much different.

Gentiles thought that Mormons and other religious en-
thusiasts were mad, wild, strange, suffering from halluci-
nations. When serious explanations were attempted, hypnosis and animal magnetism were suggested.

Animal magnetism, a faddish notion of antebellum
America, was a supposed force by which some people
thought to exert a strong quasi-hypnotic influence over
others. Against the electric rays emanating from the magnetic personality, victims were powerless. Consider the
account of Maria Ward, a sensational anti-Mormon writer
who purported to have married an elder and lived with
the Saints for many years. Supposedly unacquainted with
the doctrine of magnetic influence, she was travelling in a
stagecoach with an incognito Mormon elder:

> I soon became aware of some unaccountable power exercised
> over me by my fellow traveler. His presence seemed an irresis-
> tible fascination. His glittering eye was fixed on mine; his
> breath fanned my cheek; I felt bewildered and intoxicated, and
> partially at least lost the sense of consciousness, and the power
> of motion.[21]

Under this spell she joined the Church and witnessed miraculous cures. She subsequently explained these miracles by animal magnetism, hypnosis, and fakery.

Fanny Stenhouse, an apostate, but one who bore a
strong testimony for many years, attempted a more rational explanation. During the confirmation of a female
convert, the elder spoke with "extreme earnestness" and
then, seized with a nervous trembling, began to prophesy
great things for this sister. Fanny Stenhouse explained
why:

> When we consider the excited state of her mind, and—if the
> statements of psychologists be true—the magnetic currents
> which were being transmitted from the sensitive nature of the
> man into the excited brain of the new convert, together with the
> pressure of half a dozen human hands upon her head, it is not
> at all astonishing that when the hands were lifted off she should
> firmly believe that she had been blessed indeed.[22]

Despite her withdrawal from the Church, Sister Stenhouse did not deny the strong feelings of the man praying nor ridicule an experience that had once been so valuable to her. Rather than discount the experience, she attempted to explain the spiritual feelings it engendered.

The world's skeptical discounting of miraculous occurrences, added to the Church's hesitant acceptance of them, partly explained their declining frequency. But there were other reasons for this decline. The Saints did not always have good experiences. Tullidge explained the falling off by saying that the Saints began to fear visions and angels and prophecy and the speaking in tongues. When the power of God was manifested, he said, another power from "another source" was about equally displayed and the Saints came to regard such manifestations as "fire that could burn as well as bless."²³ Spiritual gifts were a two-edged sword. They might be from God and bless the people, but again they might be frightful and require suppression. The combination was too dangerous for the Saints to countenance.

Similarly the gift of prophecy, when abused by a budding prophet, threatened the order of the Church. One bad experience concerned a woman named Hubble who professed to be a true prophetess. She had many revelations and

knew that the Book of Mormon was true: and that she would become a teacher in the Church of Christ. She appeared very sanctimonious and deceived some, who were not able to detect her in her hypocrisy.²⁴

Hubble's manifestations caused the Prophet to remind the Saints by a revelation that "there is none other appointed unto you to receive commandments and revelations until he be taken, if he abide in me." Should the Prophet err, "he shall not have power except to appoint another in his stead."²⁵

Another reason for the decline of spiritual activity was the difficulty of controlling emotional outbursts and the official reaction against them. A rather hostile observer visited a Mormon meeting in 1831 and described his experience:

A scene of the wildest enthusiasm was exhibited, chiefly, however, among the young people: they would fall, as without strength, roll upon the floor, and, so mad were they that even the females were seen in a cold winter day, lying under the bare canopy of heaven with no couch or pillow but the fleecy snow. At other times they exhibited all the apish actions imaginable, making grimaces both horrid and ridiculous. . . . At other times they are taken with a fit of jabbering that which they neither understood themselves nor any body else, and this they call speaking foreign languages by divine inspiration.[26]

Parley P. Pratt deplored these religious excesses. He said they were disgusting, not edifying, and regretted that members would swoon away, make unseemly gestures, fall into ecstacies, fits, contortions, and cramps. He feared that a false and lying spirit seemed to be creeping into the Church.[27]

At Pratt's request Joseph Smith enquired concerning spiritual manifestations and his query resulted in Section 50 of the Doctrine and Covenants, given in May of 1831. In the section we are told that "that which doth not edify is not of God, and is darkness," and that unknown spirits will be given into the hand of the righteous if the spirits are of God, or power over them if they are not of God.[28]

Some action was taken. In 1834 Elder Curtis Hodge was tried in a Church court for his unseemly behavior. Hodge had had a spiritual experience during a Mormon meeting and was censured for his "Methodist spasm" and his "shouting and screaming." George A. Smith recalled that the Church court system had first been organized to deal with the incident.[29]

As restrained behavior was encouraged, some of the more sensational spiritual experiences tended to go underground. While they were still practiced, they were practiced privately. Much later in Salt Lake City, when Fanny Stenhouse visited Brigham Young's wives at the

Lion House to see about her daughter's wedding, one of Young's wives' faces lit up with a supernatural glow, and placing her hands on Mrs. Stenhouse's head, she poured forth a flood of eloquence in tongues.

I did not understand a single word that was uttered . . . [but the prayer] sent through me a magnetic thrill as if I had been listening to an inspired seeress. Another of Brigham's wives who was present interpreted the words of blessing to me, but added: "Do not speak of this, Sister Stenhouse, for Brother Young does not like to hear of these things."[30]

Brigham Young, the man who first spoke in tongues, preferred his wives to exercise this gift discreetly for their own comfort. Under the circumstances the declining frequency of dramatic spiritual gifts is understandable.

In the other, more active strand of religious experience, the sisters administered to the sick, gave blessings, and generally assumed the roles restricted to priesthood leaders today. This practice dated from the early days of the Church. There is no scriptural basis for their activities, but in 1837 Sister Eda Rogers was encouraged by Patriarch Joseph Smith, Sr., to bless her family in the absence of her husband. She was to lay hands on them and "Sickness shall stand back."[31] Joseph Smith gave further justification to the practice in a talk to Relief Society members given 28 April 1842. Joseph reported that he gave a lecture on the priesthood

showing how the sisters would come in possession of the privileges, blessings and gifts of the Priesthood, and that the signs should follow them, such as healing the sick, casting out devils, etc., and that they might attain unto these blessings by a virtuous life and conversation, and diligence in keeping all the commandments.[32]

Eliza R. Snow's long synopsis of his speech followed Joseph's entry in the documentary history. The thrust of the speech was a defense of an existing and harmless practice rather than an exhortation to use it more freely or discontinue it. He rebuked critics, telling them to hold their tongues, for if the sisters healed the sick it was no more than right and proper.[33] He went on to say more:

> Respecting females administering for the healing of the sick . . . there could be no evil in it, if God gave His sanction by healing; that there could be no more sin in any female laying hands on and praying for the sick, than in wetting the face with water; it is no sin for anybody to administer that has faith, or if the sick have faith to be healed by their administrations.[34]

According to Joseph, administration by women was a completely positive act that could do no harm if performed in sincerity. The effective faith could be that of the sick person as well as that of the one performing the blessing.

Although the practice was not necessarily widespread, it was performed with considerable nonchalance.[35] The sisters' results compared favorably with the elders' efforts, according to Abigail Leonard. As soon as she and her family were settled in Nauvoo, a homeless English family arrived and had to be taken in. The woman of the family was sick so the elders were summoned, but their endeavors were unsuccessful.

> I told the husband of the sick woman that but one thing was left to be done, which was to send for the sisters. The sisters came, washed, anointed, and administered to her. The patient's extremities were cold, her eyes set, a spot in the back apparently mortified, and every indication that death was upon her. But before the sisters had ceased to administer, the blood went coursing through her system, and to her extremities, and she was sensibly better. Before night her appetite returned, and became almost insatiable, so much so at least that, after I had given her to eat all I dared, she became quite angry because I would not give her more. In three days she sat up and had her hair combed, and soon recovered.[36]

This cross, hungry woman, barely snatched from death, responded to the prayers of the sisters after the elders had given her up. The sisters saved her as Abigail Leonard had been sure they would do.

Prominent Mormon Women, c. 1895; this group includes Bathsheba W. Smith, Zina D. H. Young, M. Isabella Horne, Annie Taylor Hyde, and others. #P2743, courtesy of LDS Archives.

Brigham Young encouraged the practice of female administration, admonishing mothers to bless their children. In 1844, at April Conference, he told the women so:

I want a wife that can take care of my children when I am away, who can pray, lay on hands, anoint with oil, and baffle the enemy; and this is a spiritual wife.[37]

In 1869 he addressed the women of the Church in the Salt Lake Tabernacle in a similar fashion:

It is a privilege of a mother to have faith and to administer to her child; this she can do herself, as well as sending for the Elders to have the benefit of their faith.[38]

Female blessings were common in Salt Lake. Elmina A. Shepard Taylor came to Salt Lake in 1859 and was soon made a leader in both the Relief Society and the Young Ladies' MIA. Her journal described frequent trips about Utah visiting conferences and organizing new groups. She recorded in February of 1879 after a Sunday of meetings, "Spent Monday morn in pleasant discussions and in administering to the sick." In December at the close of the afternoon of annual conference, she reported that "Being quite debilitated and sick from the effect of my heart, Sisters Eliza, Horne, Margaret Young and B. Smith laid their hands on my head and Sister Snow blessed me and rebuked the disease and I was much improved from that very time."[39]

On another occasion the next year Sister Snow administered to her, and she received a "most excellent blessing through the gift of tongues."[40] Administrations were frequently sandwiched between everyday concerns in these accounts, indicating a down-to-earth approach to gifts.

Occasionally washings and anointings took place. Sister Taylor reported that

By invitation [I] accompanied Sister Horne up to Sister Clara M. Cannon's and there met Sister Percinda Kimball, to wash and annoint Sister Hardy who lies very low with consumption. It was the first time I ever saw the ordinance administered and I felt blessed in being thus privileged. The spirit of the Lord was there.[41]

Washings and anointings were probably rarely performed if Sister Taylor, a close associate of important female Church leaders for twenty years, had not seen them before. These blessings were more than prayers for health, but differed from the temple ordinances of washing and anointing. The sisters had been instructed not to use words learned in the temple and to speak in faith in the name of Jesus Christ rather than in the name of the priesthood.

The Relief Society asked the First Presidency for guidelines on female administration. The reply they received in 1888 empowered women to administer to sick women and children. The letter quoted Joseph's early talk. In answer to the question "Have the sisters a right to seal the washing and anointing, using no authority, but doing it in the name of Jesus Christ, or should men holding the priesthood be called in?" the sisters were told they did have the privilege. "Therefore it is not necessary to call in the Brethren. The Lord has heard and answered the prayers of the sisters in these ministrations many times." This letter was circulated from 1888 to 1910. During that time women freely blessed the sick.

In 1914 the First Presidency with Joseph F. Smith as president issued a new circular letter. Most information was repeated, but in answer to the question about calling in the brethren, the letter went on to say, "It should, however, always be remembered that the command of the Lord is to call in the elders to administer to the sick, and when they can be called in, they should be asked to anoint the sick or seal the anointing." This counsel superseded the first letter and describes the situation we know today.[42]

In 1907 Joseph F. Smith had said that women might lay hands on the sick along with priesthood holders with perfect propriety. "It is no uncommon thing for a man and wife unitedly to administer to their children."[43] A considerable change of policy and tone can be noted between the above quotation and the following one from a letter Joseph Fielding Smith sent the Relief Society in 1946:

While the authorities of the Church have ruled that it is permissible, under certain conditions and with the approval of the priesthood, for sisters to wash and anoint other sisters, yet they feel that it is far better for us to follow the plan the Lord has given us and send for the Elders of the Church to come and administer to the sick and afflicted.[44]

The subject of female administrations was briefly discussed in the 1972-73 Melchizedek Priesthood manual. Joseph Smith was quoted as having said there was no harm in the practice.[45] No statements more recent than Joseph Fielding Smith's 1946 pronouncement have been found.

Though scholarly interest in spiritual experiences is increasing,[46] the subject is seldom discussed in Church meetings. The practice of administration by women has certainly declined. Few women in the Church would even consider blessing their own children today, let alone their friends before childbirth. Yet this was an honorable and accepted practice until close to our own time. Perhaps it is one that Church leaders and members might consider reviving in times of stress. As long as the prayer is given in the spirit of invocation, in the name of Christ, in faith, there can be no objection. Anxious mothers might reach the source of comfort and healing.

A consideration of spiritual experiences tells us something about nineteenth century Mormon women. Supernatural incidents happened to them. To explain away these experiences only locks contemporary readers out of their lives and into our own more rational period. Mormons of that generation saw the hand of God in their lives.

The prevailing mentality encouraged such experiences. The women were told spiritual gifts would be theirs, and they awaited them with anticipation. Leading women like Eliza R. Snow experienced all sorts of divine manifestations and publicized them well. Those who cultivated their spiritual gifts were honored. The incentives for faithful receptivity were great.

Women were full partakers of the spirit from the beginning. Spiritual gifts were not reserved to men. In fact women were more receptive than males. Women were full practitioners from the beginning. Before 1842, women were blessing each other and their sick children and continued to do so well into the present century, with the sanction of several succeeding prophets. Not until 1914 were the sisters officially discouraged from following their traditional role.

Today's Mormon woman can benefit from a study of her sister of the past. Frequently alone during difficult times, she learned to rely on herself and the Lord. She lightened her heavy cares by constant appeal to her Savior and prayed with such fervor she could pull down power from heaven.

Notes

1. Edward W. Tullidge, *The Women of Mormondom* (New York: n.p., 1877), pp. 451–52. Carol Lynn Pearson, *Daughters of Light* (Provo, Utah: Trilogy Arts, 1973) is a collection of Mormon women's spiritual experiences.

2. Fanny Stenhouse, *Tell It All* (Hartford: A. D. Worthington & Co., 1874), p. 54. Compare to Joseph Smith and others, The Doctrine and Covenants (Salt Lake City: The Church of Jesus Christ of Latter-day Saints, 1876), 84:65–73.

3. Lucy Smith, *Biographical Sketches of Joseph Smith the Prophet, and his Progenitors for Many Generations* (New York: Arno Press, 1969), throughout.

4. Doctrine and Covenants, 24:13.
5. Aurelia Rogers, *Life Sketches of Orson Spencer and Others* (Salt Lake City: G. Q. Cannon and Sons, 1898), p. 170.
6. Tullidge, pp. 128–30.
7. Hannah Cornaby, *Autobiography and Poems* (Salt Lake City: J. C. Graham & Co., 1881), p. 40.
8. Rogers, p. 332.
9. Tullidge, p. 473.
10. Ibid., p. 207.
11. Cornaby, pp. 10–11.
12. Christopher Merkley, *Biography of Christopher Merkley Written by Himself* (Salt Lake City: J. H. Parry & Co., 1887), pp. 12–13.
13. Tullidge, pp. 160–63.
14. Ibid., pp. 475–77.
15. *Woman's Exponent*, 12 (1 June 1883), 2. Presendia is spelled in a variety of ways.
16. Tullidge, pp. 208–9.
17. Personal communication, 11 April 1973, with the author's father.
18. Joseph Smith, *History of the Church of Jesus Christ of Latter-day Saints*, ed. B. H. Roberts, 7 vols., (Salt Lake City: Deseret News, 1949), 4:607.
19. Franklin D. Richards, *Narrative of Franklin Dewey Richards* (San Francisco: n.p., 1880), p. 15, Bancroft Library, Berkeley, Calif.
20. Tullidge, pp. 94–95.
21. Maria Ward, *Female Life Among the Mormons, A Narrative of Many Years Personal Experience, by the Wife of a Mormon Elder* (London: G. Routledge & Co., 1855), p. 12.
22. Stenhouse, p. 51.
23. Tullidge, pp. 56–58.

24. John Whitmer, *The Book of John Whitmer*, Library-Archives of the Historical Department of The Church of Jesus Christ of Latter-day Saints, hereinafter cited as LDS Church Archives.
25. Doctrine and Covenants, 43:3–4.
26. "M.S.C." in the *Painesville* (Ohio) *Telegraph*, 15 February 1831, p. 1, quoted in Marvin Hill, "The Role of Christian Primitivism in the Origin and Development of the Mormon Kingdom, 1830-1844," (unpublished Ph.D. dissertation, University of Chicago, 1968), p. 124.
27. Parley P. Pratt, *Autobiography*, quoted in *History of the Church*, 1:170 n.
28. Verses 23, 31–32.
29. George A. Smith, talk in Ogden Tabernacle, 1864, quoted in Brigham Young, *Journal of Discourses*, 26 vols., (Salt Lake City: Church of Jesus Christ of Latter-day Saints, 1967), 2:7. The date of the trial was 17 February 1834.
30. Stenhouse, p. 69. Another example is found in Emily Dow Partridge Young diary, 23 June 1874, Harold B. Lee Library, Brigham Young University:

    I was invited to tea to Sister Stain's. There I met several friends. In the evening several spoke in tongues. Sister E. Snow insisted on my speaking in tongues so I complied, but I am not in favor making much use of that gift. I would rather hear speaking in our own language. I think it the safest. The devil is apt to poke his nose in where there is tongues, especially among the inexperienced. And I do hope the sisters will be wise and not suffer themselves to get into a muddle, but seek those gifts that are most profitable to all. When we speak in our own tongue we know what we say, and if we speak in other tongues we have to depend on some one else to tell us what we say, yet the gift of tongues is one of the gifts of the gospel, but should not be trifled with.

31. Blessing given to Eda Rogers by Joseph Smith, Sr., quoted in Pearson, p. 65.

32. *History of the Church*, 4:602.
33. Ibid., 4:603.
34. Ibid., 4:604.
35. Female administration may not have been widely publicized. Betsy Jane Tenney Loose Simons was left a widow in Quincy, Illinois, after the Saints departed for the west. Her Church connection was limited to weekly meetings with nine other sisters. With no one to preside, they prayed and read the *Deseret News*. In 1858, when a son developed complications after the measles, she "longed for an Elder or someone holding the Priesthood, that the disease might be rebuked." Despite several days of assiduous care and prayer the boy was dying. A kindly neighbor offered to sit with her through the death. If only an elder were available, she thought, her son might be administered to:

> All at once as distinct as though someone had spoken to me, [a voice said] "Why don't you administer to him yourself?" I was anxious for my lady friend to depart that I might administer as the spirit directed. In a few moments she left. . . . Alone I could unburden my heart and pour out my soul in earnest prayer to my Father in Heaven. Kneeling by the bed on which lay my dying child, I made a covenant with the Lord if he would heal my child, it should be an evidence to me that it was my duty to sell my home and come to the valley. . . . I administered to him alone and he was healed.

Sister Simons, though a member of the Church, did not know that women were blessing their own children. The idea came to her through revelation and provided a means of saving her loved son. Had she known the procedure she would have called in some of the sisters and laid on hands. Apparently, in the fifties, instructions were not being circulated through the Church. (Betsy Jane Tenney Loose Simons, brief biography, written 24 August 1881, copy in LDS Church Archives.)

36. Tullidge, p. 169.
37. *History of the Church*, 6:322.
38. *Journal of Discourses*, 13:155.
39. Elmina A. Shepard Taylor journal in LDS Church Archives.
40. Ibid., 4 October 1880.
41. Ibid., 1 December 1879.
42. James R. Clark, ed., *Messages of the First Presidency of The Church of Jesus Christ of Latter-day Saints*, 5 vols., (Salt Lake City: Bookcraft, Inc., 1965), 4:314–17.
43. *Improvement Era*, 10 (February 1907), 308.
44. *Messages*, 4:314.
45. Joseph Fielding Smith, *Selections from Answers to Gospel Questions* (Salt Lake City: Church of Jesus Christ of Latter-day Saints, 1972), pp. 199–200.
46. Thomas G. Alexander, "Wilford Woodruff and the changing nature of Mormon Religious Experience," *Church History*, 45 (March 1976), 1–14. Alexander argues that Woodruff's strongest apocalyptical spiritual experiences clustered around the issues and periods of greatest stress—the Nauvoo period and the polygamy crisis that ended in the Manifesto. In general Woodruff's spiritual manifestations declined in fervor and frequency as he grew older.

Eliza Roxcy Snow. Negative #20021, used by permission, Utah State
Historical Society; all rights reserved.

Eliza R. Snow
Maureen Ursenbach Beecher

There was nothing unusual in a young lady writing to her mature aunt and pouring out all the hopes and hesitations, the challenges and the frustrations of her twenty-two year old heart. But when the young lady was Louisa Lula Greene and the sixty-seven year old great aunt was Eliza Roxcy Snow, the correspondence was likely to produce something more significant than usual. Their letters were full of woman talk—that might be expected. Louisa had contemplated a marriage and, with some doubts, had rejected it for the present. She confessed her decision to the older lady, apparently expecting some rebuff. After all, this was 1871, the kingdom of the Saints was growing, and the faithful were fulfilling the injunction to multiply and replenish the earth.

The anticipated rebuff was not forthcoming: "My dear Niece," responded the wise aunt, "I am just as well satisfied with your present position as I would have been with the contemplated one. There is a great deal to be done, and if we are disposed we can do good in whatever position we may be placed." She should wait awhile, being careful not to cultivate feelings which would oppose both duty and interest. "To be sure," she went on, "while unmarried, one cannot be fulfilling the requisition of maternity, but let me ask: Is it not as important that those already born, should be cultivated and prepared for use in the Kingdom of God, as that others should be born?"[1] Then followed a series of suggestions which ultimately led Louisa to the founding of the *Woman's Exponent*. With one fly-by-night exception, it was the first magazine published by and for women west of the Mississippi.

Louisa later recounted the story. Edward L. Sloan, editor of the *Salt Lake Herald*, had published some poems which Louisa had written when she was a student in Salt Lake City. Impressed with the promise she showed, Sloan suggested that the *Herald* hire her, but his colleagues opposed the plan. Anxious to see her talents put to use, he wrote Miss Greene proposing that they start a woman's paper.

Louisa wrote again to her aunt. She sought the older woman's advice, as well as the sanction of the all-powerful prophet-president Brigham Young to whom Eliza had access. President Young asked Sister Snow about the girl's qualifications for such an undertaking, and was told "that what [she] might be lacking in education [she] could learn, and that [she] was staunch." Brigham Young appointed her to the mission and blessed her in it.[2]

That winter and into the spring the two women worked to raise subscriptions for the forthcoming magazine. The support of "Presidentess" Eliza R. Snow guaranteed the success of the initial campaign. Once the publication was underway, Louisa's literary sense and writing acumen maintained the subscribers' interest.

Louisa Lula Greene married the year following the founding of the *Exponent*. Children came and home responsibilities increased until they edged out a literary career, though not literary activities. She contributed to Church publications and worked in Church organizations while raising the four of her seven children who survived infancy. She died in 1944 at the age of ninety-five.

Of the wise and supportive aunt there is more to relate. The role she played in the founding of the *Woman's Exponent* had by 1872 become a familiar one to her; she was well practiced in recognizing a need, adopting a plan, organizing helpers, and taking action. There is hardly an auxiliary organization in the present Church which does not rest solidly on the base built for it by Eliza R. Snow. Childless herself, Eliza was midwife at the birth of most Church organizations. With her good mind and position close to the leaders, her influence was immense.

Emma Smith, the wife of the Prophet Joseph Smith, was the first president of the Relief Society. Nominally, Eliza's role in the early society was secondary, but in fact her voice came through loud and clear, even in those days when she was secretary to Emma Smith and her counselors.

Consider that first "official" meeting on 17 March 1842. Willard Richards took the minutes so often reprinted by the *Exponent* and later Relief Society publications.[3] President Joseph Smith instructed the women in parliamentary procedure, and then the brethren withdrew. The women nominated and elected Emma Smith as president. When the men re-entered, the group discussed the name the new society should carry. Joseph Smith: "'Benevolent' is a popular term." Emma Smith: "The popularity of the word 'Benevolent' is one great objection." She favored "Relief." Her husband rose to state that he had no [real] objection to the word "Relief." Eliza R. Snow rose to say that she "felt to concur with the President [Emma] in regard to the word Benevolent." Joseph Smith concluded that he would "have to concede the point." Notwithstanding their love for the Prophet and their obeissance to the priesthood he represented, the two women, successive presidents of the new society, established and maintained a spirit of "counseling together" which meshed their independent concerns with the interests of a priesthood-directed Church.

In the years which followed, Eliza, appointed president of all the Relief Societies by Brigham Young in the early days of the Church in Utah, maintained that balance

between initiative and obedience which seems a moot
point within the Church still. Her comments, made after
forty years' experience in directing a Church auxiliary, revealed this skillful maneuvering. She was writing to Sister Willmirth East, an Arizona Relief Society president,
who was having difficulties with her bishop while trying
to activate the Relief Society program. "Perhaps the bishop has not been properly informed relative to the [pro-
gram]," Eliza suggested. "If so, it would be well for you or
some other judicious sister or sisters to explain it to him."
With her characteristic understanding of human nature—
note her suggestion of "some other judicious sister" as an
alternative to Sister East, whom she obviously knew quite
well—Eliza then instructed the sister that she must "not
oppose his wishes. There is no virtue in breaking one law
to keep another. *We will do as we are directed by the Priesthood.*"[4] (Italics hers).

Eliza did as she was directed, although sometimes a
little resentfully, as suggested in such slightly sarcastic
observations as that the young men needed better instruction in manners: "I have suggested," she wrote,
"that the boys be organized but of course we Ladies cannot dictate."[5]

About the behavior of the young ladies, though, she
could do something. Clarissa, one of Brigham Young's
daughters, wrote warmly of "Aunt Eliza" and her influence on life in the Lion House where she lived as a wife of
the President. "No one at the house appealed to me more
greatly than Aunt Eliza R. Snow." But through her account of the attempts made jointly by her sometimes in-
dulgent father and the strictly moralistic, almost puritan-
ical Aunt Eliza at achieving "retrenchment" came a touch
of her sister's resentment. She told the episode of the silk
sashes—the grosgrain ribbons father Brigham had given
his older daughters. Phoebe had laid hers on the bed with
her best dress in anticipation of an evening dance. It disappeared and the girl cried to her father: "I know that

Aunt Eliza has taken it." "We'll see," he comforted her. Just then Eliza came by on her way to family prayers. "Phoebe has lost a sash. Have you seen anything of it?" he queried. "Yes, President Young," she replied. "I felt that you wouldn't approve of anything so frivolous for your girls so I put it away." "Sister Eliza," said the president, "I gave the girls those ribbons, and I am judge of what is right and wrong for my girls to wear. Phoebe is to have her sash."[6]

Peace and the sash were restored for that one occasion. But the crisis left its impact, and Eliza became first lieutenant carrying out the wishes of General Brigham Young in the subsequent creation of the "Young Ladies' Retrenchment Association," forerunner of the Mutual Improvement Association. Her plea to the women, reinforcing President Young's doctrine of simplicity and a frugal economy, was for "retrenchment" in behavior, in dress, in decoration, in entertaining, in anything where increasing extravagance was taxing the economy for fashionable "imported" goods rather than plainer "home industry" products. Traveling from ward to ward establishing junior and senior societies, she spread her "organization gospel" throughout the Church. To bishops, distressed over the behavior of some of the young men of the wards, and even to the young men themselves, she urged that a similar association be set up. She felt that "As sure as the sisters arise and take told of the work, the brethren will wake up, because they must be at the head!"[7] At one meeting, to which she invited the girls to bring their beaux, she warned the young men that if they did not "have off their drinking and tobacco, where were the young girls to get husbands?" Her message had impact: before morning the young men were after their bishop to organize them.[8]

That was in 1873. The year before, in London en route to Palestine on her grand tour, she had enlightened young Junius Wells, then a missionary, with her vision.

Quite possibly that meeting began the series of events which culminated, in 1875, in Brigham Young's calling young Wells to organize the first official YMMIA in Salt Lake City. What Eliza could not do first hand, she could accomplish indirectly.

The habit of authority is an easy one to maintain, exercising it as often as Eliza R. Snow did. From 1866, when Brigham Young gave her instructions to organize Female Relief Societies throughout the Church and instructed bishops to support her, through the period of the establishment of Retrenchment Societies in the wards, she learned to circumvent the snags with which bureaucracy can trip the meeker souls among us. She gave her own account of a chance conversation which established, in less than an hour, the basis on which the Primary was founded:

In August 1878, Mrs. Emmeline B. Wells and I, after attending a conference of the Young Ladies in Farmington, Davis Co., spent an hour, waiting for the train, with Mrs. Aurelia Rogers. During our conversation, Mrs. R. expressed a desire that something more could be effected for the cultivation and improvement of the children morally and spiritually than was being done through the influence of day and Sunday Schools. After consulting together a few moments, I asked Mrs. R. if she was willing to take the responsibility and labor on herself of presiding over the children of that settlement, provided the Bishop of the Ward sanctioned the movement. She replied in the affirmative. The train was near, and no time to consult the Bishop; but directly after arriving home, I wrote the Bishop, and by return Mail received from him a satisfactory response, in which he [Bishop Hess], not only gave his permission but hearty approval accompanied with his blessing. I then informed Mrs. Rogers that she might consider herself authorized to proceed, and organize in Farmington, which she did.[9]

On it goes, the story of organizing, directing, retrenching, improving—Relief Society, MIA, Primary. Only in one endeavor where she might have led was Eliza content to be a fellow traveler: women's rights and suffrage. This acknowledged "first lady" of Utah Territory lent her support rather than her leadership to Emmeline

B. Wells and Jane S. Richards in the feminist movement of the century. When they needed her eloquent oratory or her figurehead support, Eliza Snow was on hand. In 1878 she conducted the proceedings of the largest meeting of women ever assembled in Utah, held to protest against the interference of the Ladies' Anti-Polygamy Society. Eliza had been in Box Elder County on one of her organizing tours, and had, it seems, little to do with the setting up of the meeting. But, "called to the chair," the *Exponent* reported, "she responded eloquently, although she had not had a moment's leisure to prepare herself." Her defense of plural marriage—she proudly and consistently spoke of her own marriage to the Prophet Joseph Smith— was a strong and impassioned one: she proclaimed polygamy to be "necessary to the redemption of the human family from the low state of corruption into which it had sunken." She concluded, "I truly believe that a congress composed of polygamic men who are true to their wives, would confer a far higher honor upon a nation . . . than a congress of monogamic, unreliable husbands."[10]

Eliza R. Snow was a firm defender of righteous polygamy and a less ardent, though sincere, supporter of women's suffrage. She could never be an advocate of "women's rights" nor did she need to be. Her position was ideal: the fact of her sex never prevented Eliza from achieving anything which was important to her. On the contrary, the fact of her sex, multiplied by her determination, her ambition, and her drive, had placed her in a position more prominent than any but Brigham Young. In matters touching the women she stood closer to the Prophet than did any of his counselors. As Eliza saw it, she was not the only favored one in this Zion of the Saints. In an address to a mass meeting of over five thousand women just prior to the granting of the franchise to the Utah Territory women, she reminded her audience that they were privileged above their eastern sisters, including those who reviled the Mormon women as being stupid, degraded, heart-broken vassals. "I will now ask of this [present] assemblage of intelligent ladies," she went on, "do you know of any place on the face of the earth, where woman has more liberty, and where she enjoys such high and glorious privilege as she does here as a Latter-day Saint? No! The very idea of a woman here in a state of slavery is a burlesque on good common sense."[11]

Her response to the extremes proposed by some of the more ardent feminist activists in the East may be seen in this excerpt from an address which she wrote for a Twenty-fourth of July celebration in 1871:

How very different our position from that of our sisters in the world at large, and how widely different our feelings and prospects from that class known as "strong-minded," who are strenuously and unflinchingly advocating "woman's rights," and some of them at least proclaiming "woman's sovereignty" and vainly flattering themselves with the idea that with ingress to the ballot box and access to financial offices, they shall accomplish the elevation of woman-kind.

And she added, in verse, what to her was the essential key to the whole social order:

> And all their efforts to remove the curse
> Are only making matters worse and worse;
> They can as well unlock with a key,
> As change the tide of man's degen'racy.
> Without the Holy Priesthood—'tis at most
> Like reck'ning bills in absence of the host.[12]

"Not that we are opposed to woman suffrage," she adds. In theory she put women into restricted roles, under the protection of a benign priesthood. In fact, however, neither Eliza nor the women she influenced were inhibited by that priesthood which, supposedly protecting, sometimes threatened their autonomy. Take the Women's Commission House, for example. "The women can take hold and do all of the trading for these wards as well as to keep a big loafer to do it," she had said to President Young. "It is always disgusting to me to see a big fellow handing out calicoes and measuring ribbon. I would rather see the ladies do it. Let them do this business and let the men go to raising sheep, wheat, or cattle."[13] She had organized the store, which handled home manufactures in competition with other shops, including those "Babylonish establishments" which sold imported goods. In general the store fared well, with support from the women and cooperation from the local producers and manufacturers. But there came a time when Eliza got her dander up. Brother Haslem, an employee in Brigham Young's Deseret Mills, had disagreed with her over the contracted commission on fabric from the mill. In a letter stating her case to "Dear President Young" she complained of Haslem's mistreatment. "Although we are novices in the mercantile business," she remarked, "we are not green enough for that kind of management." Her complaint duly registered, and her business concluded, she closed the letter, womanlike, "With love," and signed it, business-like, "Eliza R. Snow."[14]

If Eliza once took her president-husband to task privately, he once publicly slapped her fingers. In December of 1873 the *Exponent* published a paper which Eliza had written attempting to reconcile natural recycling of body elements with literal resurrection, a question Orson Pratt had raised during Joseph Smith's time. Nothing was said, at least not openly. But two years later, because of the popularity of the piece, the *Exponent* reprinted it. The next issue of the paper carried a prominent declaration over his name. Referring to the article "by Miss E. R. Snow," he said, "I had hoped that after its first publication it would have slept and never been awakened; but the fact of its having been so repeatedly called for, places me under obligations to correct the minds of the Latter-day Saints." Then he hit Eliza on a tender point by quoting Joseph Smith, her first and ever loved Prophet, as having said in a similar situation, "It has just one fault and that one fault is, it is not true."

Louisa Lula Greene Richards, founder of the *Woman's Exponent* and editor for the first five years. #P1700/465, courtesy of LDS Archives.

Three weeks later the congregation at October Conference heard President Young's final word: a long discourse which he had written on the subject. The work was soon published, advertised widely, and distributed among the Saints. That was late fall. In the 5 April *Deseret Evening News*, almost six months later, a small note appeared in a lower corner of the page with the notices for the coming conference: "To whom it may concern." Eliza acknowledged her error in having published a work which the President "pronounced untrue," and recanted: "Permit me to say that I fully concur in the views expressed by Pres. Young."[15]

The public disclaimer could have been predicted. Whenever Eliza's personal preferences ran counter to priesthood authority, the latter held sway. It is tantalizing, though, to ponder plausible explanations for the delay between the publication and the retraction, and to project in imagination the hot discussions—or were they cold silences?—which might have passed between the pontificating president and this penitent heretic in the intervening months.

It is not difficult to study Eliza R. Snow as a public figure. Accomplishments such as hers are easy to recount: co-founder of Relief Society, MIA, Primary; for twenty years president—"presidentess" was a title she liked—of the Relief Society, and unchallenged "captain of Utah's woman-host"; organizer of ward auxiliaries, a territorial fair, medical education classes, a silk industry, a woman's commission store for marketing home manufacturers; and founder and director of a hospital.

All along the way she was a writer and a theologian. Joseph Smith had early dubbed her "Zion's poetess," and the title remained. Eliza published two volumes of her poems and seven other works, notable among them a biography of her brother Lorenzo and her collected *Correspondence of Palestine Tourists*, an epistolary recounting of her 1871-72 journey to Palestine.[16] She also wrote many occasional poems and orations for singers and speakers to present at festive celebrations. One can hardly find a Twenty-fourth of July program without at least a toast by Eliza, or a New Year's Day newspaper without her versified summary of the year just past.

Eliza's writing fails of greatness. "O My Father" is much sung, not for its literary merit but for its theological content. The Lorenzo Snow biography, while mainly reflecting two great lives, Eliza's and her apostle brother's, is moralistic, pedantic, and ill-proportioned. There is, however, a pleasing readability to her prose, moving as it does smoothly and correctly from point to point, its comparisons parallelled grammatically and its high spots elaborated with neatly turned phrases. As a literary corpus, her whole, sadly, is something less than the sum of her parts. But her literary attributes were those of the age, and her early publishings, under such pseudonyms as Narcissa, Pocahontas, and Tullia, quite matched those of her contemporaries. The published verse exchange between Miss E. R. Snow of the *Times and Seasons* and the Shawnee Bard of the *Wabash Courier* is fine enough poetry to the nineteenth century sentimental taste.

Only a few of the private writings of Eliza R. Snow are extant.[17] In them, and in some of the poetry, we find access to a soul which, with the proud restraint of her New England ancestors, would otherwise not have revealed itself. One journal, for example, began on 29 June 1842 with a strangely disjointed entry. "This is a day of much interest to my feelings," she wrote. The understatement was poignant: 29 June was the date of her marriage to Joseph Smith, a plural marriage unknown to other Mormons, so secret she could make only veiled allusions to it, even in her journal. The day's entry continued, its prose jerky and awkward, not the smooth flow of her usual style. Her deep faith conflicted with her dread of censure for participating in this new practice. Abstractly recounting recent decisions and unspecified blessings, she lurched unaccountably into a poetic expression of what must have been a real fear: "powers of darkness . . . stand array'd like an impregnable barrier against the work of God." Rain and hail worked in her outpouring not as comments on the weather, but as gloomy forebodings of human prejudices and hatred. The prose rose to poetry, and it is in the poetry that one may find the Eliza who loved and trusted and feared and had being within herself.

The diary recounted the visit with Emma Smith to plead for Joseph before the Governor and then told of his arrest, with Porter Rockwell, for the attempted assassination of Boggs of Missouri. A poem followed the prosaic account:

> O God, thou God that rules on high,
> Bow down thine ear to me:
> Listen, o listen to my cry—
> O hear my fervent plea.

Overtly she begged succor for the people's prophet and punishment to his foes; less conspicuously, though more earnestly, she asked that God comfort her earthly lord and husband.

Journal entries showed Eliza moving into the Smith residence at Emma Smith's invitation; Joseph went into hiding; strangers bearing a forged writ for his arrest searched the house; Sidney Rigdon showed signs of returning faith; Joseph returned home; the threats continued. Life was turbulent, events succeeded each other rapidly, but in the recounting came again a poem:

> O, how shall I compose a thought
> When nothing is compos'd?
> How form ideas as I ought
> On subjects not disclos'd?

And of course her subject could not be disclosed; "celestial marriage" was still a secret practice. *"This principle* [italics hers, a veiled reference to celestial marrage] will bear us up," she affirmed, though "tempests howl / In thunders, round our feet." The final quatrain suggested more broadly the real concern: the whispered gossipings hinting of the marriage practice so foreign to the American custom.

> What though tradition's haughty mood
>   Deals out corroding wrongs;
> And superstition's jealous brood
>   Stirs up the strife of tongues.

The next entry in the journal told of Joseph's flight into hiding again, leaving Emma sick in bed. Three days later, under date of 12 October 1842, was a copy of the poem-letter by which Eliza assured Joseph of Emma's improvement and her own faith, "For the God of our forefathers, smiles on us here."

Another poem, this time of the "bliss of conscious innocence" which triumphed over the malevolence of "vile reproach" of friends withdrawing their love. I think it not an error to read into the sentiment that hurt occasioned by whispered criticism of her liaison with the Prophet. The poem was written between 9 October and 30 November 1842.

And so she wrote, her prose telling the story, her poetry revealing the soul. In those lines she recorded the inner reality which formed the outer woman.

The dated entries in the journal ended with 14 April 1844; there was no entry for 27 June 1844. The martyrdom which she could mourn in poetic outpouring she did not recount in prose.

But how does one merge them, the prose and the poetry, the sensitive poetess and the dynamic presidentess? There was no fusion; Eliza kept with her always a part of her mind into which she retired, a room of her own in which poetry expressed what experience could not explain, a place of retirement "when there's nobody here but Eliza and I."

Less and less frequently as her administrative responsibilities grew did she find time for her retirement into that private space; perhaps she needed it less. The rare confessional quality of her poems almost vanished as her literary skills were demanded for more pragmatic purposes—defending the Saints, the kingdom, polygamy; encouraging the women; celebrating the liberty of the valley settlements. Her journal-keeping ended early, but there came even to the last some one or two glimpses of the interior woman.

Eliza R. Snow died in her room in the Lion House on 5 December 1887 at the age of eighty-three. For her funeral the Assembly Hall was draped in white; right, somehow, for the leavetaking of one who deemed the world to which she would go to be the pure spirituality she sometimes sensed in the world she must leave. One of her finest lines applied: "Bury me quietly when I die." But the one which remained is the "Epitaph" which keeps her with us: "I would not be forgotten, quite."

Notes

1. Eliza R. Snow to Louisa Lula Greene, 23 April 1871, Eliza R. Snow papers, LDS Church Archives.
2. Louisa Lula Greene Richards to Zina S. Whitney, 20 January 1893, Louisa Lula Greene papers, LDS Church Archives. The history is more fully explained in Leonard J. Arrington, "Louisa Lula Greene Richards: Woman Journalist of the Early West," *Improvement Era*, 72 (May 1969), 28–31.
3. "The Story of the Relief Society," *Relief Society Magazine*, 6 (March 1919), 134–35.
4. Eliza R. Snow to [Willmirth] East, 23 April 1883, Eliza R. Snow papers, LDS Church Archives.
5. First Ward, Park Stake, Relief Society minutes 1870-1893, 5 September 1872, LDS Church Archives.

6. Clarissa Young Spencer, *One Who Was Valiant* (Caldwell, Idaho: Caxton Printers, Ltd., 1940), p. 76.

7. Ibid., pp. 78–79.

8. Senior and Junior Cooperative Retrenchment Association minutes, 15 August, 13 September 1873; 1 May 1874, LDS Church Archives.

9. Eliza R. Snow, "Sketch of My Life," in *Eliza R. Snow, An Immortal: Selected Writings of Eliza R. Snow* (Salt Lake City, Utah: Nicholas G. Morgan, Sr., Foundation, 1957), pp. 40–41.

10. E[mmeline] B. W[ells], "Pen Sketch of an Illustrious Woman," *Woman's Exponent*, 10 (15 September 1881), 57.

11. Wells, "Pen Sketch," *Exponent*, 9 (1 February 1881), 131.

12. *Deseret News*, 20 (26 July 1871), 287–88.

13. Spencer, p. 77.

14. Eliza R. Snow to Brigham Young, 10 February 1877, Brigham Young Collection, LDS Church Archives.

15. The first printing of the article is in *Woman's Exponent*, 2 (1 December 1873), 99, and the second in the same journal, 4 (1 September 1875), 54. This reprinting is followed in the next issue, 4 (15 September 1875), 60, by Brigham Young's reprimand and the publication of his pamphlet *The Resurrection* (Salt Lake City, Utah: Deseret News Steam Printing, n.d.). Eliza's retraction is from *Deseret News Weekly*, 25 (5 April 1876), 152.

16. Eliza R. Snow, *Poems, Religious, Historical, and Political*. Comp. by the author, 2 vols., (Salt Lake City, Utah: LDS Printing and Publishing Establishment, 1877); Eliza R. Snow Smith, *Biography and Family Record of Lorenzo Snow* (Salt Lake City, Utah: Deseret News Company, Printers, 1884); Eliza R. Snow, ed.,

Correspondence of Palestine Tourists (Salt Lake City, Utah: Deseret News Steam Printing Establishment, 1875).

17. The trail journals, 1846–49, the originals of which are in the Huntington Library, San Marino, California, were published serially as "Pioneer Diary of Eliza R. Snow," *Improvement Era*, 46–47 (March 1943-February 1944), and again in *Eliza R. Snow, An Immortal*. Parts have been deleted in both published versions. The Nauvoo journal is at present in the vault of the General President of the Relief Society, Salt Lake City, Utah.

Patty Sessions. Negative #13517, used by permission, Utah State
Historical Society; all rights reserved.

Pioneer Midwives
Chris Rigby Arrington

The satchel bumped against her leg as she walked, kicking up clouds of dust in the moonlight, along the deserted road. The dust settled on her shoe tops and on her hands and under her tongue. She quickened her pace and remembered again the confident pressure of his hands on her head and the sound of his voice in blessing. He had started with her name. "Sister Ann Carling . . . ."[1]

Hearing the muted cries before she rounded the corner, she saw the small house set back away from the road, and she remembered his promise. She entered the house and set her things next to the sink. From her satchel, she took, not the baby that children thought was hidden inside, but the familiar rags, a few bottles of herbs, and the assorted crude instruments that were sometimes needed during the birth of a baby.

As she prepared to work, she could hear the woman's wailing as though it were coming from somewhere far away. She washed her hands with lye soap and entered the bedroom. When the child seemed long in arriving and the mother began to tire, Ann looked down at her hands and prayed that the healing powers the Prophet Joseph had promised her were still there.

And then it was done. Another child was crying in another mother's arms, and one more night's rest was lost

forever. She looked outside and saw the darkness beginning to fade. Around the corner of the house came the father whose urgent midnight bellowings had aroused her.
He looked tired and proud as he lugged a sack of potatoes
down the road toward Ann's house in payment for her
services.

Women like Ann Carling, who struggled against the
high death toll exacted by the frontier, combined faith
healing and practical medicines, spiritual gifts and physical comforting in their ministrations.[2] Always there was
the duality of spiritual and educational influences in the
methods of the Mormon midwife. But while both forces
remained in play, there was a shift of emphasis over the
years from the spiritual gifts to the medical education.
Faith healing remained an essential tenet of Mormonism,
but as medical methods improved, the confidence of the
people rested increasingly on professional training.

Nineteenth century American medicine tended towards radical treatments such as bleeding, blistering with
hot rope coals, drenching with ice water to induce shaking, and administering cathartic drugs. In light of such
scientific horrors, the lack of confidence of Church leaders
in the usual medical practices was somewhat understandable. The full-time doctor, like the lawyer, was distrusted
because he did not earn his bread by the sweat of his
brow. Mormons were doubly suspicious of the medical
profession after a series of encounters with quacks and
unsympathetic gentile physicians and surgeons.[3]

Brigham Young made it clear that regular gentile doctors should not be consulted. People who visited these
doctors were said to be "drawing away from the simple
truths and principles of this part of our religion." One Salt
Lake stake president wrote, "I must testify to you that it is
and will be far better for our loved ones to die, and go un-
spotted to God, while we stand firmly by our principles,
than for them to be saved to us in this life, if it can be
done [only] by the skill of one not of our faith."[4]

Mormon medical practitioners were drawn to Thomsonianism, a gentler form of medicine usually condoned by the early Church leaders. Named for Dr. Samuel Thomson of New England, the Thomsonian doctors received their licenses to practice by buying a book—*New Guide to Health; or Botanic Family Physician*—and a twenty-dollar license, both of which were guaranteed to produce amazing results. Thomsonianism flourished in New York, Ohio, Missouri, and Illinois during the early years of the Church, and it was in the East that such influential Mormons as Willard Richards, apostle and second counselor to Brigham Young, first came into contact with these naturopathic medical practices. At the time of the Mormon migration to Utah, Thomsonian and botanic practitioners were also common on the frontier.[5]

The basic premise of the Thomsonians was that a cure for almost anything existed in nature—in herbs and other plants. The method was often reduced to the formula, "puke 'em, sweat 'em, and purge 'em."[6] Herb remedies relied upon in early Mormon communities often varied from one locality to the next. Herbs used in connection with childbirth and the treatment of young children included saffron tea, which was administered to the infant directly after birth to clear its skin. Ginger tea and castor oil were used to ease the pain of teething, and if the gums became inflamed they were cut with a sharp pen knife or rubbed with a silver spoon until the teeth broke through. Small children were given a cup of lamp oil to stop the croup. For diarrhea, a half teaspoonful of gunpowder was administered twice a day.[7]

More generalized Thomsonian remedies included the application of onion poultices on the chest to relieve pneumonia. Worms were cured with garlic. A common practice for both earache and toothache was the application of a poultice made from hops and whiskey. Even cancer was doctored: red oak bark was boiled to the thickness of molasses and mixed with sheep's tallow, spread on leaves of linwood and poulticed over the ulcer.[8]

Concoctions of sagebrush were probably the most common remedies. Used as a blood purifier and stimulant, sagebrush was also employed as a rinse for the ladies' hair since it was said to prevent grayness, cause rapid growth, and stop fallout. Sagebrush was also used for sores and sprains on animals and people.

As a climactic example of the Thomsonian or botanic creed, Claire Noall recorded the following story. A young boy was run over by a plowshare and had both of his legs ripped open. The farmer for whom he worked would not allow him to go home until thirteen days later. By the time he arrived home, his legs were both black from the toes to just above the knees. Catherine Davis Simmons, a reputable midwife, prepared a pot of boiling water into which she put the different parts of the sagebrush plant. The boy, who was in excruciating pain, was told to sit on a rock with his legs in the hot water. A number of days after the treatment his legs recovered their color, and he had no further problems with them.[9] But while miraculous cures were spoken of, Thomsonian methods were less helpful than harmless. They allowed the patient to recover his health without too much damage from medicine.

The medical practices of early Utah were governed by superstitions as well as published "knowledge." It was thought that tickling a baby would produce a stuttering child and that bright lights injured newborns who had just come from a dark place. Looking into a mirror before the age of one might result in difficult teething. A child would be prone to run away if her mother ate rabbit meat while she was nursing.[10]

One form of superstition involved folklore recipes. Zina D. H. Young, midwife and prominent leader in the Relief Society, had a favorite recipe to remedy caked breasts, strains, lame backs, and rheumatism. Four good-sized live toads were cooked in boiling water until soft. Then the toads were removed and the water boiled down to one-half pint. A pound of fresh butter was added to the

simmering liquid along with two ounces of tincture of ar-
nica. The result was an excellent toad ointment.[11]

In this paradoxical milieu of mystical beliefs, folklore,
natural remedies, and faith in divine intervention, the
Mormon midwife was the practicing physician. Her duties included not only birth-related activities, but every
conceivable form of medical treatment. In the isolated
Mormon settlements, the midwife was an obstetrician,
surgeon, dentist, and a homebrewed folk heroine. For her
important ministrations she charged a three-dollar fee, often paid in produce. When the family had no money to
pay, her services were free.

The maternity duties performed by a midwife extended beyond the actual birth of the child. Whenever
possible, the husband would fetch the midwife a few
days prior to the expected birth. She helped around the
house, and after delivering the baby, she would care for
the mother and child and manage the housekeeping for
ten days. People believed that a woman should be confined for nine days after birth in order for her organs to
realign themselves with her body. Folklore had it that the
mother was not to wash herself or be washed during this
period.

Although the majority of births was natural and un-
complicated, some cases required training beyond that of
the midwife. Deaths of children and mothers were not
uncommon. When difficulties developed in labor, the
cures sometimes increased the problems. If the baby was
long in coming, the midwife might drastically change the
position of the woman in order to force the child out. In
one instance a woman who had been in labor over twenty-four hours was draped across the back of a chair. The
pressure thus put on her was great, and the child was
born so fast that both of her pelvic bones were broken. On
another occasion Susannah Richards went to deliver a
baby but discovered that the child's arm was out at such
an angle that she could not possibly position the baby for

birth. She sent for another midwife, but the two still made no progress. As a last resort, they sent for a doctor, but by the time he arrived the mother and child were dead. He subsequently discovered that the child had broken through the uterine wall and was lying in the mother's abdominal cavity.[12] Midwives were simply not equipped to deal with complicated births.

The lack of the most rudimentary sanitary methods compounded the difficulties of delivery. Louella Washburn remembered, when one of her children started to come early, that she had not yet prepared for approaching winter. As her labor pains increased, she cleaned the house and dragged in an old stove from outside which she scrubbed and assembled. The child was born to a soot-covered mother just as the midwife arrived to find she hadn't time even to wash her hands. Fortunately, both mother and child survived.[13]

Considering these primitive conditions, the success of the midwives was remarkable. Reports of their successes became a matter of great pride and legend. Probably they have been exaggerated. Patty Sessions reportedly assisted in the birth of 3,977 babies with only two difficult cases.[14] Sister Hannah Sorenson from Denmark delivered four thousand babies without losing a child or mother.[15] Julina Smith delivered over 1,025 babies without losing a mother.[16] Mariah Huntsman Leavitt delivered five hundred children without losing a mother, although she admitted to some stillborn children.[17] Sarah Young Vance delivered 1,500 babies and never lost a child or mother.[18] These reports have seldom been checked against official census reports. In fact a midwife's written record was often relied upon for official purposes. If a midwife made her record look better than it was, her records were the ones that were believed. One bishop in St. George said that each month he would check the tithing record of Sister Anna Milne, the community midwife, to determine the number of births for that month.[19]

All midwives could not have been as successful as these reports indicated. Patients did die, and when they did, the midwife had the painful responsibility of acting as undertaker. The heat of Salt Lake Valley summers made it necessary to inter bodies as quickly as possible. The midwife would often be called upon to wash the body and prepare it for burial. Sometimes she sewed the burial clothes.

Because of the lack of doctors, midwives often found themselves assisting in medical cases that were far removed from childbirth. Elizabeth Ramsay, set apart by Brigham Young as a nurse, midwife, and doctor, moved with her family to St. Johns, Arizona. There her duties ranged from midwifery to autopsy. When the Mexicans and Indians in the area troubled the Mormons, she was often called upon to remove bullets. She and her son John carried the fatal cases into the back of the saloon where a quick autopsy was performed. Occasionally Elizabeth cut down bodies after lynchings to declare them dead of broken necks.[20]

Jane Johnston Black, also set apart by Brigham Young, delivered more than 3,000 babies. She was once called upon to amputate a man's leg with a butcher knife and a carpenter's saw. The man recovered.[21]

When the explosion of a powder can left one young girl with her face burned so badly that her skin hung in rags and blisters, Paulina Lyman, revered midwife of Parowan, Utah, applied a mask of linseed oil to the girl's face and covered the oil with varnish. When the mask was removed there were no scars at all.[22]

The reputation of Ann Carling reached such a point that even neighboring Indians called for her to nurse them in their illnesses. Hurrying to give aid, Ann would jump to the side of a wagon, ordering the driver to go as fast as the horses would gallop. Her career as a midwife ended when she fell from this perch at the age of ninety and broke her hip.[23]

Christine Kingborn Archibald was another midwife who did everything from pulling teeth to performing minor surgery. As she traveled to far away homes, she would often ask the driver to stop and purchase a bottle of liquor for use in the home as an antiseptic. "Of course," she said, "He'd take a wee drop to drown his sorrow, then we'd take a real fast ride."[24]

Dealing with life and death as they did, the midwives assumed heroic proportions in their communities. Their unusual feats were puffed into legends. In other societies the power of midwives was sometimes construed as threatening. Some midwives were feared for their evil power and some were called witches.

By contrast Mormon midwives were fortunate in belonging to a community that accepted death as the will of God and honored authority without question. The direction of Prophets Joseph Smith and Brigham Young in both earthly and heavenly matters was followed as a matter of course. When, in the customary Mormon manner, the Prophet called a woman to act as a medical agent, she and everyone else took that call seriously. Her connection with authority gave her status.

The link with religious power was even more important than medical training. A few of the early midwives had received medical training in foreign countries, but the majority had simply been called to the role by some religious leader.[25] The indispensable qualification, without which any medical education was considered incomplete, was priesthood sanction in the form of a blessing.[26]

Church leaders advised the midwives to rely on faith healing. The LDS ceremony of administering to the sick consists of laying hands on the head of the sick person, pouring a few drops of oil on the forehead, and saying a prayer in which the person is often promised recovery. Another prayer, a "sealing" of the anointing, is then usually pronounced. Church leaders continually urged the Saints to rely on these blessings before getting other medical help. In short, in the early days of the Church, a blessing was used by the Mormons as a universal remedy.

As has been seen, the rites of administration were eventually more specifically assigned to holders of the priesthood, but in the early years it was a common practice for women to anoint sick people. Of particular interest here was the "washing and anointing" of women by other women prior to childbirth. Zina D. H. Young lists numerous occasions in her journals when she was called upon to perform this service.[27]

Besides specific blessings, many midwives relied on the power of simple prayer. One sister from Denmark, who practiced midwifery over a period of thirty years, knelt and asked God that she might be successful in her work and return to her room content before leaving her home to attend someone.[28]

Mariah Huntsman Leavitt, a spiritually gifted midwife, called four men holding the Melchizedek Priesthood to kneel around the bed of a woman having a difficult time in childbirth. The men began to pray, but after a few moments she informed them that she could tell they were not in harmony with each other and ordered them to correct the problem. Two of the men who were brothers admitted that they had fought bitterly that day, and after apologizing to each other they began again to pray. The baby was born shortly thereafter.[29]

How all these factors merged in practice may be seen in the life and experiences of Patty Sessions, the matriarch of all Mormon midwives. Her life as revealed in her journals stands as a model of the early Mormon midwife. Patty delivered babies all the way across the plains. The first night after the Saints were expelled from Nauvoo, Patty tramped through the snow on the banks of the Mississippi River to "put Jackson Redden's [Redding] wife to bed."[30] The Redding infant was the first of several children born on the icy river bank. Patty's journal is thereafter filled with accounts of numerous deliveries, many taking place under terrible conditions.

During the summer of 1846 the births came one after another, and Patty was kept busy running up and down the wagon trains to deliver the children. Her work was so strenuous and demanding that by early August she took to her bed for nearly a month. She was told that her stomach was inflamed and that she would probably die. She made the arrangements for her death, clearly specifying how she wanted her coffin made. But when Brigham Young came to visit her, he told her she was needed on earth, and that the Saints would hold on to her until she stopped breathing and then fifteen minutes more after that. These words cheered her, and she began to recover. Soon she was up and about, working just as hard as before.

At Winter Quarters during the winter of 1846-47 there was a bumper crop of babies. On 7 November Patty delivered a woman of her twentieth child. On the eighth Patty put three women to bed within six and a half hours. In January of 1847, she was asked by President Heber C. Kimball to deliver the baby of a woman who was not married. Patty wrote in her journal, "I went to the Bishop to have a bedstead fixed up for her and to make her comfortable. Although I thought she was a bad woman, yet she was on the ground and about to be confined, and I pitied her."

Patty's birthday, 4 April 1847, was celebrated at Winter Quarters with a small party. Even on that day Patty was continually called to the bedsides of women in need of her services. Of her birthday Patty wrote:

My birthday, fifty-two years old. We had some wine and drank a toast to each other. . . . Eliza Snow came after me to go to a little party in the evening. I was glad to see her; told her it was my birthday and she must bless me. . . . I then went and put James Bullock's wife to bed, then to the party, had a good time singing and praying. I was called away to Sister Morse, then to Sister Whitney then back to Sister Morse; put her to bed at 2 o'clock.

Josephine Catherine Chatterly Wood, "Aunt Jody," an early Utah midwife. Negative #25323, used by permission, Utah State Historical Society; all rights reserved.

Two days later, the seventeenth anniversary of the Church, the Saints at Winter Quarters were told to load up and move out of the spring mud as fast as possible. They drove to the river and were ferried across. As the day ended, there was thunder and lightning. An anxious husband awakened Patty at six the next morning to request her to come and deliver the baby of a woman who had suffered a great deal that day. Patty clambered up on the man's horse behind him. Thick snow was falling. They pushed ahead through snow and mud that came almost up to the horse's belly. When they got to the little log cabin, Patty found that the baby had already arrived without help. The poor woman had ridden thirteen miles that day after labor had started. Then in the dark she had crossed the creek on a log. Both mother and child were fine.

When Patty finally arrived in the Salt Lake Valley, she had the privilege of delivering Harriet Page Young's son, the first Mormon child born there. For Patty the birth was a prophecy fulfilled. She had been promised five months earlier that she would deliver the first male child in the Valley. Patty kept very busy during the fall of 1848. A letter reported that "'Mother Sessions,' the stork's other name," had had a harvest of 248 "little cherubs" since living in the Valley. Many cases of twins were born, and in a row of seven houses joining each other, there were eight births in one week.[31]

When a deformed woman came due with her baby, Patty stayed all night with her while the doctor delivered the baby "with instruments." The baby survived, but the mother died shortly afterwards. Patty wrote, "Although I have practiced midwifery for 37 years and put thousands to bed, I never saw a woman die in that situation before."

Patty lived a long and productive life, still delivering children well into her seventies. Though she was a woman of action, her journal revealed her thoughtful piety:

Yet my trust is in God. He is my all, and in His Holy name I call for His spirit to direct me through my life and for wisdom in all things. O Lord . . . make the path of duty plain before me and give me grace to walk therein and give me patience to endure all that I may be called to pass through.

Patty Sessions was almost ninety-nine when she died on 14 December 1893.

While Mormons in frontier settlements were untouched by medical progress in the East, medical advancement did begin to quicken in the middle 1800s. The anesthetic effects of ether were first demonstrated in the United States by Crawford Long in 1846. The same year that the pioneers arrived in Utah, the American Medical Association was founded, and Simpson introduced chloroform. Pasteur and Koch developed a germ theory of disease during the same period. In 1865 Lister enunciated the principles of antiseptic surgery, and the Civil War sparked other significant advances in surgical technique and the treatment of wounds.

But while the dawn of scientific advancement was beginning to break in the East, Utahns still suffered from cholera, typhoid fever, yellow jaundice, and smallpox. Besides disease, violent injury took its toll.

The coming of the railroad in 1869 made communication with the East faster and began to break down Utah's isolation. Prejudice against outside doctors slowly faded in Utah as a transition period began in Mormon medicine. Primary dependence on faith healing gradually gave way to improved scientific methods:

Medical leadership moved from almost complete reliance upon the laying on of hands by Mormon elders for the healing of the sick to the calling upon trained medical doctors for professional advice. The transition was born of necessity rather than of choice. The encouragement and advice of Mormon leadership accelerated the transition.[32]

Though untrained midwives continued to ply their traditional trade, they were gradually supplanted. As Mormon leaders recognized the medical needs of the community, both men and women were educated to improve conditions.

Some organized efforts to improve medical care in the territory had been carried on since the early days. The first medical organization met in the valley in 1852. Spearheaded by Willard Richards, the Council of Health was set up partly in order "to learn females how to take care of themselves."[33] But it was based on priesthood leadership, and the council originally excluded women. This effort proved to be another example of the continuing medical dichotomy in the minds of Mormons. Although many sessions of the Richards group were devoted to the gathering and analysis of herbs, the meetings were punctuated with speaking in tongues, the recitation of prophetic dreams, and priesthood blessings to rebuke the power of illness.

By 1857 the influence of Thomsonianism in Utah had weakened. Some people recognized that more competent medical education could be obtained at reputable eastern schools. The next step was to persuade Brigham Young of that fact. President Young, a paragon of practicality, had opposed the extreme methods current among doctors, but he readily subscribed to any immediately useful medical practices. Brigham Young's distrust of the medical profession must be paired with another statement:

It appears consistent to me to apply every remedy that comes within the range of my knowledge, and to ask my Father in Heaven, in the name of Jesus Christ, to sanctify that application to the healing of my body; to another this may appear inconsistent. . . . But it is my duty to do when I have it in my power. Many people are unwilling to do one thing for themselves in case of sickness, but ask God to do it all.[34]

In 1872 President Young was more confident of the remedies medical schools could offer than he had been previously, and he called his nephew Seymour B. Young to study medicine at the College of Physicians and Surgeons in New York City. A year later President Young called the son of Willard Richards, Joseph S. Richards, to study medicine at Bellevue Hospital Medical College in New York City.[35]

As professionalism increased, the old-time midwives were gradually forced out of business by trained male doctors. Only gradually did women gain access to the regular medical profession. Some few women obtained medical degrees at sectarian schools in the 1850s and 1860s, but not until about 1870 did medical coeducation start to become respectable. As early as January 1868 President Young encouraged Mormon women to school themselves in midwifery. His general epistle for that period specifies that ladies should be trained in anatomy, surgery, chemistry, physiology, the preservation of health, the properties of medicinal plants and midwifery.[36] Several midwifery classes and general physiology courses were launched in Utah and some proved fairly successful.[37]

At a meeting of the Cooperative or General Retrenchment Association in July 1873, Bathsheba W. Smith remarked that President Young "had suggested to her that three women from each ward in the city be chosen to form a class for studying obstetrics."[38] Recognizing the difficulty in getting the sisters to undertake the study, Relief Society leaders made the suggestion a requirement. And they went a step further. Eliza R. Snow insisted that if women were to be considered equal with men in the medical profession, they would have to be trained at the same schools and armed with the same degrees: "We want sister physicians that can officiate in any capacity that the gentlemen are called upon to officiate and unless they educate themselves the gentlemen that are flocking in our midst will do it."[39] Mormon women felt it degrading and unseemly for a man to attend a woman in childbirth or to treat any female disorders. It was evident that women would have to be educated to provide proper medical care for their sisters. Brigham Young, persuaded of that fact, announced in 1873:

If some women had the privilege of studying they would make as good mathematicians as any man. We believe that women are useful not only to sweep houses, wash dishes, and raise babies, but that they should study law . . . or physic. . . . The time has come for women to come forth as doctors in these valleys of the mountains.[40]

The problem had been recognized and the work of educating women in the scientific art of midwifery and general medicine could begin.

The women's reaction to President Young's statement was not as enthusiastic as he had hoped. A handful of courageous women responded to the call, and President Young set them apart to go east to medical schools. Among those set apart were Ellis Shipp, Margaret Shipp, and Romania Pratt, each of whom obtained a medical degree from a reputable eastern institution. The last quarter of the nineteenth century found Utah with a greater percentage of its women studying medicine than any other state or territory. Individual Relief Societies supplied the funds to educate some sisters while other women relied on their families to send them allowances.

When the first three women returned to Utah from medical school, the results were soon noticeable. All three set up successful midwifery classes to train women from every settlement in Mormon country. Partly because of their link with the East and partly because of loosening attitudes against contact with the good things of the outside world, Utah began to benefit from ordered medical advancement. Sanitary conditions were improved. The midwives trained by Drs. Ellis and Margaret Shipp and Dr. Romania Pratt were the best prepared of any in the state. In 1892 a law was passed that made it necessary for all new practitioners of the art, whether they were midwives or doctors, to pass an exam in order to acquire a medical license. Between 1893 and 1932 two hundred and eight women were licensed to be midwives for Utah. Midwives continued to practice in rural communities even after licensing stopped.[41]

Even as training improved for midwives, many unnecessary deaths continued to occur. Concerned Mormon women urged the establishment of a public hospital that would meet the special needs of Latter-day Saint patients. Utah's Episcopal Church had established St. Mark's Hospital early in 1872, and the Catholics of Utah were operating Holy Cross Hospital by 1875. Mormons were often patients in these hospitals, but Relief Society sisters were embarrassed by non-Mormon doctors and staff members who discouraged the Mormon practice of anointing the sick within their hospitals. Eliza R. Snow spoke out. She said that a hospital was needed and that "there are women in the stakes of Zion whose lives are being sacrificed to this need."[42] The Deseret Hospital opened on 17 July 1882 in the building formerly used for health care by nuns of Holy Cross Hospital. The Deseret Hospital served as a maternity home as well as a training place for midwives. Here again a scientific advancement was accomplished without losing the old Mormon flavor.

The hospital was built with donations, and the promise of free service was extended to those who could not pay. Anointings and washings were performed within the sterile, white walls of the hospital. One woman said, "We realize that the other hospitals are excellent institutions, but we want one where our own Elders can walk freely in and perform the ceremonies of the Church without having the eyes of the curious upon them."[43] In return for a training class at the hospital, women were required to give fifty days of free charity work. The Deseret Hospital was later forced to close down for lack of funds.

As women became more firmly established in Utah midwifery and medicine, the male doctors began to complain of "petticoat domination."[44] The women advertised in the *Woman's Exponent*:

Ellen B. Ferguson
Physician and Surgeon
Office and Residence on 2nd South
between 3rd and 4th East Streets.

> Special study has been given to Surgery, Diseases of Women,
>   and Diseases of the Nose, Throat, and Lungs
>   Can be called by telephone day or night.[45]

Small communities also used the advertising services of
the *Exponent*:

> Midwives
>
> A competent midwife is wanted to locate per-
> manently at Castle Dale, in Emery County. Spe-
> cial inducements offered. Correspondence so-
> licited.[46]

Training was necessary for medical advancement in
Utah, but human elements made it difficult to obtain that
training. Ellis Shipp, teacher of a successful midwifery
class in Salt Lake City, overcame personal obstacles in her
quest for a medical degree. Ellis was the plural wife of
Milford Bard Shipp and had four small children when she
was called to study medicine at the Women's Medical College in Philadelphia, which was attracting women from
all over the world. Although it pained Ellis to leave her
family, she had a strong desire to study medicine. She
supplemented her meager home allowance with part-time
work. One job was guarding the hall of cadavers at
night.[47]

Ellis had a joyful reunion with Bard when he came to
Philadelphia in March. But she was not feeling well, and
he persuaded her to come home for the summer. She was
worried that this interruption would forever end her
studies, but she missed her children and home. When she
arrived in Utah she discovered that she was pregnant.
When fall came, Bard and the other wives could not believe that she was really determined to go back to school.
But she returned to Philadelphia. Her fifth child was born
the day after her last exam. She had asked to be delivered
in the charity ward as she had no money, but the dean of
the college arranged for very nice quarters.

When she returned to Utah, Ellis offered a series of

classes in nursing and midwifery. President Young instructed each community to call two or three women who would be supported by the Relief Society to come to Salt Lake City and take these training classes. By this time other women, Romania Pratt and Margaret Shipp among them, had also received medical degrees and started classes both in Salt Lake City and in outlying regions. After completing one of these courses the students would go to a member of the priesthood for the blessing they considered essential.[48]

In addition to delivering thousands of babies (including President N. Eldon Tanner), Ellis Shipp trained five hundred women to serve as midwives and general medical agents. In many instances, these women then trained others, multiplying Dr. Shipp's efforts.

Ellis Shipp, and women like her, having obtained the finest training available, held firmly to their religious convictions. They continued to call in the elders to bless the sick. They continued to wash and anoint women prior to delivery. They continued to pray fervently before attending the sick. Whether they were practicing faith or perfecting the latest medical advancement, their purpose was to bring comfort and healing to those in need. They firmly believed that

the prayer of faith shall save the sick, and the Lord shall raise him up; and if he had committed sins, they shall be forgiven him. Confess your faults one to another, and pray one for another, that ye may be healed. The effectual fervent prayer of a righteous man availeth much.[49]

While the Saints maintained a strong reliance on the spiritual dimension of medicine, the frontier tradition of homespun midwives gave way to professional medicine and doctors like Ellis Shipp. With the coming of the Union Pacific iron horses and increased communication with the East, pioneer midwives like Patty Sessions gradually disappeared from the West. The current return to the training of midwives in contemporary medical practice makes it particularly appropriate to resurrect the miracles and memories of these pioneer women whose work is immortalized in the sprouting branches of groves of family trees. Many present-day Mormons owe their first gasps of mortality to the sure hands and quaint midnight courage of Zion's deliverers.

Notes

1. Kate B. Carter, comp., *Heart Throbs of the West*, 12 vols., (Salt Lake City, Utah: Daughters of the Utah Pioneers, 1930–50), 3:136.
2. Claire Noall, *Guardians of the Hearth* (Bountiful, Utah: Horizon Publishers, 1974), p. 15.
3. For a discussion of some of the tensions between Mormons and Gentile doctors, see Robert T. Divett, "Medicine and the Mormons," *Bulletin of the Medical Library Association*, 51 (January 1963), 4–8.
4. "Our Sunday Chapter," *Young Woman's Journal*, 2 (March 1891), 278–79.
5. Divett, pp. 2–5. Divett indicates that all of the following Mormons were Thomsonians: Frederick G. Williams, Levi and Willard Richards, Priddy Meeks, Calvin C. Pendleton, and Silas Higgins. Willard Richards not only had a Thomsonian diploma, but had entered the Thomsonian Infirmary in Boston and studied under Samuel Thomson himself. See J. Cecil Alter, "Addendas," *Utah Historical Quarterly*, 10 (January, April, July, October 1942), 47.
6. Phyllis J. Richardson, "Thomsonian Influences in Early Mormon Utah History," p. 5 (unpublished seminar paper on file in the LDS Church Archives). Mormons readily adopted Thomsonian remedies since they believed that herbs were to be used for nursing and healing the sick. The chemicals that homeopaths and allopaths used (calomel, arsenic, the bromides

and the opiates) were considered by Mormons to be "poisonous medicines, which God never ordained for the use of men." "Seventh General Epistle of the First Presidency," 18 April 1852, in James R. Clark, *Messages of the First Presidency*, 4 vols., (Salt Lake City, Utah: Bookcraft Inc., 1965), 2:98.

7. Carter, *Heart Throbs*, 7:195–216.

8. Ibid.

9. Claire Noall, "Superstitions, Customs, and Prescriptions of Mormon Midwives," *California Folklore Quarterly*, 3 (1944), 111–12.

10. Juanita Brooks, "Mariah Huntsman Leavitt," *Forms Upon the Frontier*, ed. Alta and Austin Fife and Henry H. Glassie (Logan, Utah: Utah State University Press, 1969), p. 120.

11. Zina D. H. Young journals 1880–92, 26 June 1892, in private possession of Mary Firmage, Provo, Utah.

12. Noall, *Guardians*, p. 49.

13. Kate B. Carter, comp., *Our Pioneer Heritage*, 17 vols., (Salt Lake City, Utah: Daughters of the Utah Pioneers, 1958–74), 6:540.

14. Ibid., 6:426.

15. Young journals, 6 March 1890.

16. Noall, *Guardians*, p. 86.

17. Brooks, p. 128.

18. Leonard J. Arrington, "Latter-day Saint Women on the Arizona Frontier," *New Era*, 4 (April 1974), 44.

19. Carter, *Our Pioneer Heritage*, 6:464.

20. Ibid., 6:437.

21. Ibid., 6:429.

22. Noall, *Guardians*, p. 62.

23. Carter, *Qur Pioneer Heritage*, 6:430.

24. Ibid., 6:455–56.

25. Carter, *Our Pioneer Heritage*, 6:438.

26. *Woman's Exponent*, 10 (15 August 1881), 44.

27. Young journals, 1880–92, throughout.

28. Ibid., 6 March 1890.

29. Brooks, pp. 125–26.

30. Patty Sessions journals 1846-66, 10 February 1846, LDS Church Archives. All information in this section on Patty's life is found in her journals unless otherwise noted.

31. Thomas Bullock to Levi Richards, 24 August 1848, LDS Church Archives.

32. Noall, *Guardians*, pp. 133–34.

33. *Deseret News* (Salt Lake City, Utah), 24 July 1852.

34. Brigham Young sermon, 17 August 1856, *Journal of Discourses*, 26 vols., (Salt Lake City: Church of Jesus Christ of Latter-day Saints, 1967), 4:24–25.

35. Divett, p. 9.

36. General Epistle, January-February 1868, p. 26, Brigham Young circular letters, LDS Church Archives.

37. A physiology class in the Fifteenth Ward under the direction of Sarah M. Kimball and taught by Mary E. Cook was well-supported and publicized. The class met on Tuesdays and Thursdays and appropriate books were ordered and used. The class lasted almost a year (1872-73). See *Woman's Exponent*, 2 (1 August 1872, 15 November 1872 and 15 March 1873), 37, 93, 157. A dearth of information on other physiology classes in the *Exponent* indicates that perhaps President Young's suggestion was not acted upon with great enthusiasm.

38. *Woman's Exponent*, 2 (1 August 1873), 35.

39. Salt Lake Stake, [General or Cooperative] Retrenchment Association minutes, 1871–75, 13 September 1873, LDS Church Archives.

40. Quoted in Noall, *Guardians*, p. 104. Noall attributes this statement to an October conference address, but neither *Journal of Discourses* nor the *Deseret News* contains an October 1873 conference address for President Young.

41. Quoted in Carter, *Our Pioneer Heritage*, 6:425.

42. Noall, *Guardians*, p. 155. See also Divett, pp. 9–10.

43. Ibid.

44. Ibid., p. 145.

45. *Woman's Exponent*, 12 (1 August 1883), 40.

46. Ibid., 10 (1 February 1882), 136.

47. Noall, *Guardians*, p. 122.

48. Ibid., p. 133.

49. James 5:5–16.

Students in a patriotic demonstration at Winter Quarters School in Carbon County. George Edward Anderson, photographer. #P1 10815, Photographic Archives, Harold B. Lee Library, Brigham Young University, Provo, Utah.

Zion's Schoolmarms

Jill C. Mulvay

School teaching was a natural occupation for Mormon women. Their commitment to education was great, and, in the absence of trained personnel, young girls and mothers took on the responsibility of running schools. They saw the teaching role as a holy calling, a surrogate motherhood, by which they helped individuals to progress. Though learning was hampered by primitive conditions, disruption, and lack of training in the early years, the general movement was always towards higher standards.

"Next to the worship of our God," proclaimed Sidney Rigdon in 1838, "we esteem the education of our children and of the rising generation."[1] For a people who believed they could not be saved in ignorance, education was of the utmost importance. As the Saints moved from place to place schooling was interrupted but never forgotten. Schools were established and left behind in Kirtland, Ohio; Far West, Missouri; and wherever the Saints located. When Rigdon gathered his family to Nauvoo in 1839, he immediately provided for their education. "As soon as possible," Wandle Mace wrote, "a room was prepared for school purposes, and by the request of Sidney Rigdon I went to Lima, and brought Miss Eliza R. Snow to Nauvoo to teach school."[2]

Eliza Snow, who had conducted a select or private school for girls in Kirtland, taught in Rigdon's family school in Nauvoo for a time, and later held other schools in the growing city. In the winter of 1842, she was "entirely governed by the wishes of Prest. and Mrs. Smith" in setting up a school in the Masonic Lodge room above Henry Miller's store. Extant records indicate that she had thirty-seven students and received about $30.00 for teaching a three-month term.[3]

School in Nauvoo was held wherever a suitable room could be found. In January 1843, Joseph and Hannah Holbrook moved into their new home and within a month she was teaching school in one of the rooms. She received $1.50 per scholar per quarter, which income her husband indicated "became much assistance to me."[4] Martha Jane Coray assisted her husband Howard in his teaching, first in a rented room built for use as a schoolhouse and later in the Music Hall, which accommodated some 150 scholars.

Single and widowed as well as married women could make a living teaching school because educating children was considered proper women's work. They made up almost half the teaching force in Nauvoo and early Utah. The school term often commenced and closed according to the teacher's wishes, and she could conveniently do her teaching along with her household and family work.

As the Saints were driven from Nauvoo in 1846, teachers left music halls and lodge rooms behind for wagon boxes, tents, and other makeshift classrooms. Several schools were started in Winter Quarters in the winter of 1846-47, and Emmeline B. Wells, then nineteen, taught in one of them. "Even in crossing the plains," one author suggested, "if the camp lingered a few days, primers were brought out, children were drilled in their ABC's, and other necessary subjects were taught to the older ones."[5]

Within three months of the pioneer company's arrival in the valley of the Great Salt Lake, the first school was being held at the Old Fort in a military tent resembling a wigwam. Nine young scholars sat on rough logs and their teacher, Mary Jane Dilworth, used an old camp stool for her desk. They learned psalms and sang songs, scrawled on smooth pine logs to practice their lessons, and raced through spelling matches from the old *Blue Back Speller*.[6] School was considered essential even in those busy early days.

Once the Saints were settled in the Salt Lake Valley, women were frequently called upon to use their ingenuity in setting up the pioneer schools. Hannah Holbrook taught her first Utah school in a mud and willow wickiup near the Jordan River. Early teachers in Millcreek used dugouts for classrooms. In St. George, Mariette Calkins taught in a wagon box and tent in her back yard. Students started school at one end of the wagon box and graduated when they progressed beyond the other end. The vagaries of life in the new valley interrupted lessons—crops had to be planted, homes had to be built—but education continued.

If teachers were like mothers, students sometimes moved right in like children. Women often used their own homes as schools. Ann Clark Martin lived in a two-room home in Scipio, Utah, where each morning the beds were taken down and moved aside so the school benches could be moved in for the day. Sister Martin sometimes baked her bread while the school was in session. In Beaver County, "Grandma Pratt's" young scholars worked at sewing and churning while singing appropriate songs. They even learned "to know by the sense of smell when the 'salt rising' in a tin can in a corner of the big fireplace was ready for mixing."[7]

Some teachers were ambitious to improve their methods and materials. Charilla Abbott, setting up the first school in Ogden in 1849, tried to help children learn to read by collecting printed letters from scraps of paper and old books and pasting them on paddles. Henrietta Wall, entering her school in Glenwood, Sevier County, found a shabby room with no blackboard and one grammar book for a class of eight. The children wrote on slates. Determined to teach them to use pen and paper, she showed them how to make their own ink from kinnikinnick bark. Such teachers wanted to manage their schools as they did their tidy homes. Church leaders were aware of the lack of suitable materials and in 1848 they admonished those making the westward trek to secure a copy of "every book, map, chart, or diagram that may contain interesting, useful, and attractive matter . . . from which, the rising generation can receive instruction."[8]

Despite ambitious teachers the quality of education was generally low. At best young pioneer scholars received a "tolerable education in the common branches."[9] Lucinda Lee Dalton explained that as she grew up in Beaver, Utah, and San Bernardino, California, in the 1850s her parents tried to give her every available opportunity for education, "hoping that afterward I would be able to teach my younger brothers and sisters. "But," she wrote:

the mixed and ill-regulated schools of new countries . . . are not capable, even when supplemented by diligence, of giving that thorough and methodical training which is the great object of school life. Scattered information is certainly better than none, but in my opinion, for the purposes of life, it compares with systematic training—much like a weak crutch with a strong leg . . . but such was the best then to be had.[10]

Young Lucinda took advantage of the best at hand; at the age of twelve, a "beloved tutor and friend" began training her as a teacher. But within a few months her father opened a private school and took Lucinda as his assistant. She was a pupil no more. At age sixteen she began to teach an infant school. Soon she was teaching older children, all the time keenly sensitive to the defects in her own education. "Many an evening," she admitted, "I faithfully fathomed the few pages in the Arithmetic which the first pupil would be likely to achieve during the following day."[11] Self-training was uphill business and the results evidently frustrating:

It is most humiliating to see boys and girls yet in their teens acquiring greater proficiency than all my tedious years of self-culture have enabled me to gain. But I am glad they are not limited to my meager opportunities, and I console myself for all that I lack, with the hope and determination that my children shall have a large part of that which I sought but never found.[12]

Lucinda Dalton was typical of the scores of earnest but poorly trained teachers. In hopes that Zion would increase in knowledge, light, and power, they taught the rising generation in weeks or months the few skills they learned through years of effort.

In early Utah two school systems grew up simultaneously. A free enterprise system allowed anyone feeling qualified to open a school and recruit pupils. The other system involved Latter-day Saint Church leaders, who were also concerned with the cultivation of Zion's children. Church leaders planned an educational system similar to the one they had hoped to set up in Nauvoo— an extensive system of schools headed by a university responsible for higher education as well as teacher training.

By late fall 1850, several Salt Lake City wards were constructing schoolhouses. Since the schoolhouse was often the first public building erected in a ward, it accommodated day school as well as Church meetings and social events. As wards focused their attention on the establishment of schools, the board of regents of the University of Deseret opened a "Parent School" for the purpose of qualifying teachers. But the parent school did not flourish and faded entirely after a year. Normal training in Utah was not revived for almost eighteen years.

In 1853 Church leaders divided each Utah county into districts with each district electing three trustees responsible for building, fueling, and superintending the schoolhouse. Since district boundaries corresponded closely to ward boundaries, these schools were often called "ward schools." County courts appointed boards of examiners capable of determining qualified teachers.

There was no standard examination set for teachers, and trustees and examiners felt free to choose instructors according to their own criteria.

Fifteen year old Mary Jane Mount Tanner was unsuccessful in her first attempt to qualify as a teacher in a ward schoolhouse. She applied for and was promised a consideration. After earnestly reviewing her arithmetic, geography, and grammar, she practiced her reading, writing, and spelling. The examiners who interviewed her talked about the importance of training the minds of the youth, then proceeded to investigate the knowledge of the two applicants, Mary Jane and an older person. "The situation was new to me," Mary Jane later wrote, "and I trembled with excitement but managed to write a tolerably good copy hand."

Reading came next. I had not brought a Reader and there was not one in the house. I wanted to get one but they said it was not necessary, some other book would do as well. I shall never forget my feeling as a volume of "Josephus" was brought forward, and opened at his Dissertations on Hades.[13]

The older applicant was given the position. Mary Jane concluded that her "youth and inexperience weighed against" her; nevertheless, a year later she was teaching in the Eighth Ward schoolhouse.

Ward or district schools varied in quality depending on the financial support and concern of ward members, the diligence of the trustees and examiners, and the qualifications of individual teachers. Martha Spence Heywood found some opposition as she set up the ward school in Salt Creek (Nephi), Utah. "Some of the brethren objected to the salary of five dollars a week for the teacher" and refused to pay their share.[14] Twenty dollars per month was less than the average teacher's salary at that time. The brethren at Salt Creek relented, but the problem was typical. Qualified instructors who could not earn needed income in ward schools often turned to other employment or opened their own private schools where they could set their own fees.

Trustees and examiners were responsible for hiring teachers and opening schools in the late fall. Some engaged teachers well in advance and others waited until all "prudent and discreet persons" were "bound to other business" for the season. Because ward schools were of uneven quality, many private academies, institutes and select schools continued to exist even when public education was available. Late in the fall of 1860, Brigham Young and Heber C. Kimball built schoolhouses for their families. At various times throughout the year the advertising columns of the *Deseret News* noted the openings of private schools, such as Martha T. Cannon's "select school for ladies" held in the west wing of the Fourteenth Ward schoolhouse in the fall of 1868. Some private schools were conducted in ward schoolhouses during spring and summer when ward schools were not in session. Mrs. Cannon's school provided older girls a chance to meet together apart from the medley of ages meeting as the "ward school" elsewhere in the building.[15]

Finding qualified teachers was difficult. In 1855 the *Deseret News* lamented, "In more than one instance have we known of persons being employed as teachers, who had no other qualification excepting that they were out of employ."[16] Local boards of examiners were to recommend only qualified teachers, but there were few qualified teachers from whom to choose. Before coming to the Valley, Elmina Shepard (Taylor) had received normal training in New York, and Emmeline B. Wells had been schooled in Massachusetts. But they were exceptions. The Lucinda Daltons and Mary Jane Tanners growing up in Utah had no opportunities for normal training. As professional standards were upgraded, the self-taught mother substitutes were in less demand.

It is no wonder that Louisa Lula Greene (Richards) was acutely conscious of her lack of training in educational method and material. In May 1867, shortly after Louisa's eighteenth birthday, she and her older sister opened their first school in Smithfield, Cache County, Utah. "I want to be a very good School teacher," she wrote at the close of her first day, "and do not know how. I feel that I am not competent as yet to do justice in this respect and so [I] am not satisfied with what I do."[17] Louisa could teach sums and the alphabet, but of classroom management and curriculum development she knew nothing. For a young girl with little sense of how time should be apportioned or how students should be drilled, teaching was a difficult chore.

Louisa's journal reflected the feelings of an involved and sensitive young teacher. "If my days were all to be spent as a happily as this has been I think I would be a school maam' all my life & and not be very anxious for the end to come," she decided one Monday. But on Friday Louisa found "My school is done for this week and I am not sorry for it. No!"[18] She was committed to teaching "the precious lambs," and could not help loving some of her scholars. But she had to cope with the fact that they were "full of fun and mischief, and so ungenerous, ungrateful and tantalizing," that "the better they are treated, the worse they act."[19]

The process of coping involved Louisa in a kind of growth she might not have experienced in a pedagogy course. With new awareness she asked herself: "Must I not bear with their failings even as I ask my Heavenly Father to bear with mine?" And there was the gratifying recognition of her own progress. "I wonder if I improve any in teaching," she puzzled at the end of her first month. "I have an idea that I do. [I] am satisfied the children learn some."[20]

Louisa's overriding concern, however, was with her own learning, and she longed to leave the ranks of the amateurs and become a professional teacher. "Oh if I was but competent to teach and control! Oh how I long for the education that would fit me to be a school teacher in Zion! But this blessing I may never know. Still, it is not impossible that it may be mine."[21]

While the teachers were bemoaning their inadequacy, the administration was planning an institution for further training. Robert L. Campbell, the superintendent of common schools, indicated in his 1868 annual territorial report that "the universal interrogatory by School Trustees from every part of the Territory . . . is: can you send us a qualified teacher?"[22] He urged the legislature to establish and maintain a normal school, and in March 1869 the University of Deseret, under the direction of President John R. Park, began a collegiate course and a normal course with studies in English, mathematics, commercial business, and natural science. Of the 223 pupils enrolled, 103 were women, and among them—Louisa Lula Greene. "Prof. Park commenced school to day," reads the 8 March 1869 entry in her journal, "and I started to go to his school; think I shall be very well satisfied with it."[23]

By 1870–71, the University of Deseret consisted of a collegiate department, a model school, and an academic department. Superintendent Campbell had proposed setting up a model school, after which the best common schools of the territory might be patterned. The academic department was actually a high school, since at the time there were no schools which adequately prepared students for college work.

Two sisters, professional educators, added significantly to the progress of education in Utah. Mary and Ida Cook were better trained than most Utah teachers. They were raised in Lafayette, New York, where their father was a prominent doctor. Both had graduated from New York normal schools, Mary from the State Normal School at Albany, and Ida from Oswego State Normal School. While teaching school in St. Louis, Missouri, the Cooks were converted to the Church. They arrived in Salt Lake City in the late sixties. Thirty-five year old Mary Elizabeth Cook was quiet and dependable and had experience in directing graded schools. Ida Ione Cook, barely twenty when she first came to the Valley, was particularly capable of working with advanced (teen-aged) scholars. Their advent marked the beginning of the professional teacher in Utah. As in all increasingly professionalized areas, the poorly trained amateurs began to retreat.

President John Park, committed to strengthening the growing University of Deseret, immediately took advantage of the talented pair. In 1870 Ida Cook was named a faculty member in the university's academic department and Mary Cook was designated principal of the primary department in connection with the model school. At the close of the 1870–71 school year, funds for the university were cut significantly and John Park was called on a mission. For two years the only functioning aspect of the university was the model school, which continued under the principalship of Mary Cook, and the advanced classes under Ida Cook. As "acting presidents" they kept the university alive until John Park returned.

The University of Deseret's emphasis on normal training lessened after 1872, and the university's model school at Social Hall became Mary Cook's private school. For six years no school year opened or closed without the press rendering "encomiums of praise and commendation" to "M. E. Cook's Graded School." It was divided into senior, junior and primary grades. Several assisting teachers were able to observe Mary Cook's methods in action. In 1876 Miss Cook held five weeks of summer school "to accommodate pupils from the country and others who are desirous of pursuing their studies without cessation."[24] At last the systematic schooling Lucinda Dalton had longed for was available somewhere in the territory. The *Woman's Exponent* commented that Mary Cook had "taken great pains and been untiring in her efforts to establish this system of school here."[25] That system proved effective according to some editorial praise in the *Salt Lake Herald*: "From her school the University of Deseret has probably secured as many scholars as from all others put together and satisfaction has been the result."[26] In the fall of 1878 Mary Cook moved to St. George in an effort to work out a system of graded schools there.

After leaving the University of Deseret, Ida Cook taught at the Social Hall in connection with her sister. One of her teen-aged scholars was Feramorz Young, son of President Brigham Young and candidate for the U. S. Naval Academy. His diary provides a brief account of some of his studies with "Miss Ida." Colborn's arithmetic, Cornell's geography, Greene's grammar, Quachenbo's composition, Anderson's U. S. history, and Wilson's speller are listed in Fera's diary as his course of study. Fera confessed to his diary that he had "nearly lost spirit in school it being very dull." Ida Cook impressed Feramorz as a thorough teacher, and when she was ill and her sister Mary took the class, he simply commented that "Miss Cook is not well enough acquainted to teach us as Miss Ida does."[27]

One contemporary called Ida Cook a "gifted original thinker" of "somewhat erratic temperament,"[28] and perhaps it was in a burst of brilliance that Ida moved to Logan in 1875. She proposed to set up a high school (still something of an anomaly in the territory), and was engaged to teach at $90.00 per month if the school succeeded and $80.00 per month if it did not. The lower salary was much higher than most male teachers were receiving, and signified the high regard held for the tall black-haired teacher whose piercing black eyes made her such an effective disciplinarian. It must have delighted twenty-five year old Ida, known for her "scorn of male dominance," to be a step ahead of most men on the pay scale. The high school did succeed; one hundred and fourteen pupils were enrolled in 1877, while most ward schools had from fifty to seventy-five students.

If the Cook sisters were out of place among other early teachers, it was because they represented a new attitude toward teaching. "Teaching today has become a profession," announced the bulletin of one of Utah's new normal schools.[29] A teachers' institute was organized at the Timpanogas Branch of the University of Deseret in Provo. In 1874, a normal school was established in St. George. In the new territorial Teachers' Association, teachers concerned themselves with instructional methods and graded schools, and they sponsored summer institutes for normal training. Mary Cook was one of the professionals called to head the first institute in 1873. Appropriately enough, Louisa Lula Greene, *Woman's Exponent* editor, ran an editorial praising the program: "When we reflect that Utah has had to use in the school room as teachers, many whose opportunities for acquiring a thorough education have been very limited indeed, we hail the inauguration of the Institute."[30] Significant changes had occurred in the six years since Louisa had opened her first little school in Smithfield.

As education itself became increasingly professional, the women who attempted to keep pace encountered considerable prejudice. Lucinda Dalton met it in Utah's country schools. "Well I remember my disgust," she wrote to Emmeline B. Wells, "when I asked a gentleman teacher if, in his opinion, I was sufficiently advanced in mathematics to study algebra with profit; and he replied that it would be a waste of time for me to ever study it, because I already had more learning than was necessary for a good housekeeper, wife, and mother, which was a woman's only proper place on earth."[31] Similar discrimination was common throughout the United States. Male teachers were usually paid more than twice as much as female teachers.[32]

Women were accepted as teachers and principals, but it would be years before a woman's professional future in education extended further. Mary Cook had been praised as a "woman eminently qualified in all respects," and in 1874 the People's Party slated her for Salt Lake County superintendent of common schools. But there was one respect in which she was not qualified: she was not a male.

Spurred by the inquiry of "A Citizen" as to whether or not Mary Cook was eligible for the office, the *Salt Lake Herald* made an unofficial examination of the current statutes and concluded that "males only are eligible to offices in this Territory. . . . If Miss Cook were elected the courts would be compelled to decide she could not exercise the functions of the office."[33] Her name was withdrawn from the ticket.

Three years later in August 1877, the *Woman's Exponent* celebrated "A Woman's Victory—Miss Ida Cook has been elected Superintendent of District Schools for Cache County."[34] She conducted a successful month-long normal training session for Cache Valley teachers before schools opened that fall. All seemed to go well, but when attention was drawn to the statutes which rendered her ineligible for a territorial office, she was forbidden to continue in the capacity of superintendent.

Meeting in 1880 to elect the trustees for their schools, twenty ladies in Beaver County wished to elect two ladies as trustees, but the brethren opposed and defeated their idea because there was "no law for it."[35] Shortly thereafter, seventeen women petitioned the legislature to remove the political disabilities of the women of Utah and to grant them the right to hold public office. The legislature responded, but the non-Mormon governor refused to sign the bill into law.

The doors were apparently barred, but a few windows opened. In connection with his concept of a cooperative economy, Brigham Young encouraged women to pursue whatever occupations they could learn. And he gave them some propitious opportunities in education. In 1875 he endowed the Brigham Young Academy at Provo. Martha Jane Coray was called to serve on the board of directors and the executive committee. Ida Cook was named one of three trustees for the Brigham Young College at Logan. The school opened in the fall of 1878 and Ida Cook served as principal for the first six years. These early academies operated on primary and secondary levels, not at

college level. Even so, the women who served as trustees
and faculty of these institutions set a precedent of prestige
for women in education and assured new opportunities
for women such as Maude May Babcock and Susa Young
Gates, who later served on university faculties.

Windows opened in the common or public schools as
well. The statutes regarding county superintendents were
changed in 1890 so that registered voters, not just males,
qualified. In 1892 Ida Cook became principal of the Logan
schools and when the offices of principal and superintendent were combined, she was elected superintendent of
the city schools with a salary of $1,500.00 per year—a
higher salary than any Logan teacher received.[36]

To say that Mormons supported education is not to
say that the children enjoyed it or were cooperative. A
teacher's day-long proximity to a score of students could
be, in the words of Elmina Shepard, "a most interesting
study."[37] Or, as young Louisa Lula Greene complained
one Friday evening, "Five days shut up in the house with
a lot of little children that cannot keep quiet is enough to
weary the stoutest heart I think and make any one thankful to be released in a couple of days."[38]

Mary Jane Tanner wrote glowingly of her teaching
days—in retrospect. "We were very merry. I loved [the
children] very much and they returned my kind feelings,
bringing flowers and trimming my hair until I must have
looked like a miniature flower garden. . . . I found it hard
to assume the dignity necessary to my calling."[39] Ida
Cook would have frowned upon such loss of dignity and
aplomb and the subsequent loss of authority which could
be fatal to a teacher. "First become, yourselves, what you
would have your pupils become," she advised those in
her normal school, "then you have reason to expect progress."[40] But one "Old Maid," complaining in the columns
of the *Woman's Exponent*, found it difficult to become anything but frustrated:

Here I am in the schoolroom with my spectacles awry, and a half-dozen little urchins pulling at my capstrings to attract my attention; and one of the little wretches actually had the audacity to plant a solid little foot exactly on my worst corn! Oh, but didn't I give him a good shaking! He was aware that he had a pair of ears for sometime afterwards.[41]

Even the most capable encountered occasional conflict. A student of Mary Cook's recalled "one day when she kept her whole arithmetic class in during the entire noon hour."[42] Age and experience were not always insurance against severe discipline problems.

Martha Jane Coray taught school in the Provo First Ward in 1875. She had earlier assisted her husband teaching school in Nauvoo and in Provo's first schoolhouse. One might expect a woman of fifty-five years, the mother of twelve, to preside regally over an ordered, obedient class. But her school was "horrid noisy." One Thursday the boys set off a blast in the classroom and Mrs. Coray determined that she didn't "intend to be imposed upon much more by such a set of geese." The next day all the boys ran off and she returned home sick. "School awful—outrageous girls," she noted the following week. She did receive "a note of apology from [the] girls committee," but the combination of problems caused her to seek out one of the school trustees.[43]

"The trustees decided that the teacher must enforce order according to her best judgement and pupils must abide the rules or leave the school," explained Mary Jane Tanner after a dispute with one of her pupils.[44] Sometimes it was a contest to see who would leave first, pupil or teacher. Sensing, perhaps, a losing battle, Elmina Shepard once reflected, "I have many trials, and unless I change my mind, I shall not teach another season."[45]

Elmina taught four subsequent seasons. Something in her teaching experience must have offset the trials. Perhaps it was the income granting a young girl some degree of independence. But teaching had other rewards. At least it kept a woman thinking. Lucinda Dalton studied to keep ahead of her pupils lest she have to acknowledge herself "vanquished by some industrious boy or girl." Though her study was far from the liberal education for which she longed, she conceded it "sharpened my wits" and "advanced my knowledge of the common branches."[46] Louisa Lula Greene, also anxious for a good education, determined, "I can learn some here attending to the little ones."[47]

Teaching provided the stimulation of interaction with people, even if they were small people. Elmina Shepard found it "an excellent opportunity for reading human nature."[48] And for a woman lonely in the wilds of southern Utah, it did something else. Martha Spence Heywood wrote that she found it "to be of much benefit to me as the activity of the operation and its responsibility prevented lonesomeness that otherwise would have been disagreeable."[49]

Practically forced into teaching in the early days by a need to earn a living and a dedication to universal education, Mormon women found rich rewards. Within the gospel framework teaching took on special significance. As a teacher, a Mormon woman could fulfill her traditional home role outside of the home, and without filling the requisite of maternity, she could still, in a sense, be a "mother in Israel." Keeping school was an extension of traditional huswifery for many women.

This idealistic goal warred with reality when untrained teachers found difficulties imparting their own scant knowledge to unwilling students. The conflict led teachers who had sought the job because of financial necessity or a desire to serve others to seek practical training to help them become better teachers. The move towards professionally oriented schools was a mixed blessing. School curricula and methodology were doubtless improved, but the vitality of the lay element was forced out as standards rose.

By the turn of the century, teaching was institutionalized. Some of the early schoolteachers kept pace with new educational systems and continued teaching in the growing number of grade schools and high schools. Many who had kept school during their teens and twenties steered their careers toward the less traditional professions then opening to women. Whatever other courses they pursued, the Mormon women who had once taught the three R's and the gospel in their homes and adobe ward schoolhouses maintained their commitment to cultivate the children of Zion. As public schools became increasingly secularized, these women fulfilled that commitment through teaching in the expanding Relief Societies, MIA's, Sunday Schools, and Primaries. Perhaps in that sense, the role of "schoolmarm" remains a part of every Mormon woman's heritage.

Notes

1. Sidney Rigdon, "Oration," 4 July 1838, Far West, Caldwell County, Missouri, as quoted in John Clifton Moffitt, *The History of Public Education in Utah* (n.p., 1946), p. 5.
2. Wandle Mace autobiography, p. 44, LDS Church Archives.
3. Eliza R. Snow journal 1842–44, 12 December 1842; "Schedule of common school kept by Eliza R. Snow." Nauvoo School Records, LDS Church Archives.
4. "The Life of Joseph Holbrook," p. 40, LDS Church Archives.
5. Susa Young Gates and Leah D. Widtsoe, *The Life Story of Brigham Young* (New York: Macmillan Company, 1931), p. 283.
6. Levi Edgar Young, "What the Mormon Pioneers Did for Education in Early-day Utah," *Young Woman's Journal*, 31 (July 1920), 358.

7. "The University of Utah and Other Schools of Early Days," Kate B. Carter, comp., *Heart Throbs of the West*, 12 vols., (Salt Lake City: Daughters of Utah Pioneers, 1939–51), 12:18.

8. General Epistle from the Council of the Twelve, *Latter-day Saints' Millennial Star*, 10 (15 March 1848), 85.

9. Mary Jane Mount Tanner autobiography, p. 46, LDS Church Archives.

10. Lucinda Lee Dalton to Emmeline B. Wells, 27 December 1876, p. 4, LDS Church Archives. Original at Bancroft Library, University of California, Berkeley, California.

11. Ibid., p. 6.

12. Ibid., p. 7.

13. Mary Jane Mount Tanner autobiography, pp. 54–55.

14. Martha Spence Heywood journal 1850–56, 12 July 1852, LDS Church Archives.

15. "Schools," *Deseret News* (Salt Lake City), 12 November 1853; "Select School for Ladies," ibid., 9 September 1868. The distinction between a ward school and a private school was based on who enlisted the students and collected the funds. If trustees did so, it was considered a ward school. If the teacher did so, it was considered a private school. Evidently some trustees relegated their school responsibilities to ambitious teachers, and schools functioning in their wards were private, though they may or may not have been open to all ward members and/or students from outside the ward. (See Moffitt, pp. 18–28.)

16. "Education," *Deseret News*, 26 December 1855.

17. Louisa Lula Greene journal, 8 April 1867 to 27 March 1869, 6 May 1867, LDS Church Archives.

18. Ibid., 27 and 31 May 1867.

19. Ibid., 7 May and 11 June 1867.

20. Ibid., 3 and 11 June 1867.

21. Ibid., 6 May and 21 June 1867.
22. Robert L. Campbell, *Annual Report of the Territorial Superintendent of Common Schools, for the Year 1868* (Salt Lake City: Deseret News Printing, n.d.), p. 4.
23. Louisa Lula Greene journal, 8 March 1869. The male-female ratio in Louisa's collegiate course approximates sex ratios in the public schools. Between 1862 and 1875 the number of male scholars (4–16 years old) enrolled in schools slightly exceeded the number of female scholars enrolled (9870 to 9408 in 1875), reflecting the preponderance of younger males in the territorial population (18,094 to 17,602 in 1875). (O. H. Riggs, *Biennial Report of the Territorial Superintendent of Common Schools, for the Years 1874–75* [Salt Lake City: Deseret News Printing, 1876], p. 20.)
24. "Home Affairs," *Woman's Exponent*, 1 July 1876.
25. Ibid., 1 September 1876.
26. "Closing Exercises," *Salt Lake Daily Herald*, 21 June 1878.
27. Feramorz Young journal, 2 January 1872 to 25 February 1872, 24 January and 2 February, LDS Church Archives. At the beginning of February, Fera boasts that he is "thoroughly established in the following lessons: Grammar—Punctuation and Analysis of Sentences; Geography—History of the Map & Physical Geog. of North America; Arithmetic—Fractions, Brockerages; History—U.S. General History Just Beginning; Reading—Extracts from National 5th Reader; Spelling—Extracts from Wilson's Speller." Entry for 1 February.
28. Untitled typescript dealing with Karl G. Maeser, John R. Park and Ida Ione Cook, p. 7, Susa Young Gates Collection, Box 17, Utah State Historical Society, Salt Lake City, Utah. Mrs. Gates also attributes to Ida Cook a "scorn of male dominance."

29. Announcement of Morgan College, Salt Lake City, Utah, for 1870, p. 9, as quoted in Ralph V. Chamberlin, *The University of Utah: A History* (Salt Lake City: University of Utah Press, 1960), p. 55.

30. "Territorial Normal Institute," *Woman's Exponent*, 15 July 1873.

31. Lucinda Lee Dalton to Emmeline B. Wells, 27 December 1876, p. 8.

32. In 1875, a tally of eighteen counties reporting to the territorial superintendent shows that 220 male teachers received salaries totaling $61,985.70, while 238 female teachers received salaries totaling $33,547.00. (Riggs, *Biennial Report 1874–75*, p. 21.) Moffitt indicates that male teachers in Utah, particularly in the secondary schools, have been given a distinct advantage in salary far into the twentieth century, even though a law was passed in 1896 assuring females "the same compensation as is allowed to male teachers, for like services, when holding the same grade of certificate." (Moffitt, *Public Education in Utah*, pp. 322–24.)

33. "Is a Woman Eligible to the Office of County School Superintendent?" *Salt Lake Daily Herald*, 15 July 1874.

34. "Home Affairs," *Woman's Exponent*, 15 August 1877.

35. L. B. Pratt to Emmeline B. Wells, 2 January 1880, "Correspondence," *Woman's Exponent*, 15 February 1880.

36. Joel E. Ricks, ed., *The History of a Valley: Cache Valley, Utah-Idaho* (Logan, Utah: Cache Valley Centennial Commission, 1956), p. 339.

37. Elmina A. Shepard journal, 29 April 1850 to February 1851, 6 May 1850, LDS Church Archives. At the time she kept this journal, Elmina was teaching school at Middlefield Center, Otsego County, New York. In 1856 she was baptized a Latter-day Saint, having heard the gospel through a school trustee, John

Druce. He also introduced her to George Hamilton Taylor whom she married shortly after her baptism. The Taylors came to Utah in 1859 and in 1880 she was named president of the YLMIA.

38. Louisa Lula Greene journal, 31 May 1867.
39. Mary Jane Mount Tanner autobiography, p. 72.
40. "The Normal School at Logan," *Salt Lake Daily Herald*, 18 September 1877.
41. "Serious Reflections of the Old Maid," *Woman's Exponent*, 15 May 1876.
42. "The University of Utah and Other Schools of Early Days," p. 40.
43. Martha Jane Knowlton Coray journals, July 1875 to August 1877 inclusive, 3 January; 24 and 25 February; 9, 15, and 16 March 1876, LDS Church Archives.
44. Mary Jane Mount Tanner autobiography, pp. 72–73.
45. Elmina A. Shepard journal, 14 August 1850.
46. Lucinda Lee Dalton to Emmeline B. Wells, 27 December 1876, p. 6.
47. Louisa Lula Greene journal, 6 May 1867.
48. Elmina A. Shepard journal, 6 May 1850.
49. Martha Spence Heywood journal, entry for October 1854.

Ira Eldredge and his three wives, c. 1864. Eldredge (1810-1866) was bishop of the Sugar House Ward when this image was taken. He was married to Nancy Black (1812-1895), Hannah Mariah Savage (1832-1905) and Helvig Marie Andersen (1844-1939). #P4248, courtesy of LDS Archives.

Plural Wives

Stephanie Smith Goodson

Courtship, in Mormon country one hundred years ago, was riding in a buggy with the first wife along. Courtship was dancing with young girls at balls while first, second, and third wives looked on. Courtship was marrying the governess or the new immigrant who happened to be living under one's roof. Courtship and marriage in the days of polygamy were anything but courtly. But, as Nels Anderson points out in *Desert Saints*, "Frontier life itself was not romantic." He went on to say, "Pioneer people were motivated by elementary survival interests, and none were more practical than some of these pioneer women, many of whom favored men who were most secure economically and able to provide the substance for living."[1] Although practicality was not the only motivating force behind the acceptance of polygamy, it played a large part in the decision of many women to enter plural marriage. Practicality also figured largely in the life styles of the polygamous families.

At its inception, however, nothing could have been more impractical for the fledgling Mormon Church than this seemingly outlandish doctrine. The commandment resulted from a revelation given to Joseph Smith sometime in 1831.[2] Not surprisingly, Joseph was forbidden to make the commandment public or to teach it as a doctrine at that time. But eleven years later he was commanded to instruct the leading members of the priesthood on the Principle. Polygamy remained an unwritten law until 12 July 1843, when a portion of it was written. The practice was not openly acknowledged until Orson Pratt gave the first public justification on 29 August 1852, after the Saints were in far-off Utah.

Contrary to popular belief, the early Church leaders were as shocked as anyone else by the commandment. Joseph Smith reported that he tried to ignore the commandment but was visited by an angel with a sword who threatened him "with destruction unless he went forward and obeyed the commandment."[3] Members of the Quorum of the Twelve were no less dismayed, as John Taylor reported:

I had always entertained strict ideas of virtue, and I felt as a married man that this was to me . . . an appalling thing to do. . . . Hence, with the feelings I had entertained, nothing but a knowledge of God, and the revelations of God . . . could have induced me to embrace such a principle as this. . . . We [the Twelve] seemed to put off, as far as we could, what might be termed the evil day.[4]

Brigham Young, the most famous polygamist of them all, said, "I was not desirous of shrinking from any duty . . . but it was the first time in my life I had desired the grave."[5] When Joseph Smith explained the Principle to Benjamin Johnson, whose sister he had asked for in marriage, Brother Johnson told Joseph he would kill him if his intentions towards his sister turned out to be less than honorable.[6] When the High Council of Nauvoo was presented with the Principle and asked to sustain it, two of the stake presidency and one of the high councilmen rejected it.[7]

Nor did the early plural wives seem particularly honored with the privilege of becoming the second or third wife—even of an apostle. When Joseph Smith taught the doctrine to Sarah M. Kimball, proposing to her at the same time, she asked him to go teach it to someone else.[8]

But most of the early polygamous women, after the initial repugnance—and, often, refusal—went through a period of questioning, doubt, and prayer and then felt that they had received a testimony of the truthfulness of the doctrine. Lucy W. Kimball's reaction is a typical one:

When the Prophet Joseph Smith first mentioned the principle of plural marriage to me I became very indignant, and told him emphatically that I did not wish him ever to mention it to me again, as my feelings and education revolted against any thing of such a nature. He counseled me, however, to pray to the Lord for light and understanding . . . after I had poured out my heart's contents before God, I at once became calm and composed; a feeling of happiness took possession of me, and at the same time I received a powerful and irresistible testimony of the truth of plural marriage, which testimony has abided with me ever since.[9]

A few of the sisters seemed to comply out of fear for their immortal souls. Mercy Thompson, who became the plural wife of Hyrum Smith, said, "I dared not refuse to obey the counsel, lest peradventure I should be found fighting against God."[10]

Polygamy was even more of a trial to the first wives, mostly daughters of New England with the strictest convictions about monogamy and virtue. However, they too went through the pattern of horror, questioning, prayer, testimony and, finally, acceptance of the doctrine. One apostle's first wife said this of her experience:

I went into the cellar and prayed, but it seemed that the more I prayed, the more my feelings became wrought up. But I did not give up. . . . First I'd weep; then I'd rage in anger and then I'd pray. . . . When I was about to give up the effort a great calm settled my soul. Then I knew that polygamy was a true principle of the Lord.[11]

She gave her consent to her husband, but her real feelings about polygamy still prevailed, for she told him, "I know I will not be able to control myself. If I see any of your children running around, I'll feel like wringing their necks."

Some of the sisters did not seem to falter at all; indeed many of them encouraged hesitant husbands or took the first steps in wife selection themselves. One wrote, "I feel crippled as we now stand. I want only to be able to walk uprightly like the bravest and best of our people when we have chosen another companion to be one with us."[12] Some of these early plural wives became the strongest defenders of the practice. The strong testimonies they developed during the difficult period of secrecy helped them through the trials that were to come later.[13]

After the public announcement in 1852, great pressures were brought to bear on the members to enter polygamy. The greatest pressure of all was the doctrine itself. William Clayton concluded that "the doctrine of plural and celestial marriage is the most holy and important doctrine ever revealed to man on the earth, and . . . without obedience to that principle no man can ever attain to the fulness of exaltation in celestial glory."[14] During the Reformation period of 1856, when all basic doctrines were stressed, members were commanded to rectify their laxness towards polygamy. That many members took the exhortation of their leaders to heart is evident. More polygamous marriages were contracted in the years 1856–57 than any other time during the fifty-year period polygamy was practiced.[15]

The Reformation coincided with the great drought of 1855. The crop was reduced to famine levels and many Saints were near starvation. Utah emigration reached a peak the same year; many unmarried women arrived in Utah.[16] Men who were financially able were urged to take more wives.[17] Those were also urged to marry polygamously to save the women from the wiles of gentile men, particularly the soldiers and "winter Mormons" (unconverted "converts" who feigned sincerity in joining the Church so that they could marry Mormon girls, only to abandon them and their children when they moved on).[18] An understanding of these economic factors indicates that marrying was not done out of religious fervor alone.

With all the pressures on Church members to enter polygamy, it seems more surprising that ninety percent did *not* practice polygamy than that ten percent did![19] One reason for this paradox is that the pressures evidently were not applied equally to all members. Polygamy seemed to be a requirement for Church advancement. Apostle George Q. Cannon said in a talk in St. George that he "did not feel like holding up his hand to sustain anyone as a presiding officer who had not entered into the patriarchal order of marriage."[20] Joseph F. Smith said in a meeting that Church leaders should either become polygamists or relinquish their positions to those who were willing to accept the Principle.[21] A few were threatened with release from positions if they did not enter polygamy and some were advised to enter it as a preparation for being promoted to some position of authority.[22] Another reason that more did not marry polygamously was that a man had to be interviewed by his bishop and stake president to see if he was suited, especially financially, for polygamy. Many applicants were turned down.[23] Since the greatest pressure was on the leaders and the wealthy in the Church, it is quite likely that the ninety percent who did not enter the Principle breathed a sigh of relief and only gave the doctrine lip service. It would be interesting indeed to be able to survey the monogamists of the period to assess their feelings on their status in relation to the polygamists and to explore how they felt about not participating in a commandment that was necessary for celestial advancement.

There were in reality few large harems. Joseph Smith is reported to have married twenty-seven women; Brigham Young, twenty-seven (although he is said to be sealed to 150 with whom he never lived); Heber C. Kimball, who lived with the largest number of wives, had forty-five; John D. Lee, nineteen; and Orson Pratt, ten (sealed to 200). Some of these wives were older women and widows who entered into polygamous marriages for financial support. Brigham Young, for example, married several of Joseph Smith's widows. Some of these women were wives in name only and never actually lived with their husbands. From these five many-wived men, the figures on number of wives per husband decrease rapidly.

In a study of 2,000 who practiced polygamy, Stanley Ivins found that 66 percent of the male membership had taken one additional wife, 21 percent had taken a third wife,[24] 66 percent a fourth wife and 6 percent five or more wives. Half of the men were through marrying by the age of forty. Teen-aged brides accounted for 38 percent of the women, 67 percent married under twenty-five years of age, and 30 percent married when they were over thirty. From the statistics, Ivins compiled a picture of an average man who engaged in polygamy. At the age of twenty-three, he married a wife of twenty. Thirteen years later he took a second wife of twenty-two. Chances are two to one that he had finished marrying then; if he did take a third wife, it would be four years later, and she would be twenty-two to his forty. Chances are three to one that he would not take a fourth wife; if he did, he would be forty-four and she would be twenty-two. A fifth wife, age twenty-one, might be added when he was forty-six. This would be the end of his marrying unless he belonged to a 3 percent minority.[25]

Usually the entrance into plural marriage was humane and orderly. There were many different styles of courtships. Some men were encouraged by revelation to take wives. John Manning said that on a business trip to Salt Lake, "The Lord showed four women to me and also the places where to find them."[26] He went directly to their homes, and they all later married him. John W. Taylor dreamed that he and his wives and children met the Savior at the resurrection day. He saw the faces of women he had not yet met and felt that he had to marry them all, even though the Manifesto stopped polygamous marriages before his family was complete. Brother Taylor's third wife also had a revelation about one of these future wives and many years later fainted when she actually saw her.[27] There is at least one case of revelation discouraging a plural marriage. One man told his wife he had received a revelation to marry a certain girl. The next morning the wife told him she had received a revelation to shoot any woman that became his plural wife. He decided not to enter into polygamy.[28]

The authorities counseled husbands to be careful of the feelings of their wives, particularly of the first wife. For this reason, the choosing of a wife was sometimes a team effort. Barnard and Diana Mary White had a difficult time obeying the counsel to take an additional wife. When they finally decided on the step, they considered the available girls together. They invited their choice, Sarah Jane Fife, into their home to help Diana Mary with some sewing. The trial was successful, and they decided that Barnard should try to win the hand of Sarah Jane.

Visits were made to the Fifes, and as the winter went by, it became the custom for Barnard and Diana Mary to call for Sarah Jane when they were going to meetings and parties. The high seat on a lumberman's dray may not seem like a very romantic spot—especially when the man's wife was along—but there was an air of courting about these occasions, anyway.[29]

Sometimes the first wife did more courting than the husband. Nephi King's second wife said that not only did his first wife do most of the courting, but "she was the one to first ask me if I would be willing to be a polygamist's wife."[30] One man who let his wives have a hand in mate-selection had an interesting technique. He would organize a sleighing party of young girls and afterwards would take them home for his wives to observe.[31]

Technically, the approval of the first wife was required before a marriage could take place. Oftentimes, after counseling with the first wife, marriage plans would be abandoned. Sometimes, however, the husbands disobeyed counsel and did not consult their wives at all. One man, who had been married sixteen years, asked his wife to get his temple clothes ready. When she inquired about the occasion, he replied that he was taking another wife. The son of the first wife recorded, "Ma never got over that."[32] Even though the approval of the first wife was a requirement, sometimes first wives were thought to be "just stubborn," and the authorities would override their objections. Later, when polygamy went underground because of governmental persecution, courtships took place in secret; often the wife not only did not give her consent but, for security reasons, did not know that the marriage took place at all.

Sometimes a jealous wife discouraged prospective wives. Juanita Brooks reported that when her grandfather went to court a new wife, the first wife arrived a few minutes later. She remarked that the children were asleep, she was lonesome, and she thought she would come to chat. After a short while, the first wife remarked, "Well, John, let's go home." He acted a little nettled and answered, "You go ahead; I'll be along in a few minutes." The first wife hurried out, slamming both the door and the gate. This action disheartened the prospective second wife. The next time he courted without the knowledge of his first wife. One day he simply left for a trip north with a load of dried fruit and his wife-to-be.[33]

In some cases, women took the first steps in marriage proposals. Some polygamists were "much sought after." The twelfth wife of John D. Lee boldly told him she wanted him to "take charge of her and her effects."[34] Brother Lee graciously acquiesced. Sometimes, as in this case, these forward women were unattractive, older, or widows, but often they were young girls. It may seem strange that young girls should be interested in men twice their age, but older, established men had status, and often the charm and stature that comes with age. They also had financial security. These practical pioneer girls seemed to find the security of a home more desirable than marrying a younger, ostensibly more romantic, bachelor.

Plural marriage absorbed many single female converts. As mentioned above, many foreign-born female converts flooded into Utah, especially in the 1850s.[35] They were often older, between twenty-five and thirty-five years of age, making it hard for them to compete with the younger women for husbands. These girls were usually sent to live with families of their own nationality, with the hope that proximity would take care of the problem. More often than not, this process worked. Sometimes men were asked to marry specific women. A Dane living in Parowan, Utah, already had two Danish wives. When another Danish emigrant came to town, the bishop said, "Brother Bayles, take this sister into your house where she will have someone to talk to. I suggest that you marry her." Brother Bayles obeyed and took a third Danish wife. The situation was repeated with a fourth Danish wife.[36]

The efficaciousness of propinquity is also illustrated by the number of men who married domestic servants, governesses, and seamstresses in their homes. The second wife of Isaac Lambert said, "I nearly raised the Lambert family before I married Isaac, working for the first wife and doing everything in the house. I scrubbed this kitchen floor until it is worn out right now."[37] John W. Taylor hired a girl he was interested in to work in his home; he later married her.[38]

Other practical considerations encouraged polygamy. Joseph M. Tanner's first wife was reluctant to have him take a second wife. But she had been married for five childless years and she felt she must allow her husband to have a family.[39] Another wife insisted that her husband take a wife to provide a family for him. She picked out the seamstress who worked for her. Later the sister wife gave the childless first wife two children to rear.[40] One son said that his father "selected his wives with consideration of their natural function in mind—bringing forth children. . . . His wives were selected with attention to heredity, education, and absence of defects."[41]

That love, romance and even companionship were only minor motivations for marriage is illustrated in this marriage proposal of Parley P. Pratt:

Prest. Young,
Dear Brother,

I have in my own mind selected another assistant missionary to assist me in my mission for time and all eternity. It only requires *your sanction*, the *Lady's Consent*, and the *seal of God* to complete the appointment.

The candidate is a sister from Manchester England heretofore known as Sister Hill. What say ye?

Your Bro. P. P. Pratt

Dear Sister Hill,

I hope you will excuse the liberty I have taken in presenting the above to Prest. Young. He gave his ready sanction, to the selection, and it now remains for you to say whether you will undertake such a mission, of your *own free will and choice*.

Count well the cost. I can promise you nothing but Poverty, hard work, and many burdens in this work which few can bear.

And be assured your decision either way will never lessen our friendship.

Your Bro. P. P. Pratt

P.S. excuse the name of hill.
your name I do not know.⁴²

This particular young lady did not consent to become another "assistant missionary."

A most unromantic proposal was made by John W. Taylor to his third wife. He mentioned in passing that he had had his mind set on a double wedding and was disappointed that it hadn't worked out. The prospective wife was as stunned to learn he was courting another girl as she was to discover he had planned on marrying them both on the same occasion.⁴³ Another girl, who became the second wife of her sister's husband, complained that most of her courting was done "in the corral, milking the cows."⁴⁴

One reason that so many courtships seemed so unromantic and usually so well-chaperoned was that the men were counseled by John Taylor and other authorities that courtships should be short and direct. They thought it would be "unseemly" for married men to appear to be chasing after younger girls. As the fourth wife of Hyrum Stratton said, "Married men didn't do any courting of their plural wives. Why, we would have thought it dishonorable for a mature married man to go sparking around like a young man. They just came and asked us, and if we wanted them, we agreed."[45]

The plural marriage ceremony itself had some interesting and emotional twists to it. The first wife stood in between her husband and the bride during the ceremony and, after agreeing to give the woman to her husband, she was instructed to place the bride's right hand in her husband's.[46] The secrecy of the Underground days added some unusual variations on the theme of marriage. John W. Taylor and his third wife were married on a carriage ride through Liberty Park.[47] Annie Clark Tanner's marriage ceremony was also performed in secret. After the ceremony, Brother Tanner and his two wives took the train to Annie's parents' home, where she was dropped off. Her sister asked cheerfully, "Did it happen?" as she sat down to a wedding feast of bread and milk. Not only did she spend her wedding day alone, but two weeks later Brother Tanner failed to keep his first "appointment" with her.[48]

After courtship culminated in marriage, a variety of living arrangements was established. In general, marriages seemed happiest when each wife had her own home. Having sufficient means to provide comfortably for all the families also contributed to marital success. The well-off families of John Taylor, Apostle Erastus Snow and Joseph F. Smith had entirely separate homes with little interaction among the families. The affluent did not always have separate homes, however, a notable example of this being the famous Lion House, residence of Brigham Young and his wives.

Even though well-off families seemed to have the most success, less affluent families could also manage well. Hans Olson married four Swedish girls between 1850 and 1860, all about the same age. For ten years they all lived in an adobe house in Logan. Each wife had a large room where she lived with her children. The families shared a kitchen and dining room. Although they were able to live peaceably in one home, they were more content when each family was provided with a house. Each wife eventually had her own home, most of them on one block.[49]

The first wife of John W. Taylor was completely separated from the other five. "You and May will simply have nothing to do with one another," he told his third wife before their marriage. The third wife of Samuel W. Woolley could have had her own home but preferred sharing her time between the households of the other two.[50]

If the wives had separate households, the husband worked out some system for dividing his time. Samuel W. Woolley spent Monday and Tuesday with the first wife, Wednesday and Thursday with the second wife, Friday and Saturday with the third wife and divided up the Sundays. Children were on their best behavior when their father was there; they could relax the rest of the week.[51] A husband with several households saw the best of each and could escape to another whenever he wished. Orson Smith established his three families in separate homes, but the lots were joined together. Margaret Smith Watson wrote of the arrangement, "Orson provided all sorts of amusements and sports for his twenty-seven children, and they had their pleasures in the home." He spent a week with each family, but visited every family daily for prayers. Family meetings were filled with instruction, counsel and advice, and with participation in a program by family members. The children grew up without knowing of differences among the trinity of mothers.[52]

Note that it is in retrospect that one gets such glowing testimonials of polygamy. Opinions about what it was like to live in polygamy range all the way from Fanny Stenhouse's and Ann Eliza Young's tirades against the indignities suffered by the women to the often saccharine "never-a-cross-word-was-uttered" accounts of some of the descendants of polygamous families. As the many books written on how polygamous families got along attest, the truth lay somewhere in between and was a matter of the interpretation of the doctrine by each family.[53]

Some men swore their marriages were heavenly. Elder H. W. Naisbitt stated that there had been no better time in thirty years of married life than when there were three wives in one house. Describing his home, he said, "There is a spirit of peace and intelligence. From the condition of plural marriage came a discipline of life, a power of self-restraint, and tender regard for each other's feelings, a jealousy for each other's rights—tempered by a consideration that relations were meant to be enduring." Elder Naisbitt remarked that plural marriage could have more love, interest and soul than monogamy under the best conditions.[54]

On the other hand, Brigham Young's address during the Reformation in Salt Lake City pointed out that polygamy was not always "sweetness and light." In this address he stated that he was tired of complaints from polygamous wives. During the following two weeks he asked the women to decide whether or not they wished to stay with their husbands. He declared he would set every woman at liberty if she wished. He asked them either to round up their shoulders to endure the affliction of the world and to live their religion, or to go to heaven alone.[55] There was no exodus of women asking for release from their polygamous marriage ties. Polygamy had its problems, but apparently they were not severe enough to cause general dissolution of the marriages.

Jealousy, obviously, was the greatest single problem. As mentioned earlier, men of forty would marry girls in their teens or twenties. The wives men married in their youth were twenty years older than subsequent wives; physical comparisons were natural. Some husbands showed their partiality. One first wife said in jealous rage, "O.K. Go to your darling, then, if you wish."[56] Wives competed for their husbands' attention and also by producing the most and best children. However, most jealousy was caused by inequality of treatment. Annie Clark Tanner was the daughter of a second wife. The first wife lived across the street. There were noticeable differences in the two households. "Aunt Mary" had a hired girl and a larger house. She entertained the Church authorities and other guests who came to visit her husband. She also packaged provisions for both families, and not too fairly. The second family was glad when their father was there to divide the supplies.[57] Aside from having to share the husband, inequality of material possessions brought most unhappiness to plural familes.

Difficulties were overcome in most cases. Divorce was rare during the pre-Manifesto period.[58] One plural wife credited religion with helping families solve their problems. "The religion of Christ teaches us to overcome natural selfishness in all respects. We become nobler and happier as we overcome selfishness and become like the Savior."[59] Abigail Gardner, in writing to her sister, said, "But best of all, we live generally in peace and union, loving each other like sisters, but this could not be done without the spirit of our God which we received by obedience to the everlasting gospel."[60]

Other women, tormented by jealousy, were advised to forget themselves in service to their husbands and especially their children. Brigham Young counseled, "Sisters, do not ask whether you can make yourselves happy, but whether you can do your husband's will if he is a good man." He continued, "Where I find women jealous of each other, and watching their husband, I would ask, 'Where are your children?' They are nearly all the time in the mud or in some mischief."[61] On another occasion, he told the sisters it was their duty to bear children. "Do you look forward to that? or are you tormenting yourselves by thinking your husbands do not love you? I would not care whether they loved a particle or not; but I would cry out, like one of old, in joy of my heart, 'I have got a man from the Lord! Hallelujah! I am a mother! I have borne an image of God.'"[62] He thought motherhood should compensate for any lack of romantic attention. Women were counseled to rise above petty difficulties and think religiously.

Despite the difficulties of polygamy, there were many advantages in having several women living close together or under the same roof. Practical division of labor was possible. In the David Cannon household, each of the wives did the part of the work she liked best. "Aunt Joe" always milked the cow and did other outside work while "Aunt Rhoda" did the dishwashing and other housework. Washing and ironing they did together. The older children helped whichever mother needed them:

We went from one home to the other freely and were always welcomed by the mother. There were quarrels between us children, but no different than those between other brothers and sisters. This was largely due to the justice of our father. He was so absolutely just in his treatment of our mothers and their children, there was never a tinge of jealousy in the family.[63]

The children learned the special skills of several women. On the Henry Reiser lot, which housed three families in three homes, each mother shared her store from her own garden with the other two, and each mother taught her arts to all the children. "How well I remember when I was but ten years old," a descendant wrote, "Aunt Margaret taught me to knit a pretty pattern of cotton lace, speaking in German, and paid me for embroidering a little baby dress. My mother was of literary inclination and a student, and Aunt Catherine a fine seamstress and cook of a radiant and happy disposition."[64]

The presence of another woman was a comforting security in case of a mother's illness or death. Charles Terry's wife never recovered from the shock of losing a child, and her health failed. The husband sought the assistance of a twenty-one year old neighbor, who showed an interest in the children. He married her later, with his wife's consent, since the first wife was fearful of the future of her three children.[65] Phoebe Ann Covington was nineteen when she married John Ezra Pace. His first wife Caddie Ivins passed away six years after this second marriage, leaving four children under eight years of age. By that time, Phoebe had three of her own, but she mothered the seven children under eight years of age. As time went on, nine more children were born to her. Fifteen years after the death of his first wife, Pace married Caddie's sister Julia, who bore him three children. When Julia also died, three more children were added to Phoebe's sixteen. There were five babies under three years of age and eight under seven.[66] This, of course, was an extreme case, but there are many cases which record sister wives raising the children of wives who had died. Or, surprisingly often, a childless sister wife was given a child to raise as her own. At the least, childless wives benefited from being around children.

Polygamy developed independent women who bore much of the financial responsibility for their families. It was not uncommon for men to leave their wives with little money while serving missions for the Church. The women were required to support themselves and rear their children alone. Annie Clark Tanner's husband abdicated his financial responsibilities, telling her that he never planned to visit her again, and that she must "look to [her] brothers for help." Singlehandedly Annie raised and educated her seven children.[67]

Even when their husbands were in residence, these matriarchs often managed their households alone. Polygamy forced women to be resourceful. Many women developed home industries to meet expenses and support husbands who were away. Some combined their home duties with money making jobs in the community. Childcare problems for polygamous wives away from home for one reason or another were virtually eliminated with the help of other sister-wives.

As can be seen, the advantages of polygamy often offset the problems of the system. Because the Principle was new and there were no established patterns of behavior, the Saints practiced it with great diversity. Personality and preference shaped the style of living, as well as the success of the venture. There was often a greater determination to make a polygamous marriage succeed than a monogamous one. One polygamous wife said she'd get along "if it killed her."[68] Mormons were aware that plural marriage was a religious principle and perhaps found it easier for that reason to work hard at making the marriage succeed. There was also no question that polygamists felt the eyes of the world firmly riveted upon them to see how they practiced this strange belief.

The unromantic and exotic nature of the commandment seemed impractical for a young Church seeking new members. But while the Principle was unromantic to most of those who practiced it, it was certainly not impractical. Frontier people sensed the practical advantages of polygamy. Samuel Taylor thought polygamy was "only feasible in a frontier environment"—and the frontier in the latter half of the nineteenth century was fast disappearing.[69] The strong practical applications of polygamy, coupled with the even stronger religious feelings about it, made the Principle, an anomaly in the modern civilized world, surprisingly successful.

Notes

1. Nels Anderson, *Desert Saints* (Chicago: University of Chicago Press, 1942), p. 403.
2. Doctrine and Covenants (Salt Lake City: Church of Jesus Christ of Latter-day Saints, 1920), 132:239–45.
3. Lorenzo Snow, as quoted in "Plural Marriage," *The Historical Record* (Salt Lake City: n.p., 1887), 6:222.
4. B. H. Roberts, *Life of John Taylor* (Salt Lake City: Bookcraft, Inc., 1965), p. 100.
5. Brigham Young, *Journal of Discourses*, Orson Pratt and others, eds., 26 vols., (Liverpool and London: Orson Pratt and others, 1966), 3:103.
6. Benjamin F. Johnson, as quoted in *The Historical Record*, 6:221.
7. Thomas Grover, as quoted in *The Historical Record*, 6:227. The two members of the stake presidency who rejected the revelation were William Marks and Austin A. Cowles and the high councilman was Leonard Soby. All three later apostatized.
8. Sarah M. Kimball, as quoted in *The Historical Record*, 6:232.
9. Lucy W. Kimball, as quoted in *The Historical Record*, 6:229–30.
10. Mercy R. Thompson, as quoted in *The Historical Record*, 6:229.
11. Anderson, pp. 131–32.
12. Susa Young Gates, *The Young Woman's Journal*, 2 (1890–91), 212.
13. Roberts says that Joseph Smith was commanded not to make public the revelation because of the "traditions and prejudices" of the members themselves, especially because of their newness in the gospel, and because it would be an advantage to their enemies. (B. H. Roberts, *A Comprehensive History of the Church*,

6 vols., [Provo, Utah: Brigham Young University Press, 1965], 2:103.) There are indications that he felt the time would be ripe to reveal the doctrine to the public after they had reached the Rocky Mountains. For example, he told his wife Lucy Walker that their marriage would be made known then. (Anderson, p. 393.) But the news of polygamy did leak out, both through rumor and because several of the brethren preached the doctrine who were not supposed to. Some of these were reproved and one was disfellowshipped. (Roberts, 2:104–5.) All Church authorities and many of the women indignantly denied that polygamy was being practiced. In the *Millennial Star*, Joseph Smith said emphatically that Mormons did not believe in "a community of wives," and that such a thing was "an abomination in the sight of the Lord." (Kimball Young, *Isn't One Wife Enough?* [New York: Henry Holt & Co., Inc., 1954], p. 91.) And yet enough mystery surrounded the movements of the Church leaders to confuse many of the members and feed fire to the accusations of such apostates as John C. Bennett, William Law, and others. Thomas B. H. Stenhouse and some others have tried to make a case for the number of excommunications in England and other foreign missions rising at this time, but it was not proportionately larger than at other times, nor were the reasons for various members' apostatizing shown to be directly related to polygamy. (Roberts, 4:58–61.) That some apostatized both in foreign missions and in the States because of rumors of polygamy is probable.

14. William Clayton, as quoted in *The Historical Record*, 6:226.

15. Sixty-five percent more of such marriages took place during 1856–57 than any other two-year period. (Leonard J. Arrington, *Great Basin Kingdom* [Lincoln: University of Nebraska, 1966], pp. 152, 459, n. 88.)

16. Emigration was high during the 1850s; 1856 was the peak year. Between 4,000 and 5,000 emigrants arrived in Utah during this year. (Anderson, p. 142.)

17. Much has been made of the fact that census figures for the years 1870 and 1880 show that the number of males and females in Utah was about equal, thus dispelling the idea that the great excess of women encouraged the practice of polygamy. However, these census figures include the gentile men in Utah, mostly soldiers and miners. Not only were marriages outside the Church out of the question for most Mormon women, but mere friendliness with gentile men was frowned upon. Anderson tells of one married woman who was disfellowshipped because she was "cordial" with some men who boarded with her and was on a first-name basis with them. (Anderson, pp. 400–1.)

18. K. Young, p. 137.

19. There is a problem with estimating the number of plural marriages since, especially during the Underground period, many of them were not recorded. Visitors to Utah at the time were told that approximately 10 percent of the Mormons were polygamists. Stanley Ivins says that information at the Smoot hearings indicates that about 10 percent of the Utah Mormons were involved in polygamy at the time of the Manifesto. A Church statement, however, indicates that the percentage was lower than this: "The practice of plural marriage has never been general in the Church and at no time have more than 3 percent of the families in the Church been polygamous." (Stanley Ivins, "Notes on Mormon Polygamy," *The Western Humanities Review*, 10 [Summer, 1956], 232–33.) Of course, 3 percent of the families could easily mean the same as 10 percent of the members. And it is possible that the number of members of the Church outside of Utah, where polygamy was not practiced, could have brought the figure down from 10 percent to 3 percent.

But it appears that during certain periods the percentage went even higher than the estimated 10 percent. During the 1856 period mentioned above (see note 15), probably as much as 15 to 20 percent of the population practiced polygamy. The figure undoubtedly rose with the increased marriages during 1862 and 1882–85 in defiance of the anti-polygamy legislation.

20. K. Young, p. 107.
21. Ibid.
22. K. Young, p. 107; Anderson, pp. 402–3.
23. Ivins, pp. 232–33.
24. One doctrine which was preached about polygamy was that if one wanted to attain the very pinnacle of glory in the next world he must have at least three wives. Interestingly enough, this doctrine was called the "trinity" by Mormons. (K. Young, p. 184.)
25. Ivins, pp. 229–35.
26. K. Young, p. 110–11.
27. Samuel Woolley Taylor, *Family Kingdom* (New York: McGraw Hill, 1951), pp. 47, 150.
28. K. Young, p. 122.
29. Ruth Johnson and Glen F. Harding, *The Barnard White Family Book* (Provo: Brigham Young University Press, 1967), p. 42.
30. K. Young, p. 114.
31. Ibid., pp. 129–30.
32. Ibid., p. 122.
33. Juanita Brooks, "A Close-up of Polygamy," *Harper's Magazine*, 168 (December-May, 1933, 34), 307.
34. Anderson, p. 404.
35. In Anderson's study, 59 percent of the plural wives were foreign-born. (Anderson, p. 400.)
36. Ibid., pp. 162, 400.
37. K. Young, p. 115.

38. Taylor, pp. 150–54, 157–58.
39. Annie Clark Tanner, *A Mormon Mother* (Salt Lake City: University of Utah, 1969), p. 57.
40. K. Young, p. 114.
41. Ibid., p. 69.
42. Parley P. Pratt to Sister Hill, 21 December 1853. Italics are Pratt's.
43. Taylor, pp. 41–42.
44. K. Young, p. 135.
45. Ibid., p. 129.
46. Ibid., p. 44.
47. Taylor, p. 50.
48. Tanner, pp. 58–59.
49. K. Young, p. 290.
50. Taylor, pp. 10, 39.
51. Ibid., pp. 10–11.
52. Kate B. Carter, *The Other Mother* (Salt Lake City: Daughters of the Utah Pioneers, 1937), p. 15.
53. Kimball Young rated 175 polygamous families in terms of their success or failure. He set up five categories—highly successful, reasonably successful, moderately successful (some conflict, but mostly successful), considerable conflict, and severe conflict (often involving divorce or separation). Of these nearly 53 percent fell into the first two successful categories, one-fourth into the moderate section, and 23 percent fell into the two conflict groups. (Young, pp. 56–57.)
54. B. Young, 26:142.
55. Ibid., 4:55.
56. K. Young, p. 77.
57. Tanner, p. 11.
58. Anderson, pp. 349 ff.; K. Young, pp. 226–40.
59. Gates, p. 211.
60. Abigail Gardner to her sister, 4 February 1861.

61. B. Young, 1:38.
62. Ibid., 1:37.
63. Carter, p. 7.
64. Ibid., p. 4.
65. Ibid., p. 11.
66. Ibid., p. 12.
67. Tanner, pp. 205–6.
68. Taylor, p. 54.
69. Ibid., p. 9.

Bishop Oveson of Cleveland, Utah, in front of his fine house with his wives. George Edward Anderson, photographer. #P1 12374, Photographic Archives, Harold B. Lee Library, Brigham Young University, Provo, Utah.

Mormon Haters
Carrel Hilton Sheldon

During the second half of the nineteenth century the national media featured exposés of the Mormons. An incongruous coalition of non-Mormon businessmen and politicians, their wives, clergymen, federal officials stationed in Utah, and reporters bombarded the nation with tales of Mormondom, usually shocking, sometimes amusing. Though the primary goal of most of these critics was the termination of the Mormon monopoly of power in Utah, the focus of their propaganda was polygamy. As a result, Mormon women frequently bore the brunt of the criticism and were the victims of anti-Mormon satire and scorn. The basis of anti-Mormon sentiment and the motives and aims of the various protagonists will be considered here along with the solutions proposed to deal with the "Mormon problem."

Utah historian Hubert H. Bancroft blamed the troubles of the Mormons on their exclusiveness:

Thus, notwithstanding the iniquities of the saints, together with their impudence and arrogance, as charged upon them by their enemies, the impossibility of others living with them as members of one community, of one commonwealth, is the real difficulty. . . . The trouble is this, and this will continue to be the trouble, in Utah or elsewhere in the United States, and that whether polygamy stands or falls—the saints are too exclusive industrially and politically, for their neighbors.[1]

He went on to point out that they held to one another and banded against all societies and interests except their own. They owned all the agricultural lands, cooperated in commerce and manufacture, and voted all one way. No other people could compete with them. In fact, gentile merchants were ridiculed and condemned in public Church meetings, for the Church leaders disliked their presence and resented the fact that gentiles absorbed the small amount of floating capital available in the valley. Mormons who trafficked with gentiles were considered weak in the faith.[2]

Many non-Mormons feared that Mormon political power seriously threatened the surrounding states and the nation. The Honorable John Cradlebaugh of Nevada gave a speech in the House of Representatives in 1863 in which he described a "People in our midst who are building up, consolidating and daringly carrying out a system, subversive to the Constitution and laws, and fatal to morals and true religion."[3] A front page article in the *New York Times* in November 1865 under the title "Preparing for Resistance to the Government" carried a similar message, claiming:

This people, under the advice of their leaders, are preparing for resistance, even to war, against any interference with what they call their religious faith. They anticipate no interference, except from the United States. The burden of their speeches and sermons everywhere is to arm for the coming contest. They are arming.[4]

Almost twenty years later in January 1881, a *New York Times* editorial was still saying the same thing. "An element is permitted to exist unmolested in our midst that openly defies and derides the Nation; scoffs and spits at its rulers, disgraces and pollutes the name of civilization. 'How long, oh Lord, how long' must we endure it?"[5] In Congress three years later Senator Cullom from Illinois denounced the Mormons vigorously, charging that they disliked the United States government, and imported paupers from Europe whom they taught to hate it, too.[6]

This fear of Mormon power was not unfounded. In 1856 Brigham Young had said, "The sound of polygamy is a terror to the pretended republican government. Why? Because this work is destined to revolutionize the world and bring all under subjection."[7] And Orson Pratt said, "It is not consistent that the people of God should organize or be subject to man-made governments."[8]

Though the Mormon Church's exclusivism was the basis of fierce opposition among Utah gentiles, and their growing political power frightened some observers, neither cause could arouse the nation against the Mormons. In order to marshal national support to overthrow the Mormons, polygamy was made the scapegoat upon which the anti-Mormon population of Utah piled its combined grievances.

Stories describing the horrors of polygamy were spread over the country, intentionally rousing the citizenry to end this threatening custom and, hopefully, to end the power that the Church held over civil affairs in Utah. The Church seemed most vulnerable on the polygamy issue, and it was thought that the end of polygamy would mean the end of Mormonism. "Root out polygamy, and Mormonism would die of itself, the one great incentive and strongest influence being gone."[9] "True stories" supposedly written by run-away wives, travelers' first-hand descriptions of Utah's grievous conditions, and moral diatribes were some of the forms of attack. In addition, polygamy was an excellent source of material for humorous writers and cartoonists. Stories, songs, and verses were written to describe polygamy's hilarious aspects as well as its somber ones. "Mormoniad," a lengthy poem by an anonymous author, exemplified this mode of attack:

> Nor these alone;—even women, too,
> (Without whose aid Polygamy,
> 'Tis thought by some, would never be!)
> To the great Prophet's banner flew;

> The married, and the widow, and
> The maiden who was never manned!
> The first, to solace thus their grief;
> The last, in hopes of some relief,
> Relief from apprehension lest
> She never, never, should be blessed!
> ....
> All these—full of connubial glee,
>   Be-Mormonized, infatuated,
>   And madly bent on being mated—
> Gladly embraced Polygamy;
> And godly Elders, full of pity,
> Received them in the Salt Lake City.[10]

Mark Twain satirized polygamy in his oft-quoted report in *Roughing It*:

With the gushing self-sufficiency of youth I was feverish to plunge headlong and achieve a great reform here until I saw the Mormon women. Then I was touched. My heart was wiser than my head. It warmed toward these poor, ungainly, and pathetically "homely" creatures, and as I turned to hide the generous moisture in my eyes, I said, "no—the man that marries one of them has done an act of Christian charity which entitles him to the kindly applause of mankind, not their harsh censor—and the man that marries sixty of them has done a deed of open-handed generosity so sublime that the nation should stand uncovered in his presence and worship in silence!"[11]

A selection of verse from "Saint Abe and His Seven Wives, A Tale of Salt Lake City" by Robert W. Buchanan showed how a new wife "Sister Anne" was regarded by the previous six:

> Already she saddens and sinks and sighs,
> Watched by the jealous dragonish eyes.
> Even Amelia, sleepy and wan,
> Sharpens her orbs as she looks at Anne;
> While Sister Tabby, when she can spare
> Her gaze from the Saint in his easy-chair
> Fixes her with a gorgon glare.[12]

These humorous writings ranged all the way from vicious to very funny. They served to keep the problem of polygamy on the minds of the public in an easy and pleasant way. As the samples above so aptly indicate, it was the women who most felt the ridicule such wit inspired.

Those interested in focusing national concern on polygamy whether by humor or polemics varied in motives and composition. As has been suggested, the gentile men of Utah were resentful of the Church's domination of government and business. Gentiles were not treated as part of the community and had less chance of success than Mormons. Glen Miller, an Eastern observer of the Church, writing an article for *Forum* magazine in 1894, said:

Deeper than the resentment felt by the gentiles of Utah against polygamy was that aroused by the union of Church and State in the Territory. The Church authorities have always strenuously denied that they exercised political power. Whether they did or did not, the effect was the same. In politics the Church was a unit. In business . . . most Mormon trade went into Mormon channels. [13]

The gentile women of Utah also criticized the Church and were an effective force influencing the opinions of the nation. These ladies shared the resentments and fears of their husbands and added to those their own dislike of plural marriage. They felt that the supposed unhappiness among the Mormon women proved that polygamy was wrong.

Some apostate women felt a calling to expose Mormon evils to the world. Fanny Stenhouse and Ann Eliza Young wrote accounts of their experiences and lectured throughout the country. Their books were sensational in style and appealed to the emotions of the readers. Many similar books were written. [14]

In 1878 the gentile women organized the Anti-Polygamy Society in Utah. Mrs. Sarah A. Cook, an apostate Mormon, was chosen as president. The women sent lecturers throughout the East to arouse interest and to organize The Women's National Anti-Polygamy Society. They published a newspaper, the *Anti-Polygamy Standard*, and appealed to clergymen, Congress, and the people of the nation for support. For a decade the Anti-Polygamy Society continued to send lecturers to the East to arouse the public and demand strong legislation.

The "Woman's Industrial Home" was created in 1886 by a group of philanthropically-minded women throughout the nation to "provide homes and employment for homeless and destitute polygamous wives and their children."[15] The Home closed shortly after its inauspicious beginning due to lack of interest on the part of polygamous wives. Very few women ever stayed there and not one was polygamous. The building, which became a joke in Salt Lake City, was auctioned off by the government at a great loss, first becoming a "family hotel," and currently housing the Ambassador Club.

Sectarian ministers also took up the battle. It was popular and safe to dislike the Mormons. According to a *New York Times* editorial, the Mormons were "a class of sinners that seemed to be providentially supplied for the purpose of enabling eloquent ministers to preach powerful sermons without offending any possible pewholder."[16] But quite possibly their main motivation for being in the forefront was jealousy and revenge.

In the early 1850s to 70s many ministers thought that Christian missionaries sent to Deseret would soon do away with the offensive sect. When the efforts of those ministers ended in dismal failure, the result was rage and disappointment in the vexed souls of the ministers. They concluded that Mormonism was a thing not to be reasoned with, but to be stamped out by force.[17]

In early 1882 protestant churches sponsored mass meetings in nearly all the large cities in the country in order to adopt resolutions urging Congress to act against the Mormons. The following is a list of charges made at a meeting in St. Louis:

1. It was alleged that the Mormon Church interfered in political affairs; and that a recent vote for Delegate to Congress in Idaho had been carried by a brief order from George Q. Cannon, directing the Mormons to vote for a certain man;
2. That its numbers are daily recruited by cunning appeals to the ignorance and base passions of men;
3. That the number of polygamous felons in Utah is strongly increased by the importation from abroad of thousands who are ignorantly seduced or licentiously attracted to this shameful institution;
4. That a large proportion of the whole number of polygamists are unnaturalized foreigners who owe no allegiance to the United States or its laws;
5. That it openly derides the authority of the national government, preaches treason publicly, and makes polygamous rebellion a religious duty;
6. That it degrades women, blotting out of their speech the very notion of home and all the sacred associations which it calls up, making a parody of religion;
7. And lastly it foolishly assumes to be defiant to and stronger than the government.[18]

Even objective Mormons had to admit to some truth in these charges, though the truth was often twisted to fit the facts.

Theodore W. Curtis, writing an article for *Arena*, an eastern intellectual magazine, said, "These petitions to Congress . . . are the work of conclaves of ecclesiastics headed by the orthodox, whose enmity pursued the Mormons before polygamy was any part of their creed, and who are moved more by the angry jealousy of a prosperous rival, than by fear of the disruption of the home from that source."[19] Another non-Mormon reported, "It is not polygamy that disturbs them, but envy and jealousy. If polygamy were permitted to die a natural death the Evangelical Churches would lose their last foothold against the rising tide of Mormonism."[20] Nevertheless, the efforts of the clergy worked up a spirit of indignation throughout the country. Congress was flooded with resolutions to pass anti-Mormon legislation.

A fourth group of Mormon haters was constituted by federally-appointed government officials. As a group they supported demands for anti-Mormon legislation. Many of them criticized the Church in their speeches and made no effort to get along with the people or to rule them justly. These officials "found indiscriminate denunciation of the Mormons an excellent method of perpetuating political power."[21] In an 1894 article in *Forum* Glen Miller claimed:

Not a few who came to Utah poor men enriched themselves at the expense of the Mormon Church. The shrinkage of the Church property escheated by the government would itself unfold a tale of official rapacity. Even the bench has not been free from charges of blind partisanship continued to the present hour, with here and there ugly hints of corruption.[22]

In 1872 the *California Alta* reported that polygamy would have ended years before, but that it was useful for "demagogues to bring themselves notoriety."[23] Government leaders wanted to "rob the Mormons of their property, deprive them of the protection of the courts, and drive them into banishment or rebellion. Their purpose was not order but revenge."[24]

Reporters also flocked to Utah to get a "hot" story on the Mormons. Most of these reporters were probably introduced to the "evils" of polygamy by the anti-Mormon writers or by accounts read in the East. The reporters tended to expect and find the worst. Favorable reports were looked upon with suspicion. One very positive account of the Mormons first published in the *World* was reprinted in the *New York Times* followed by the question, "What can [the editor's] object be in making his paper the apologist for a false and degrading religion?"[25] The response then given was that the only plausible reason was that the editor must be planning to become a Mormon in order to provide "himself with as many wives as he now holds shares of stock."[26] Attempts to defend Mormons were suspect.

All five anti-Mormon interests, the gentile men, gentile women, clergy, federal officials, and reporters denounced plural marriage as a crime, an evil, an abomination, a stigma. They used sensational stories or humorous anecdotes to depict the various evils of polygamy. Many of the stories were true—just not the whole truth. And the bad experiences of some were used to indicate the conditions of all the Mormon people. The attacks centered around four themes: the degradation and enslavement of women; lust, incest and the consequent congenital defects of polygamous progeny; disharmony in the home and the destruction of the family; and deceit.

The degradation and enslavement of women was an important theme. Easterners thought that the Mormon women of Utah were no better off than the black slaves of the South. Mrs. Froiseth, a sensational anti-Mormon writer, declared, "The cornerstone of polygamy is the degradation of woman, and it can flourish only where she is regarded and treated as a slave."[27] This was a sensitive issue as women's rights and equality were becoming topics of national discussion. Ann Eliza Young, Brigham's wayward wife, appealed to the women of the nation:

And you, happier women,—you to whom life has given of its best, and crowned right royally,—can you not help me? The cry of my suffering and sorrowing sisters sweeps over the broad prairies, and asks you, as I ask you now, "Can you do nothing for us?" Women's pens, and women's voices pleaded earnestly and pathetically for the abolition of slavery. Thousands of women, some of them your country-women, and your social and intellectual equals, are held in a more revolting slavery today. Something must be done for them. The system that blights every woman's life who enters it, ought not to remain a curse and a stain upon this nation any longer.[28]

Another apostate Mormon, Fanny Stenhouse, wrote that when she read the revelation on polygamy for the first time, "I felt that that new doctrine was a degradation to womankind. I asked myself, 'Why did the Lord wish to humiliate my sex in this manner?' though at the same time I believed, as I was told, that the 'revelation' was indeed sent from God."[29]

Another favorite topic of the critics was the exaggeration and abuse of sexual impulses on the part of the Mormon men. *Harper's New Monthly Magazine* reported that, "What they call their religion offers a perpetual premium for men's lusts; their teachings kill the germ of chastity in the hearts of childhood before it is ever warmed into life, and destroy the honor and sacredness of the home."[30] And a *New York Times* article said:

The shrewd and cunning appeal to the brutal and sensual instincts, constituting the strongest element in their pretended faith, is the master influence that brings converts to their standard. Men see in it an opportunity for unrestricted license of the grosser passions, and women are deluded into a fanatical idea of becoming spiritual wives of saints.[31]

Related to lust was the immorality of polygamy with regard to incest. Ann Eliza Young, a noted sensationalist, pursued this theme, saying, "Relatives intermarried in a manner that would shock even the most lax-moralled community."[32] The gentiles were understandably shocked by any hint of intermarriage.

Prevalent at this time was the belief that what a woman thought, felt, or looked at during her pregnancy and delivery would "mark" her child. Consequently, the evil emotions felt by pregnant women for their husbands' other wives would adversely affect Mormon offspring. J. H. Beadle cited a high infant death rate in Utah and remarked that "The Asiatic institution was never meant to flourish on American soil, and has resulted here in a 'slaughter of the innocent' which is saddening to contemplate. . . . The effects of their social bias are seen in a strange dullness of moral perception, a general ignorance and apparently inherited tendency to vice."[33]

Robert Barthelow, an assistant surgeon in the United States Army, reported that he had observed that the Mormon system of marriage was already producing a people with distinct racial characteristics:

The yellow, sunken, cadaverous visage; the greenish-colored eye; the thick, protuberant lips; the low forehead; the light, yellowish hair, and the lank, angular person, constitute an appearance so characteristic of the new race, the production of polygamy, as to distinguish them at a glance. The older men and women present all the physical peculiarities of the nationalities to which they belong; but these peculiarities are not propagated and continued in the new race; they are lost in the prevailing type.[34]

Dr. Samuel S. Cartwright, presenting a paper at the New Orleans Academy of Sciences in 1861, observed that the Barthelow report went far "to prove that polygamy not only blights the physical organism, but the moral nature of the white or Adamic woman to so great a degree as to render her incapable of breeding any other than abortive specimens of humanity."[35]

Today these reports are easily recognized as nonsense, but at that time the people of the nation accepted the reports that Mormon women, far away in the west, were living in the greatest misery, poverty, and enslavement imaginable. This belief, together with the conviction that a mother's life strongly affected her unborn children, made it possible for strangers to swallow the wildest tales about the children of polygamy.

Polygamy was also charged with causing disharmony in the home, introducing enough hatred and jealousy to induce illness, insanity, and suicide. It was said that when a second wife was taken, the first often became ill, "the very ghost of her former self, with no interest, no animation, no pleasure in anything."[36] Sometimes the first wife would commit suicide, "a victim of polygamy rather than of her own hand."[37] One first wife "grew nearly insane under this trouble and was wrought up to such a frenzy by jealousy and despair that she committed the most flagrant acts of violence."[38] Horror stories of this kind were common fare. Those who survived were "worse than slaves; where not their bodies, perhaps, but their very souls, their hearts, are crushed."[39]

An extension of this disharmony in the home was the destruction of the family. The polygamous husband left the wife with all the responsibilities of the home. Reports claimed, "The children of such marriages are generally growing up like wild animals, without training, instruction, or parental care."[40] Furthermore, love was assumed to be nonexistent in polygamous marriages. It was claimed that "For a man to love six women, equally well, is manifestly impossible; but it is possible for him to be equally indifferent to all."[41] It was commonly believed that without love fathers would be indifferent to the welfare of their families.

To its debunkers polygamous life seemed cold and calculating. While the average American home may not have succeeded in completely fulfilling the romantic ideal, perfect family life was still a cherished goal. Mormons swept aside the accepted view of the home and family and offered one that was totally unacceptable to most Americans.

Another complaint was that polygamy necessarily resulted in deceit. In the beginning the practice was officially denied from the pulpit. The Saints attempted to keep polygamy a quiet affair until after they were in Utah. Its existence was denied in Europe even after its disclosure in Zion. Fanny Stenhouse was in Europe when polygamy was kept secret. Then she discovered that:

After all the prevarications and denials then of the Apostles and Elders, Polygamy among the Saints was really a fact. . . . I began to realize that the men to whom I had listened with such profound respect and had regarded as the representatives of God, had been guilty of the most deliberate and unblushing falsehood, and I began to ask myself whether if they could do this in order to carry out their purpose in one particular, might they not be guilty of deception on other points?[42]

In addition to this conscious misrepresentation of Church policy, it was charged that husbands concealed from their wives the existence of previous wives or their intentions of taking additional ones. Some Mormon women did suffer from such tactics, but to say that polygamy caused such deceit and that it was widespread among Mormons is refuted by the bulk of Mormon literature.

The solutions offered for the "Mormon problem" were many and varied. Suggested solutions ranged all the way from educating the ignorant Mormon people to exterminating them. Although the brutal verbal war waged by the strongest critics neutralized some people, the general consensus among the American people was that *something* should be done.

Some people felt that missionary efforts would be effective in dealing with the Mormon problem. An article in the *Nation* in 1884 quoted Senator Brown as saying:

The Christian Church is the true medium to deal with the Mormon question. Millions of dollars are sent out yearly to convert the polygamists of India and China to Christianity. Some of this money spent at home, among people who speak our language, might result in producing a great change in the condition of the Mormon problem.[43]

The author of the article went on to caution that "Wholesale punishment for obnoxious opinions, by what are essentially acts of attainder, is a dangerous precedent to introduce into the conduct of our Government, even if it could succeed in making the 12,000 Mormon polygamists give up their extra wives."[44]

Some other moderate solutions were also suggested. Pastor Walter M. Barrows of the Congregational Church in Salt Lake City thought that "enough gentiles in Utah will destroy Mormonism for it is a plant that grows in the basement and cannot abide the light of day."[45] He encouraged people to move to Utah, which he described in glowing terms. He especially asked for school teachers because after a few months at the non-Mormon schools the children are "spoiled for Mormonism."[46] And Lester

Ward felt that "popular education, the panacea of all social as well as political evils would be the only form of national interference that any circumstances could justify."[47]

Other anti-Mormons took a militant approach. In 1879 Secretary of State William M. Evarts issued an official letter instructing the United States representatives in various European nations to assist in suppressing Mormon emigration to this country. He justified this action because Mormons were polygamists and prospective violators of the Federal Statutes.[48] In 1883 an article in the *Nation* echoed this approach asking that emigration of Mormon women be stopped until polygamy died out for lack of materials. It quoted as precedent the halt in Chinese emigration because the Chinese worked for small wages.[49]

Legislation which directly outlawed the practice of polygamy in the territories was initially ineffective. In 1879 a *New York Times* editorial said, "Such people [Mormons] are not to be dealt with by soft-hearted and goody-goody sentimentalists. They despise the law . . . and they will adhere to polygamy unless they are severely shaken up by an enforcement of the Statutes."[50]

As early as 1865 Representative Ward from New York introduced a bill in the House of Representatives stating that polygamy "should be swept from the territories of this republic if it take the whole power of the government to do so."[51] In 1883 the Reverend Mr. Talmage asserted that "nothing will ever put a stop to the spread of the Mormon 'heresy' except the sword," and he demanded that "General Phil Sheridan should be put at the head of an army and sent to Salt Lake on a mission of extermination."[52] If polygamy was to be ended severe measures were necessary.

In contrast to such militance there were some exponents of a *laissez-faire* approach to polygamy. Few outsiders thought Mormonism a good way of life, but some felt the critics were overdoing it. One man, writing his Massachusetts congressman, said he thought the excitement was a manufactured one. He had "not yet seen any clear and candid arguments against the Mormons, or their polygamy, that justify the censures so profusely and ministerially showered upon them. Epithets, used as weapons of offence, disclose, unconsciously to these themselves, the real character of those who utter them."[53]

Many gentiles felt polygamy was a sorry situation for those involved, but since the members had entered voluntarily, there was nothing the government could or should do. John Stuart Mill wrote:

It must be remembered that this relation is as much voluntary on the part of the women concerned in it . . . as is the case with any other form of marriage institution. . . . I cannot admit that persons entirely unconnected with them ought to step in and require that a condition of things with which all who are directly interested appear to be satisfied, should be put an end to because it is a scandal to persons some thousands of miles distant, who have no part or concern in it.[54]

Such voices were not to prevail. The statements and efforts of each group of anti-Mormons reinforced those of others in a way that continued to build public resentment against polygamy. The majority of the people in the country were sincere in their hatred of polygamy and its evils, but they were misled about actual conditions and enflamed by propaganda. Since women were portrayed as the innocent yet accepting victims of polygamy, the focus of polygamy propaganda was often on the Mormon women. By the end of this propaganda campaign, the moral sense of the nation had finally been sufficiently outraged to allow very strong legislation to be passed against the Mormons.

Not only was polygamy eventually abolished, satisfying the gentile women, but the Church's economic and political dominance of Utah was severely diminished, thus accomplishing the goal of the gentile businessmen and politicians. However, the Church remained unified and strong socially and religiously, defeating the aims of the clergymen. Furthermore, the successful elimination of polygamy permitted the achievement of Utah's statehood and the end of the federal officials' influence. Perhaps the anti-Mormon group which reaped the greatest benefit from the whole campaign was the reporters who undoubtedly sold many periodicals to a scandal-hungry populace.

Notes

1. Hubert Howe Bancroft, *History of Utah: 1840–1887* (San Francisco: The History Company, 1890), pp. 366–67.
2. Ibid, pp. 393, 651.
3. Hon. John Cradlebaugh, *Utah and the Mormons, A Speech on the Admission of Utah as a State delivered in the House of Representatives, 7 February 1863* (Washington: L. Towers & Company), p. 1.
4. *New York Times*, 27 November 1865, p. 1.
5. "The Curse of Mormonism, A Flagrant Despotism in the Heart of America," *New York Times*, 2 January 1881, p. 2.
6. "Another Solution of the Mormon Difficulty," *Nation*, 38 (17 January 1884), 49.
7. *Handbook on Mormonism* (Salt Lake City: Hand-book Publishing Co., 1882), p. 42.
8. Bancroft, p. 368.
9. *New York Times*, 2 January 1881; p. 2.
10. Anonymous, *Mormoniad* (Boston: A. Williams & Co., 1858), pp. 9–10.
11. Mark Twain, *Roughing It* (2 vols., New York: Grosset & Dunlap, 1913), 1:101.
12. Kimball Young, p. 10.
13. Glen Miller, "Will Polygamists Control the New State of Utah," *Forum*, 18 (December 1894), 463.

14. For example see:

Maria Ward, *Female Life Among the Mormons: A Narrative of Many Years Personal Experience, by the Wife of a Mormon Elder, Recently From Utah* (New York: J. C. Derby, 1855).

Mrs. T. B. H. (Fanny) Stenhouse, *A Lady's Life Among The Mormons* (New York: Russel Brothers, 1872).

Ann Eliza Young, *Wife #19, A Life in Bondage, A Full Expose of Mormonism* (Hartford, Conn: Dustin, Gilman & Co., 1875).

Jennie A. Bartlett, *Elder Northfield's Home; or Sacrificed on the Mormon Altar, A Story of the Blighting Curse of Polygamy* (New York: The J. Howard Brown Co., 1883).

Mrs. Jennie A. Froiseth, *The Women of Mormonism, or the Story of Polygamy as Told by the Victims Themselves* (Detroit, Mich: C. G. G. Paine, 1887).

15. B. H. Roberts, *A Comprehensive History of the Church*, 6 vols., (Provo, Utah: Brigham Young University Press, 1965), 6:184–86.

16. *New York Times*, 9 October 1883, p. 4.

17. William E. Berrett and Alma P. Burton, *Readings in LDS Church History*, 3 vols., (Salt Lake City: Deseret Book Co., 1958) 3:68.

18. Ibid., p. 69.

19. Theodore W. Curtis, "A Word for the Mormons," *Arena*, 21 (June 1899), 734.

20. "By a Non-Mormon Ten Years in Utah," *Mormons and Mormonism; Why They Have Been Opposed, Maligned and Persecuted,—Inside History of the Present Anti-Mormon Crusade* (Salt Lake City: n.p., 1899), p. 22.

21. Miller, p. 464.

22. Ibid.

23. Kimball Young, *Isn't One Wife Enough?* (New York: Henry Holt and Co., 1954), p. 350.

24. Ibid.
25. *New York Times*, 13 June 1882, p. 4.
26. Ibid.
27. Kimball Young, p. 11.
28. Ann Eliza Young, p. 604.
29. Stenhouse, *A Lady's Life Among the Mormons*, p. 34.
30. "The Mormon Situation," *Harper's New Monthly Magazine*, 63 (1881), 763.
31. *New York Times*, 2 January 1881, p. 2.
32. Ann Eliza Young, p. 310.
33. Kimball Young, p. 24.
34. Stanley S. Ivins, "Notes on Mormonism," *The Western Humanities Review*, 10 (Summer 1956), 238.
35. Ibid.
36. Bartlett, p. 120.
37. Ibid., p. 101.
38. Ann Eliza Young, p. 144.
39. Bartlett, p. 77.
40. Kimball Young, p. 362.
41. Ibid., p. 15.
42. Mrs. T. B. H. (Fanny) Stenhouse, *Tell It All; The Story of a Life's Experience in Mormonism* (Hartford, Conn.: A. D. Worthington and Co., 1890), p. 130.
43. *Nation*, 38 (17 January 1884), 49.
44. Ibid.
45. Walter M. Barrows, *The New West: The Mormon Problem* (Boston: Reprinted from The Home Missionary, December 1878), pp. 8, 14.
46. Ibid.
47. Kimball Young, p. 80.
48. Berrett and Burton, p. 63.
49. "A Radical Remedy for Polygamy," *Nation*, 37 (20 December 1883), 502–3.

50. *New York Times*, 22 January 1879, p. 4.
51. Ibid., 21 December 1865, p. 4.
52. Ibid., 9 October 1883, p. 4.
53. *The Mormon Problem; A Letter to the Massachusetts Members of Congress on Plural Marriage; Its Morality and Lawfulness, by a Citizen of Massachusetts* (Boston: James Campbell, 1882), pp. 9–10.
54. John Stuart Mill, *On Liberty* (Chicago: Regnery, 1955), p. 113.

Emily Kennedy and children in front of her house in rural Utah. George Edward Anderson, photographer. #P1 30665, Photographic Archives, Harold B. Library, Brigham Young University, Provo, Utah.

Victims of the Conflict
Nancy Tate Dredge

The last two decades of the nineteenth century were a
time of great trial for the polygamists, particularly for the
women. The anti-polygamy acts—the Morrill Act of 1862,
the Edmunds Act of 1882, and the Edmunds-Tucker Act of
1887—certainly represented mistreatment to the Mormons. Besides prohibiting polygamy, these laws disincorporated the Church, disfranchised all polygamists and
declared them ineligible for public office, and denied
them the right to serve on juries or be tried by a jury of
their peers. Many of the thousands of emigrants who
came to Utah were denied the right of citizenship because
of their beliefs.[1] Women's suffrage, which had existed in
Utah since 1870, was abolished. Women were made to
testify against their husbands in court, taking from them
the protection of a basic constitutional right. Perhaps the
most devastating punishment for the polygamous wives
was the disinheriting of them and their children, leaving
them to their own financial resources. However, if the
anti-polygamy acts were meant to destroy the spirit of the
Mormons, they failed resoundingly. Groups tend to become more unified in their feelings and their actions
when treated unfairly or persecuted. The immediate effect
of the laws was to spark an increase in plural marriages,
both in defiance of the law and in fear that members
might soon be unable to comply with the commandment.

Another reaction to the bills, particularly to the Edmunds Act, was to take polygamy underground. Throughout the ten-year period "on the Underground" and the time immediately after the demise of polygamy, the polygamous wives were truly the Victims of the Conflict.

And a conflict it was. As one polygamist noted in his journal, "In the spring of 1885, the air was heavy with rumors, that the Edmunds law was to be enforced. And ere long the great raid commenced."[2] The beginning of the "great raid" or "crusade," as it came to be called by the Mormons, was marked by the arrival of Judge Charles S. Zane in Utah in 1884. Few were acquitted during Zane's tenure; "to be tried was, in effect, to be convicted."[3] In the years 1885–86 alone, there were 151 convictions in Utah.[4] The Church's official position to its members concerning the crusade was not to fight—but to run. In a very strong statement made in 1885, John Taylor said:

What! won't you submit to the dignity of the law? Well I would if the law would only be a little dignified. But when we see the ermine bedraggled in the mud and mire, and every principle of justice violated, it behooves men to take care of themselves as best they may. That is what I have told people . . . to take care of their liberties, to put their trust in the living God, to obey every constitutional law [note that he emphasized constitutional as opposed to statutory laws, such as the Morrill, Edmunds, and Edmunds-Tucker Acts, which he considered unconstitutional], and to adhere to all correct principles. But when men tamper with your rights and with your liberties, when the cities are full of spies and the lowest, meanest of men are set to watch and dog your footsteps; when little children are set in array against their fathers and mothers and women and children are badgered before courts and made to submit, unprotected, to the gibes of libertines and corrupt men, when wives and husbands are pitted against each other and threatened with pains, penalties, and imprisonment, if they will not disclose that which among all decent people is considered sacred, and which no man of delicacy, whose sensibilities had not been blunted by low associations, would ever ask; when such a condition of affairs exist, it is no longer a land of liberty, and it is certainly no longer a land of equal rights, and we must take care of ourselves as best we may, and avoid being caught in any of their snares.[5]

Another document passed out to the members in St. George instructed the Saints not to wait to be approached by federal officials but to "take time by the forelock and keep out of the way":

We must be wise and not stop around home until an officer comes around. When there are two wives living in the same house, it is better to separate them. Our enemies do not want to put the laws into force, but to grind down the people.[6]

Indeed, the leaders set the pace for the members to follow. The members of the Quorum of the Twelve were either sent discreetly on missions abroad or went into hiding. John Taylor himself died after three years in hiding, with a $500 price on his head.

The members—both polygamous and monogamous—responded by hiding the polygamists in their homes or barns, where they grew beards, dyed their hair, and assumed other disguises. Many houses and barns during this period were equipped with trap doors and secret rooms. In one successful hideout, called Camp Serene:

One secret room was cut out of the hay in the barn, reinforced so that no one could accidently fall into it, and equipped with a secret panel as an entrance. No one except [the parents] and those on "The Underground" knew of its existence, and certainly the children never suspected that there was anything unusual about the barn, for they never found this room until years after the "Crusade" was over.[7]

Camp Serene sheltered several Church leaders as well as regular members of the Church.

There were no polygamy laws in Mexico and Canada and many members immigrated to these countries. Others went across the border to Wyoming. Franklin, Idaho, became a regular community of women living under assumed names. Pipe Springs, Arizona (known to the local ranchers as the "the Lambing Ground"), became a place to send women to have their babies.[8] In southern Utah, men hid from time to time in the St. George temple, and one woman, an Alice Yates, spent considerable time living in a church steeple in Panguitch.[9]

Children were instructed to tell strangers nothing about themselves or their families, not even their names. As in the case of Camp Serene, most parents told their children as little as possible so that they would not have to lie and so that they would not let information slip accidentally. Even adults preferred to know little about the guests in their homes so that they would be unable to testify against them at a later date. Many of the children thought it was all "fun and games," and some were taught to act as spies, but others found the period full of trials. A daughter of Edward Gilbert said:

I had a very happy childhood except for the years of the Underground. That was terrible. The officers sometimes came at three in the morning to search the house. At night if we opened the door, people would go scurrying—people who had been looking in the windows to see if father was there. . . . We never knew where father was so if the officers asked us, we couldn't tell them.[10]

Many of these children were not even allowed to play with other children, for fear they would "give something away."

The period was fraught with worry, heartache, and loneliness for the men and women who endured it. Many of the journals of the polygamists show these intense worries. George H. Taylor's account of how he and his first wife tried to protect his second wife is typical:

We had taken precautions as early as April to keep Louie out of the way. She went first to American Fork, and stopped at the Shipleys where our son John Marlow was born [in] April. From there she came home, and as we thought circumstances warranted, kept moving from place to place, stopping at Kaysville, No. Colebrook, Sr. Weinels, and at home, nearly always travelling in the night. Often in the storm, and sometimes with a crying baby.

When these trying times are over, we may probably look back and smile at the pains we took to keep her concealed, but we can never forget the anxiety, care, and constant fear and worry we were subjected to, knowing that persons were on her track to arrest her as a witness against me. Whenever we left, or came into the house, it was with a fear that some one was spying upon us. She generally made her visits back or forth late at night, and every person we met upon the street, we dodged and avoided as much as possible.[11]

This passage is interesting not only because it shows the suffering of the second wife, but also because it shows the love and concern of the first wife for her sister wife. Such concern was also demonstrated by Angelina Baxter, who drove all night to the farm where her husband was hiding with his second wife to warn them that their hideout had been discovered.[12]

There were many secret courtships and marriages during this period. A new wife would usually remain with her own family or at her job as school teacher or seamstress, often living with other secret polygamous wives. Sometimes the new wife was already working in the home of her husband as a domestic or governess, which made the transition easier. She was safe from detection—until she became pregnant. Then, when she particularly needed rest and care, she had to go on the Underground, where so many births occurred without adequate midwives. Annie Clark Tanner, who was living alone, writes about delivering her second child by herself, since she was hiding out and couldn't get help in time.[13] One author described his grandfather's ranch as a station on the Underground:

As a way station on the underground, the ranch saw mysterious visitors come and go. . . . In the upstairs bedrooms of Maria's house were pregnant girls who admitted to no marriage, staying in seclusion as they grew big. Midwives in the night delivered babies without names.[14]

Babies posed other problems for plural wives. Annie Clark Tanner was on the Underground in a home where Wilford Woodruff came as a dinner guest. She refused to respond to his compliment and innocent query of "Who is the father of this handsome child?" A mother would not divulge such information even to the Prophet of the Church in those days! And indeed President Woodruff was gently reprimanded for asking.[15] The second wife of Samuel Spaulding said of the time:

When my babies was young I couldn't live like a normal human being. I had to hide in the granary out there all day long and when my baby cried, I had to feed it and try to cover its head. At night I had to lie in that little bedroom and stifle my baby's cries while the Lord's teachers called. And that was a Mormon community and all was supposed to believe that polygamy was a holy principle. There was no one you could trust in them days.[16]

Some of these women lived in hiding for as long as ten years. Although people on the Underground were generally helpful to them, so many years of having no means of their own took their emotional toll. Annie Clark Tanner wrote with joy about two rooms of a house which, after six years of wandering, she finally had as her very own. As she noted in her diary:

The first day of my housekeeping is over. I have been extremely happy. . . . what a treat to enter one's own home after an absence of but two hours. . . . I sometimes wonder if people enjoy anything if they have not at sometime been denied it. Who realizes the advantage of going to the door to shake a duster or throw out a little water or using all they want of it without carrying it upstairs?[17]

Of course, she did not share this home with her husband, but kept it for herself and her two children.

Although it was difficult for these women to rear their children alone, their lot was better than some who had to leave their children for months at a time. Sometimes the grandparents took care of the children, but more often than not the children were cared for by the legitimate first wife, who didn't have to worry about hiding out.

When they were able to live on their own, like all the "single" women in Franklin, Idaho, they often lived in poverty, since their husbands were either in jail, in flight, or unable to communicate with them. One girl wrote of her mother taking in wash to support them. Many farms deteriorated, and what little money the husbands had was tied up in legal fees. The Church tried to help raise money for legal fees. A circular sent to all bishops and stake presidents dealing with raising money for legal fees also charged that "the families of those brethren who are imprisoned, and those who have been compelled to flee, should be looked after."[18] Many non-polygamists were in financial straits because of their generosity to the polygamists.

The prevalence of spies and "spotters" created the atmosphere of distrust mentioned by Sister Spaulding above. In addition to the increased number of United States marshals, even then called "the feds," a class of informers grew up who made a profession of helping the deputies. These "skunks" and "Mormon-eaters" were usually apostates or gentile neighbors of the polygamists.[19] "Cohab-hunting" could be profitable at the going rate of twenty dollars per polygamist.[20] As evidenced by the statements of John Taylor and others, the marshals got bolder and began to make their raids in the middle of the night. They were not very careful about the legal aspects of their actions and often neglected to obtain search warrants. Church members were constantly advised of their rights concerning illegal search and seizure in the *Deseret News* and other places.

Since the trials themselves were regarded as flagrantly unfair, they too acted to unify the Saints.[21] Many injustices were allowed in unlawful cohabitation trials not normally allowed by the United States Constitution or statute law. The Mormons thought that the 1862 law itself would be declared unconstitutional since it interfered with their right to worship as they pleased. For this reason, George

Reynolds, Brigham Young's secretary, volunteered to go to trial in a test case against the act. To the surprise of all, Reynolds was judged guilty, jailed and fined, and the act's constitutionality was upheld. Rudger Clawson was the first of many to be indicted for polygamy and unlawful cohabitation simultaneously. Since these two charges were really the same thing, Clawson was placed in double jeopardy—a constitutionally illegal action.[22] Lorenzo Snow was one of several tried under Zane's favorite ploy, the principle of "segregation." Segregation neatly sidestepped the maximum penalty of six months in jail and a $300 fine for unlawful cohabitation by dividing the period up into any desired number of days, weeks, or months, counting each time period as a separate offense with a separate indictment. President Snow was charged and convicted with three indictments of unlawful cohabitation, with only the time periods differing.[23]

Several men who had given up living with their plural wives were indicted on the basis that they had at one time lived with these wives (i.e., they were tried under *ex post facto* laws). This brought up a perplexing question: Just what could polygamists do with wives married before the Edmunds Act to show their good faith to the court? They could not divorce these wives, since the marriages were not legally recognized to begin with. To abandon their wives financially and to cease visiting their children would be irresponsible, treating them as even less than divorced women. A Brother Musser provided all of his wives with separate homes and their own deeds and lived only with his first wife, but he did support the other wives financially and did their heavy chores. This action was enough to convict him. Joseph F. Smith was convicted because he had been seen at a funeral which was held at the home of one of his plural wives and at other times in her yard. The court would not solve this problem for the polygamists; one judge remarked, "If the defendant has been unable to find any way to cease living with his polygamous women, it is not the fault of the law that he suffers from his imperfect knowledge."[24] As one writer put it, unlawful cohabitation was interpreted broadly to mean that a man and woman "dwelled together, with sexual intercourse; dwelled under the same roof, but without sexual intercourse; lived in different towns, but visited each other occasionally, with no sexual intercourse; exchanged acts of kindness and attention over a period of years, although not living together and without sexual intercourse."[25]

Women had an especially difficult time during the trials. Many refused to admit that they were married to the men on trial, were badgered by lawyers, and humiliated themselves by declaring that they did not know the fathers of their own children.[26] Although many more men than women were put in jail, some women were imprisoned for contempt for refusing to answer "indelicate questions" about their sexual lives. Some were in prison for several days, some for several months. One woman's treatment especially aroused the general disgust of the Mormon public. Annie Gallifant served only one day in prison, but she was tried and convicted during the advanced stages of pregnancy, delivering her child only days after her release.[27]

The men and women who were imprisoned, approximately 1300, were treated as heroes and heroines by other members of the Church. As one author said, "It's no longer a disgrace to go to prison. It's an honor these days. The very best men of Utah are there."[28] A typical prayer of the period was "God bless those of our brethren who are in prison for righteousness' sake."[29] George Taylor's description of the "farewell reception" held for him on the eve of his imprisonment sounds much like a missionary send-off:

On the 10th of February the people of the ward, tendered me a farewell reception in the ward hall, at which there was a crowded house. The usual programme of singing, recitations and speeches was gone through with. Some poetry composed for the occasion by Sr. Emily Woodmansy, was nicely read by Nellie Colebrook. The verses were nicely printed on large cardboard afterwards and several copies presented to me by W. C. Morris. Of course I had to make them a speech. I enclose a brief notice of the affair as published in the *Deseret News*.[30]

At the Deputy Marshal's office, while awaiting the "Pen Wagon," he and the others convicted were "visited by quite a number of our friends." Upon entering the gates of the prison yard, "we were met and surrounded by our friends who had proceeded us."[31]

Those who did renounce and promise not to break the law had the advantage of lighter sentences, or they were pardoned. However, these men were looked down upon and often lost status and even Church positions in their communities.[32] George Taylor indicated this attitude in his journal:

It was an established fact (from the time of my arrest) in my mind, that I would have to go to prison, as there was no escape, except by promising to give up my wife Louie, which I did not, nor ever intend to let the consequences be what they may. Some few cowards, had made such a promise, and gone back on their covenants and families in order to retain their liberty. But I do not think there was any one who knew me, that ever gave a thought that I would be a traitor.[33]

By the latter half of the 1880s, things in Utah were in a terrible state. The Church was virtually not functioning, having been disincorporated and all its leaders in hiding. Wilford Woodruff summed up the problems in the following statement:

Which is the wisest course for the Latter-day saints to pursue— to continue to attempt to practice plural marriage, with the laws of the land against it and the opposition of 60,000,000 people and at the cost of the confiscation and loss of all the temples, and the stopping of all the ordinances therein, both for the living and the dead, and the imprisonment of the First Presidency and Twelve and the heads of families in the Church and the confiscation of all personal property of the people (all of which of themselves would not stop the practice) or after doing and suffering what we have through our adherence to this principle to cease the practice and submit to the law.[34]

There were also pressures from within the Church. As mentioned above, many members had been financially ruined by their years of hiding or jail, during which farmlands or businesses had been left unattended, or through their generous efforts to help others on the Underground. Many Church members were simply tired of the strain. As one member put it, "People all over Utah were upset and harried and there was beginning to be a different feeling about polygamy."[35] More and more men were giving themselves up and accusing themselves in court in order to receive lighter sentences. This was the beginning of the six-cent fines—quite a contrast to $300 and six months in jail.[36] Because of the railroad and the vanishing frontier, the people sensed that the time of isolation, so necessary to the early Utah Church, was over. So anxious were they for statehood that the Constitution for their 1887 petition for statehood even barred polygamy. However, despite these pressures from within and without the Church, President Woodruff was quite emphatic in his insistence that he would not have abolished polygamy if it had not been revealed to him:

But I want to say this: I should have let all the temples go out of our hands; I should have gone to prison myself; and let every other man go there; had not the God of Heaven commanded me to do what I did do.[37]

When the Manifesto was issued at October Conference in 1890—and sustained unanimously—the reaction of the members seemed to be one of surprise rather than dismay.[38] It had not occurred to the great body of the Church that polygamy would be given up after all they had been through. Reactions varied. Many questioned the authenticity of the revelation. Revelations customarily began, "Thus saith the Lord." The Manifesto began, "To whom it may concern." Wilford Woodruff admitted the problem when he said, "I know there are a good many men and probably some leading men, in this Church who have been tried and felt as though President Woodruff had lost the spirit of God and was about to apostatize."[39] He felt the need to visit various stakes to explain what led up to the Manifesto and assert that it was a revelation. Many were confused because they had thought polygamy was to last forever. One man reconciled the problem in his own mind in this way:

I will say that when polygamy was done away with it was a great blow to me . . . the thing that bothered me was that the Lord had said to the Prophet Joseph that it should be a standing law. . . . Could it be that the Lord has made a mistake? This question bothered me for a long time but it came to me all at once. That it is still a standing law and will be so forever, but we are not allowed to practice it for a while. I can now rest easy about it.[40]

Still others seemed to feel a great wave of relief that something definite had been done, no matter how adversely it affected them. Annie Clark Tanner said:

With the long years of sacrifice just back of me, I was easily convinced that it was from the Lord . . . I can remember so well the relief that I felt when I first realized that the Church had decided to abandon its position. . . . I suppose its leaders may have realized, at last, that if our Church had anything worthwhile for mankind, they had better work with the government of our country rather than against it.[41]

Some, particularly the polygamous wives, were distressed, not relieved. The plural wife of Samuel Spaulding bravely, but resignedly, said:

I was there in the tabernacle the day of the Manifesto, and I tell you it was an awful feeling. There Pres. Woodruff read the Manifesto that made me no longer a wife and might make me homeless. . . . But I voted for it because it was the only thing to do.[42]

Some felt initially that the Manifesto was just a ruse made to pacify the outside world. Not until one year later did Elvira Day note in her journal, with some incredulity:

The Manifesto is real. President Woodruff in court also added that he never hoped to see plurality revived, so I must try to gather faith to stand alone in the Church and all other things.[43]

James Chandler concluded that polygamy's suspension was due to the lack of faith of the members as much as from pressure from the outside world:

The principle is eternal in its nature but God has required His Saints to suspend the practice because of the suffering of His Saints and it may be because it was not obeyed with due sense of its Divine character and the purity and love that should be connected with it.[44]

In the confusion that followed the publication of the Manifesto, polygamists were not sure how to proceed. The Manifesto said that plural marriages were not to be permitted, but said nothing about those already in existence. President Woodruff said that a man was not required to break his covenants with his plural wives but should provide properly for them and his children, but he did not say anything about whether they should continue to live together.[45] The following letter from Chandler to his plural wife shows some of the confusion and heartache of this period:

I can almost see you in my imagination, and I know you are worrying considerably over the thoughts of what I may do since the manifesto of Pres. Woodruff and the action of the Conference; but my advice to you is try and be patient. I have not forgotten the solemn and sacred covenants we have made, nor the love that you have shown for me. . . . It is evident now that if a person is convicted of violating the law he will be punished to the full extent and regarded as not only breaking the law of the land, but disregarding the action of the Church; and though considerable sympathy for him may be felt, it will not be prudent to make any outward display of the same.

We thus are required to manifest our faith and the sincerity of our convictions and the question is, can we stand it? How do you feel? Have you love and confidence enough for me and in me to endure whatever may come and trust to the Lord to hasten the day when these barriers shall be broken that are now erected between us? Or do you feel that is too much. . . . 'Tis

useless for us to talk about what we will do. It would be impru-
dent to write any covenants or agreement. What we have done
is I trust engraven on the tablets of memory and woven into every fiber of our hearts; our dear little children are living evidence of the ties that bind us and I pray God that we may remain firm in our faith, true to our convenants, and faithful to
each other in life, in death, and throughout eternity.[46]

Since prosecutions diminished after the Manifesto,
many polygamists continued to live together. But instead
of seeking them out as in earlier days, the federal officials
just ignored them. This attitude was summed up in a
statement made by the Senate Investigating Committee in
the Smoot hearings some years later:

The conditions existing in Utah have been such that non-Mormons and Mormons alike have acquiesced in polygamous cohabitation on the part of those who married before the Manifesto of 1890, as an evil that could best be gotten rid of by simply
tolerating it until in the natural course of events it shall have
passed out of existence.[47]

But there were many who did give up living with
their spouses. Sometimes the men interpreted the Manifesto to mean that they were relieved of financial responsibilities as well as emotional and physical ties; sometimes girls in unhappy polygamous marriages used the
Manifesto as an excuse to escape. Many heretofore acqui-
escent first wives, secure in their positions as legal
spouses, became real tyrants and ordered other wives out
of their homes. When the high council of one stake reminded one first wife of her duty towards her sister
wives, she retorted, "I am willing to share my cow and
my flour, but not my house and my husband."[48] Such
talking back to the brethren would have been unthinkable
a few years before. As might be expected, the divorce
rate, which had been surprisingly low during the previous forty years, went up (although most couples who
separated did not do so legally). Several cases of neglect
and non-support came up before the high councils. Many
members, especially other polygamists, were upset at this
desertion of families. As Jonathan Baker said:

Some faint-hearted men who have entered into plural marriage have taken advantage of these sayings in the lawyers' courts and put away their plural wives that were given them of the Lord, and deserted them to shift for themselves, taking President Woodruff's statement as a good excuse for so doing.[49]

New feelings about polygamous families also arose. The Underground period had encouraged feelings of solidarity and support in polygamists and non-polygamists alike. When there was no longer any need of rallying around, non-polygamists became critical to the point of pettiness and cruelty, perhaps as a reaction against the long years when they had felt inferior in status to the polygamists. The ones who felt that the Manifesto justified only financial support were scandalized about the families that continued to live together; other neighbors were equally scandalized by those who did not. Everyone seemed willing to judge others and speak his mind. For example, one neighbor persuaded a plural wife of Allen Tiffin to leave her husband. Ironically, Tiffin was the one who lost status in the community and even his Church positions because he had instigated a divorce.[50]

Some plural wives came to be treated as little more than mistresses. One woman wrote that her life after the Manifesto was no different from the Underground days since she continued to live in secret "like I was living a life of sin."[51] Polygamous children were often mercilessly ridiculed and teased by other children, which had not happened before the Manifesto. One plural wife's son in the Morton family recorded his feelings about the post-Manifesto period in the following statement:

After the Manifesto came the hardest time. Up until then people practiced polygamy because of their religion. No matter what happened they had the consolation that they were doing right and living their religion. The persecution did not matter—but when the Church renounced polygamy all the heroism was gone. The whole thing seemed to be in vain. Family life after that was a sort of extended Underground. The attitude of the people changed and in a way there was a stigma attached to polygamous families that had not been there before.[52]

Despite the Manifesto, marriages continued to take place. Samuel Taylor wrote that post-Manifesto marriages were so common that secret plural wives existed in every neighborhood of his home town.[53] These members apparently felt that since the Principle was true and the Church had been more or less forced into renouncing it, the authorities would not be upset if more marriages were performed. Some felt that the Manifesto was issued merely to calm the agitation of the outside world, and that the Church did not really mean it. Others felt that the Manifesto applied only to those Church members living in the United States. Many of these took their families to Canada or to Mexico, where they supposed they were free to live and take more wives. Ironically, some Church members condemned these marriages as harshly as their gentile enemies had a few years before.

The whole issue came to prominence again nationally when Reed Smoot won the 1904 senatorial election. Whether he should be allowed to take his seat in the Senate became a matter of much debate by his colleagues, who had heard, mostly from accusations in the *Salt Lake Tribune*, that polygamy was still rampant in Utah. These Senators felt that even though Smoot was not a polygamist himself, he should not be seated since he was a representative of the Mormons. There followed a year of hearings, in which Smoot denied that any leaders of the Church had taken wives since the Manifesto. The first witness, President Joseph F. Smith, announced that although he had taken no new wives since the Manifesto, his five pre-Manifesto wives had presented him with eleven children since 1890. It was further revealed that two apostles had indeed taken wives and, since this implied sanction from the First Presidency, the men had to be released from the Quorum.[54] This whole episode brought about the more stringent "Second Manifesto" by Joseph F. Smith in 1904, which said in part:

I hereby announce that all such marriages are prohibited, and if any officer or member of the church shall assume to solemnize or enter into any such marriage he will be deemed in transgression against the church, and will be liable to be dealt with according to the rules and regulations thereof and excommunicated therefrom.[55]

To further clear itself in the eyes of the world, the Church actively sought out those who disobeyed the Manifesto rather than relinquishing the offenders to legal action as they had done before 1904. Several men who worked for the Church in educational or other capacities were dismissed for taking post-Manifesto wives.[56] Plural marriages outside the United States were no longer sanctioned. Flagrant disregard of the law brought disfellowship or excommunication.

Although in 1910 the *Salt Lake Tribune* published a list of 220 men "of standing in the Church" who had taken wives since 1890,[57] time was definitely taking its toll. When the Manifesto was first published, 2,451 families were reported. Nine years later, 1,543 remained, and in 1902 there were only 897.[58] It seemed indeed as if polygamy was dying a natural death.

In the history of the Church, attitudes about polygamy have run full circle. At its initial introduction, polygamy was greeted with horror and repugnance, although eventually the members testified fervently of its truthfulness. During the days of persecution, the Principle was defended vigorously by polygamists and non-polygamists alike; after the Manifesto, non-polygamists condemned those families who practiced it, causing them to live in shame and disgrace. Strong opinions still exist in the Church today about the practice of polygamy. In a survey taken in 1962 the general consensus of members was that they would not practice plural marriage under any circumstances.[59] Part of the vehemence against the practice is a reaction against the apostate off-shoots of the

Church who still surreptitiously live it. But to most modern members who are called upon to explain it to incredulous outsiders, it is merely an embarrassment of Mormon history, a skeleton in the family closet. One farsighted plural wife's saddened reaction to the Manifesto was to think how her descendants would ridicule her for having lived the Principle. Not only had she and her fellow plural wives suffered and prevailed as the true heroines of their Mormon culture, but they were in fact and are still victims of the conflict which originally centered on an unbending Church and a crusading, punitive government, and today centers on lack of understanding. In light of the deprivations these staunch upholders of the faith endured, it is a sad commentary on the lack of empathy of Church members today that this woman's prophecy has indeed come true. Perhaps the only defense one can offer of his era's seeming indifference is that polygamy was such a strange and confusing commandment—so foreign to Christians trained in monogamy for hundreds of years and especially repugnant in these days when the whole concept of womanhood is changing—that to fathom what our forefathers *and* foremothers went through or to think what it would be like to practice polygamy ourselves stretches the imagination to realms we do not wish to enter.

Notes

1. Nels Anderson, *Desert Saints* (Chicago: University of Chicago Press, Phoenix Books, 1966), pp. 311–12, 319; Orma Linford, "Mormons and the Law: The Polygamy Cases," *Utah Law Review*, 9 (Winter 1964, Summer 1965), 543–91.
2. George H. Taylor journal, Harold B. Lee Library, Provo, Utah, p. 62.
3. Linford, p. 348.
4. Anderson, p. 318.

5. John Taylor as quoted in B. H. Roberts, *A Comprehensive History of the Church*, 6 vols., (Provo, Utah: Brigham Young University Press, 1965), 6:122–23.

6. Anderson, p. 332, n. 7.

7. Ruth Johnson and Glen F. Harding, eds., *Barnard White Family Book* (Provo, Utah: Brigham Young University Press, 1967), p. 89.

8. Kimball Young, *Isn't One Wife Enough?* (New York: Henry Holt & Co., Inc., 1954), p. 388.

9. Ibid., p. 380.

10. Ibid., pp. 402–3.

11. George H. Taylor, p. 62.

12. Young, p. 289.

13. Annie Clark Tanner, *A Mormon Mother* (Salt Lake City: University of Utah Press, 1969), pp. 111–12.

14. Samuel Woolley Taylor, *Family Kingdom* (New York: McGraw-Hill, 1951), p. 18.

15. Tanner, p. 97.

16. Young, p. 390.

17. Tanner, p. 108.

18. Anderson, p. 314.

19. Not all gentile neighbors were heartless. George Taylor says, "One of the Grand Jurors, Sam Levi was my next door neighbor, but I will give his wife credit for letting us know that they were hunting after Louie because she come and informed us to that effect." (George H. Taylor, pp. 63–64.)

20. Linford, p. 349. Polygamy was enforced by law as "unlawful cohabitation," hence the nickname "cohabs."

21. Some of the jurors made jury duty a profitable business. Linford quoted an S. A. Kenner, who said that the jurors were "men who, by means of a regular routine, are made to know what kind of findings are expected from them and that failure to so find means

immediate dismissal." (Linford, p. 556.) George Taylor noted that his trial took six minutes; with several such trials a day, a juror made good money.

22. Ibid., pp. 350–51.
23. Ibid., pp. 360–64. Lorenzo Snow served his first term (his total sentence was eighteen months and $900) and then was released on an appeal to the Supreme Court, which ruled that unlawful cohabitation was a continuous offense and could not be broken up into individual offenses. President Snow was an elderly gentleman at the time.
24. Ibid., p. 357.
25. Ibid., p. 366.
26. Tanner, pp. 68–9.
27. Young, p. 359.
28. Samuel W. Taylor, *Family Kingdom*, p. 19.
29. Johnson and Harding, p. 90.
30. George H. Taylor, p. 67.
31. Ibid.
32. Bishop John Sharp of Salt Lake City shocked the Mormons when he confessed his guilt (living in polygamy). He was not sent to prison, but paid the $300 fine. Even though he had been a good friend of Brigham Young, his action was condemned and he lost status thereby. (Anderson, p. 317.)
33. George H. Taylor, p. 64.
34. Wilford Woodruff, *Deseret Evening News*, 7 November 1891, p. 4.
35. Young, p. 132. See also Roberts, 4:217–18.
36. Anderson, pp. 324, 333, n. 17; Young, p. 18.
37. Woodruff, *Deseret Evening News*, 7 November 1891, p. 4.
38. The text of the Manifesto follows:

To Whom it may Concern:

Press dispatches having been sent for political purposes, from Salt Lake City, which have been widely published, to the effect that the Utah Commission, in their recent report to the Secretary of the Interior, allege that plural
marriages are still being solemnized and that forty or more
such marriages have been contracted in Utah since last
June or during the past year, also that in public discourses
the leaders of the Church have taught, encouraged and
urged the continuance of the practice of polygamy—

I, therefore, as President of the Church of Jesus Christ
of Latter-day Saints, do hereby, in the most solemn manner, declare that these charges are false. We are not teaching polygamy or plural marriage, nor permitting any person to enter into its practice, and I deny that either forty or
any other number of plural marriages have during that period been solemnized in our Temples or in any other place
in the Territory.

One case has been reported, in which the parties allege
that the marriage was performed in the Endowment
House, in Salt Lake City, in the Spring of 1889, but I have
not been able to learn who performed the ceremony; whatever was done in this matter was without my knowledge.
In consequence of this alleged occurrence the Endowment
House was, by my instructions, taken down without delay.

Inasmuch as laws have been enacted by Congress forbidding plural marriages, which laws have been pronounced constitutional by the court of last resort, I hereby
declare my intention to submit to those laws, and to use my
influence with the members of the Church over which I
preside to have them do likewise.

There is nothing in my teachings to the Church or in
those of my associates, during the time specified which can
be reasonably construed to inculcate or encourage polygamy; and when any Elder of the Church has used language
which appeared to convey any such teaching, he has been
promptly reproved. And I now publicly declare that my advice to the Latter-day Saints is to refrain from contracting
any marriage forbidden by the law of the land.

President Wilford Woodruff in The Doctrine and Covenants (Salt Lake City: The Church of Jesus Christ of
Latter-day Saints, 1960), pp. 256–57.

39. Woodruff, *Deseret Evening News,* 7 November 1891, p. 4.
40. Young, p. 411.
41. Tanner, pp. 114–15.
42. Young, p. 411.
43. Elvira E. Day diary, 4 November 1891, p. 48, LDS Church Archives.
44. James J. Chandler diary, 28 October 1891, pp. 172 –73, LDS Church Archives.
45. Young, pp. 415–16; Anderson, p. 415.
46. Chandler, 19 October 1890, pp. 155–57.
47. Roberts, 6:399.
48. Anderson, p. 416.
49. Young, p. 412.
50. Ibid., pp. 412–13.
51. Ibid., p. 407.
52. Ibid., p. 439.
53. Samuel W. Taylor, "Out of Limbo," *Dialogue,* 7 (Summer 1972), 85.
54. Elders John W. Taylor and M. F. Cowley resigned their apostleships when it was discovered they had performed secret plural marriages, had taken plural wives themselves since the Manifesto, and had misled some members into thinking this behavior was condoned. Elder Taylor said in his letter of resignation that although President Woodruff and others had assumed the Manifesto to prohibit all marriages, he had not considered marriages performed outside the United States to be included in the Manifesto, especially since this interpretation had never been presented to the body of the Church. Brother Cowley was later reinstated as an apostle, but Brother Taylor was subsequently excommunicated for taking yet another wife. (Roberts, 4:399–400.) John Taylor was reinstated as a member in full standing by President David O. McKay in 1965. (Taylor, "Out of Limbo," pp. 86–87.)

55. Roberts, 6:401.
56. Benjamin Cluff and Joseph M. Tanner, for example, were "obliged" to resign their positions at Brigham Young Academy. (Young, p. 420.)
57. Taylor, "Out of Limbo," p. 85.
58. Anderson, pp. 416–17. The census for the 1890 figures was not taken until 1899. Of the families broken up between 1890 and 1899, 750 were due to deaths, ninety-five to divorce and sixty-three to immigration to Mexico, giving a total of 1,543 remaining from the original figure of 2,451.
59. John R. Christiansen, "Contemporary Mormons' Attitudes Toward Polygamous Practices," *Marriage and Family Living*, 25 (May 1963), 167–70.

Susan B. Anthony and intermountain-states suffrage leaders, 1895. The picture includes Utah leaders Emmeline B. Wells, Zina D. H. Young, and Sarah M. Kimball. #P2296, courtesy of LDS Archives.

Practical Politicians
Heather Symmes Cannon

On a gloomy January thirteenth in 1870, Eliza R. Snow inaugurated Utah women's campaign for statehood. Before more than 5,000 women of all ages packed into the Salt Lake Tabernacle, she protested against the United States government:

Our numbers, small at first, have increased, until now we number one hundred and fifty thousand; and yet we are allowed only a territorial government. Year after year we have petitioned Congress for that which is our inalienable right to claim—a State government; and, year after year, our petitions have been treated with contempt. Such treatment as we have received from our rulers, has no precedent in the annals of history.[1]

This speech came between the third petition for statehood filed in 1862 and the fourth petition in 1872. Not until 1896, after six unsuccessful petitions filed over a forty-seven year period, did Utah achieve statehood. Many of the reasons for this unusual delay were closely related to the causes for the unprecedented involvement of women in the statehood struggle.

During this time, when woman's role did not normally include political participation, Mormon women became active politicians; they held mass meetings, lobbied Congress and the President, voted *en masse* from 1870–87, and employed the pressure of the press through the editorial columns of the *Woman's Exponent*. This essay will examine the historical developments leading to the women's involvement in the fight for statehood, their consequent motives and methods, and the impact of their political participation.

For the entire country the years between the Saints' entrance into the Salt Lake Valley in 1846 and the admission of Utah as the forty-fifth state in the union in 1896 were marked by national expansion and homogenization. Geographically, the United States finally reached the Pacific Ocean to achieve its "manifest destiny." Politically, the Civil War and Reconstruction immensely increased federal political power and control. The confederation of states became a union which Lincoln proved could not be divided. Economically, eastern industry, midwestern agriculture, and western natural resources were linked by the Union Pacific Railroad, completed in 1869. The completion of this railroad introduced the era of national trusts and conglomerates, a period of unbridled capitalism and national integration.

In contrast to the rapid unification and homogenization taking place throughout the rest of the country, the "Mormon Kingdom" in Utah was a theocracy characterized by economic self-sufficiency and political, economic, and social exclusiveness. The peculiarities of the Mormons had caused tensions with neighbors resulting in migrations from Ohio to Missouri and then to Illinois in order to escape persecution. Finally the Mormons moved to the great desert, a place no one had wanted. The hope of asylum by isolation was eroded in 1848, however, when the Treaty of Guadalupe Hidalgo terminated the Mexican-American War and extended United States sovereignty to the Pacific coast. The California gold rush with its trail of fortune seekers passing through Utah, the final delineation of the Canadian border, and the completion of the Union Pacific Railroad rendered the hope for separatism futile.

The contention associated with granting Utah statehood was largely generated by the same idiosyncrasies that had caused earlier tensions. Antagonism derived from Mormon economic exclusiveness, the close alliance between church and state, and after 1852, polygamy. As Leonard Arrington stated in the *Great Basin Kingdom*:

That the Mormon Kingdom should continue as a permanent enclave in the American commonwealth was unthinkable to a large segment of American opinion. The system of plural marriage, though admittedly practiced by a small minority of Mormons, was an unspeakable vice; the theocratic economy interfered with the spread of capitalistic institutions; and the supposed church control of political life was thought to be inconsistent with democracy.[2]

Horace Greeley vividly portrayed the severity of the fears these Mormon peculiarities generated. Writing for the *New York Tribune* from Utah in 1859, Greeley stated:

"Popular sovereignty" has such full swing here that Brigham Young carries the territory in his breeches' pocket without a shadow of opposition; for there is no real power here but that of "the church," and he is practically the church. The church is rich . . . the church settles all civil controversies which elsewhere cause lawsuits; the church spends little or nothing yet rules everything; while the federal government, though spending two or three millions per annum here, and keeping up a fussy parade of authority, is powerless and despised.

Whether truly or falsely, this army [at Camp Floyd, Utah] probably without exception, undoubtingly believes the Mormons as a body to be traitors to the Union and its government, inflexibly intent on establishing here a power which shall be at first independent of, and ultimately dominant over that of the United States.[3]

Though the Civil War did in fact provide fleeting visions of total independence from and even dominance over the rest of the United States,[4] the rapid organization of the West into United States territories virtually prohibited secession.

Anticipating the dangers of territorial status which allowed federal intervention in local affairs, Utah petitioned for statehood immediately after the signing of the Treaty of Guadalupe Hidalgo. This initial petition was for a State of Deseret which encompassed one-seventh of the existing United States territory. A constitutional convention had drafted a constitution and slate of officers which were approved by popular vote at the next election, but Congress rejected this first petition with its proposed constitution and officials. The slave state-free state issue determined this decision with little attention paid to the local situation in Utah. Thus, the Compromise of 1850 ignored the statehood petition and made both Utah and New Mexico territories.[5]

Utah women did not participate in this initial attempt for statehood. However, its failure and the consequent territorial status of Deseret had a profound effect on their eventual role; for it was Utah's territorial status that permitted the national legislature to enact laws relating to marriage in Utah. Traditionally, each state held the right to determine its own marital laws, to have a militia, to incorporate organizations, and to govern without federal interference in all areas not explicitly designated as national. Territories did not have these rights. Any territorial law could be overturned by national legislation, and federal courts could take over all local adjudication. Ironically, the political independence the Mormons had sought by moving beyond the reach of established gentile control eluded them, because the territorial status of Utah still left Mormons under the jurisdiction of gentiles.

By 1856, when Utah again applied for statehood, the Utah theocracy had attracted national attention. The Republican Party's platform in 1856 announced that the practice of polygamy had to be destroyed. Furthermore, the Church's Reformation of 1856 threatened disloyalty to the United States when leaders called for self-sufficiency and purged alien influences, even boycotting gentile businesses as well as ostracizing non-Mormons socially and politically. At a time when the South was rumbling of secession, the Mormon echo heightened national indignation towards the Mormons and this second statehood petition died in committee.[6] In fact the Utah War in 1857 can be viewed as a show of strength by the national government to the South. The war provided proof that the Democrats who conducted the campaign against Utah were as determined to defend the union as the Republicans.[7]

Utah next applied for statehood in 1861, after Nevada was carved from the Utah territory. The constitution proposed and the officials elected for this petiton served as a ghost government until 1872. This ghost government met at the close of each territorial legislative session and passed identical laws. Addressing the first ghost legislature, Brigham Young explained the motivation for this procedure as a preparation for the time when the United States government would fall apart. He warned:

But I do not want you to lose any part of this Government which you have organized. For the time will come when we will give laws to the nations of the earth. . . . We should get all things ready.[8]

Implied in this statement is the thought that the impending Civil War would dissolve the Union, paving the way for the Kingdom of God with government emanating from Zion. The successful preservation of the Union dashed these hopes.

The failure of this third statehood petition in 1863 left the Mormons still vulnerable to national legislation. The passage of the Morrill Act prohibiting polygamy in 1862 reaffirmed the national intent to exert power over the territories. This act was not enforced during the war since there was no desire to fight on a second front, and the national government needed to keep Utah open as a passage to California. However, with the end of the Civil War a rash of bills was presented to Congress aimed at enforcing the Morrill Act.

The Morrill Act had presumed that Congress had a right to outlaw polygamy as it had slavery. Later bills, based on further reconstructionist tenets, assumed the federal government had the right to suspend voting privileges, to exact oaths of loyalty, and to overhaul or oversee local government by the appointment of federal commissions supported by the military. The constitutionality of these post-Civil War bills was questioned by the national press and none was passed immediately. However, the essential features of these bills were finally enacted during the eighties in the Edmunds and Edmunds-Tucker Acts, after the nation was sufficiently aroused by anti-Mormon propaganda to apply these extensions of federal power against Utah.

The Cullom Bill was the most threatening of the post-Civil War bills. This bill gave federal officials responsibility and broad power for enforcing polygamy laws. It also deprived wives of immunity as witnesses and made cohabitation a misdemeanor. This threat to polygamy and to the Church's political and judicial power in Utah elicited strong feminine protest. In 1870 the women held the first of many mass meetings protesting the impending passage of this bill.

Mass meetings were the most dramatic form of feminist political action. Meetings were held in the prominent cities and towns of Utah in 1870, 1878, and 1886. The speakers protested against national legislation and judicial abuses and injustices, debated anti-Mormon propaganda and misrepresentation of their situation, and defended their religion and themselves. Resolutions were drafted and sent to Congress and the President. Generally, a series of meetings was inaugurated by a huge meeting in the Salt Lake Theatre or Tabernacle. In 1886 the Church-owned railroads issued half-fare tickets to women wishing to attend the-Salt Lake meeting, and the Church newspaper, the *Deseret News*, strongly encouraged attendance. The rural meetings featured local speakers, but usually passed the resolutions drafted at the Salt Lake meeting without modification. Utah women who had traveled from their New England or European homes, suffering the persecutions and trials of the exodus for the sake of their religion, were distressed by the attempts to restrict or suspend altogether the practice of their religion. In her introductory remarks before the Salt Lake Mass Meeting in 1870, Mrs. Sarah M. Kimball said, "We have been driven from place to place, and wherefore? Simply for believing and practicing the counsels of God, as contained in the gospel of heaven."[9] Harriet Cook Young reemphasized this point of view, stating in response to the threatened Cullom legislation:

We, the ladies of Salt Lake City, have assembled here today . . . to express our indignation at the unhallowed efforts of men, who regardless of every principle of manhood, justice, and constitutional liberty, would force upon a religious community, by direct issue, either the course of apostasy, or the bitter alternative of fire and sword. Surely, the instinct of self-preservation, the love of liberty and happiness, and the right to worship God, are dear to our sex as well as to the other; and when these most sacred of all rights are thus wickedly assailed, it becomes absolutely our duty to defend them.[10]

Since attacks on the Mormon theocracy focused on the inflammatory polygamy issue, the women's duty to defend their faith involved a defense of this practice. Critics of Mormonism asserted that women and children living under the autocratic Mormon patriarchy had not learned to make the independent choices and judgments basic to democracy. Mormon women were typically described as degraded, miserable, and bitter; and the mental and moral competence of the women and their offspring was questioned. In their defense the women praised polygamy as conducive to the "elevation and independence of women."[11] In an "unspoken speech" in her journal, Emily Dow Partridge Young, widow of Brigham Young, wrote in 1879, "The Principle [of] Polygamy or 'Plural Marriage' is as pure as the Gods. It is not that, that causes the foul stench that taints the air. It is the corruption of our assailants that breeds pestilence."[12]

Legislative threats to the Mormon faith and insults to the women's honor, virtue, and intelligence spurred the women to political activism. The following statement of Eliza R. Snow epitomizes this motivation for female involvement:

Were we the stupid, degraded, heartbroken beings that we have been represented, silence might better become us; but as women of God, women fulfilling high and responsible positions, performing sacred duties—women who stand not as dictators, but as counselors to their husbands, and who, in the purest, noblest sense of refined womanhood, are truly helpmates—we not only speak because we have the right, but justice and humanity demand that we should.[13]

The vehemence of Utah's objection to this legislation and particularly the women's mass protest meetings were conducive to the ultimate failure of the Cullom Bill.[14]

Some claim the Cullom Bill also inspired the Mormon-dominated Utah legislature to enact female suffrage, assuming the women would support their husbands in opposing similar legislation on the state level. A female suffrage bill for the territories was presented to Congress in 1857 by George Washington Julian, Republican Congressman from Indiana. The bill had been suggested by the New York Times as a means to eliminate polygamy. Enactment of female suffrage in Utah in 1870 actually reinforced the Church's stand by doubling the faithful electorate. Though Church leaders expressed no opinions on female suffrage previous to its unanimous approval by both houses of the territorial legislature, they heartily supported it thereafter.

Some Mormon women in 1870 expressed mixed feelings as to women's role in politics. Mrs. M. T. Smoot said:

We are engaged in a great work, and the principles that we have embraced are life and salvation unto us. Many principles are advanced on which we are slow to act. There are many more to be advanced. Women's rights have been spoken of. I have never had any desire for more rights than I have. I have considered politics aside from the sphere of women; but, as things progress, I feel it is right that we should vote though the path may be fraught with difficulty. [15]

Such political reticence probably explained the temperance with which Mrs. Sarah M. Kimball described the purpose of the 1870 meetings:

The object of this meeting is to consider the justice of a bill now before the Congress of the United States. We are not here to advocate woman's rights, but man's rights. The bill in question would not only deprive our fathers, husbands and brothers, of enjoying the privileges bequeathed to citizens of the United States, but it would deprive us, as women, of the privilege of selecting our husbands; and against this we unqualifiedly protest. [16]

Other 1870 speeches emphasized the persecutions of the Saints and the women's disgust with the "manifest degeneracy of the great men of our nation" who were proponents of the bill. [17] The resolutions voted by the meeting and sent to Congress emphasized the unconstitutionality of the Cullom Bill, the women's belief in and defense of polygamy, and their right to "exert all our power and influence to aid in the support of our own State government." [18]

Despite these separatist hints in 1870, the constitution adopted for the fourth statehood petition in 1872 gave some indication that Mormons might be willing to compromise. The fifth article of this constitution agreed to "such terms . . . as may be prescribed by Congress as a condition of the admission of said State into the union." [19] The gentile Liberal Party in Utah opposed this petition as it had all others; statehood would guarantee it a minority status. These efforts, coupled with a national lack of faith in Mormons, who were still ignoring the Morrill Act, resulted in the defeat of this statehood attempt.

The failure of this fourth statehood petition coincided with the passage of the Poland Bill in 1874, which enacted the previously defeated provision to take jurisdiction for polygamy cases out of the Mormon-controlled territorial courts and put them in the federal courts where some convictions could be obtained. This law paved the way for an intensified anti-polygamy campaign by Utah gentiles, who now hoped to gain political control of the territory.

In 1878 mass meetings were held in response to a militant gathering sponsored by the Anti-Polygamy Society. Gentile women founded this Utah organization in response to the notorious Carrie Owens Case. Carrie Owens married John Miles who, the same day, married another wife. Though forewarned of the arrangement, Miss Owens rebelled later in the day, reported her husband to the United States Marshal, and asked the gentile ladies for their support. The ladies sent a statement to President Hayes' wife and the women of the nation denouncing polygamy. They asked Congress for further laws to enforce existing anti-polygamy legislation and to delay the admission of Utah as a state until enforcement was accomplished.

The Mormon women responded by protesting *en masse* "against the misrepresentation and falsehood now against our people."[20] The gentile paper, the *Daily Tribune*, estimated the attendance at the Mormon meeting at 12,000 (total Salt Lake population was 23,000 at that time), but claimed this was proof of Mormon women's weakness, for "the part of the helpless and deluded Mormon wives is to obey and at the call of the holy priesthood they turn out without a murmur to testify to the bounties of a system which has wrecked their happiness."[21] The *Deseret News* cited the large attendance as a proof "that the best way to consolidate and give stronger activity to a religious cause, is to persecute and seek to destroy it."[22]

A dominant theme of these 1878 meetings was a criticism of the gentile ladies for trespassing on the homeland the Mormon women had created out of the desert. Emily Dow Partridge Young mused about the gentile ladies' motivation in her journal:

They look upon our pleasant homes with greedy eyes. Their fingers itch to lay hold of our possessions. It grieves them to think of so many millions of dollars spent in building temples; and then they can't find out what is done in those temples. They have waited long, and worked hard to overthrow Mormonism and to oust this people that they might take the spoils. They begin to be tired of waiting; and fearful it may slip through their fingers, if they don't make a desperate effort, and rouse all hell to work with them.[23]

The resolutions passed at these 1878 meetings defended the free exercise of religion and protested laws depriving citizens of their rights. The women avowed their faith in plural marriage. They called for the passage of a women's suffrage amendment currently being circulated in the United States and thanked the Woman's Suffrage Association for their support in opposition to bills designed to nullify Utah's Woman's Suffrage Act.

In 1879 the Reynolds Decision in the Supreme Court, which substantiated the legality of the Morrill Act, inaugurated the period of the "raids" and the "Underground." Another statehood petition was sent to Congress in 1882. Three women were elected to the convention which prepared the state constitution included with this petition. The failure of this fifth statehood attempt, which had been actively supported by Utah women, was inevitable at a time when even the President was determined to punish Utah for the continued practice of plural marriage.[24] Furthermore, the Republican-Democrat balance of power in Congress was so tenuous that no new states were admitted from 1876–89. With the rejection of this fifth Utah statehood attempt died the last hope for escape from severe national legislation. The Edmunds-Tucker Act passed in 1887 added insult to injury by abolishing women's suffrage in Utah.

The last series of mass meetings held in 1886 protested the imminent passage of this act. Because Mormon women had not voted to overthrow their leaders, their ability to exercise independent judgment was questioned. When the Edmunds-Tucker Act abolished female suffrage in Utah, the justification was that the women voted only as instructed by their husbands. Delegates at the 1886 mass meeting protested:

Resolved, By the women of Utah in mass meeting assembled, that the suffrage originally conferred upon us as a political privilege, has become a vested right by possession and usage for fifteen years, and that we protest against being deprived of that right without process of law, and for no other reason than that we do not vote to suit our political opponents.

Resolved, that we emphatically deny the charge that we vote otherwise than according to our own free choice, and point to the fact that the ballot is absolutely secret in Utah as proof that we are protected in voting for whom and what we choose with perfect liberty. [25]

These meetings also protested the legal excesses practiced since the passage of the Edmunds Act in 1882 and their potential expansion by the passage of the Edmunds-Tucker Bill. Resolutions objected to the "cruel and inhuman proceedings in the Utah courts," to "compelling legal wives to testify against their husband without their consent," to "questions concerning [women's] personal condition . . . and the paternity of their born and unborn children," and to the treatment of women who "have gone to prison and suffered punishment without crime, rather than betray the most sacred confidence." [26] Included with the resolutions sent to Congress was a series of case histories delineating these abuses.

It is interesting that the mass meetings evolved from defenses of polygamy and threats of national defiance in 1870 to legalistic protests against judicial excesses and abuses of female rights in 1886. The succession of petitions sent by Utah women to Congress and the President followed the same trend. Early petitions, such as one in October 1871, signed by 2,500 women, demanded the repeal of the Morrill Act and admission to statehood. In 1874, 30,000 women demanded the repeal of the Morrill and Poland Acts. Later petitions appealed for relief from law-breaking officials. In 1879 the Supreme Court had ruled that the Morrill Act was legal. Thereafter, the petitions of the Mormon women addressed themselves to the protection of women and children who had lost their legitimacy and inheritance rights by the decision. Many of the petitions were taken to the White House personally by feminine leaders. Emmeline Wells met directly with President and Mrs. Hayes and came away with a very favorable view of the first lady despite her husband's opposition to the Mormons.

After their suffrage was rescinded in 1887, the women turned to the *Woman's Exponent* as their main political forum. *Exponent* editorials protested the injustice of disfranchising the women and continued the objections to the mistreatment of women by officials and courts. Articles also emphasized Utah's desire for statehood and kept the women abreast of the progress of the statehood struggle.

In 1887 the sixth statehood petition was filed. This legislation forbade polygamy and the union of church and state. All members of the constitutional commission took a "test oath" swearing they were not practicing polygamy, but even this was not acceptable to Congress. When the Supreme Court declared the Edmunds-Tucker Act constitutional in 1890, it was obvious that the Church could not long survive. The leaders were in perpetual hiding, the Church property was rapidly dissolving, the performance of temple ordinances had been suspended, and there was no hope for judicial redress.

The issuance of the Manifesto terminated this intolerable situation. The Manifesto was the first step in Mormon acceptance of the need for accommodation to national norms. There is no indication that women were anxious for this move and the *Exponent* reported it without comment. With the Manifesto the era of persecution ended. The dissolution of the Mormon political party—the People's Party—and the establishment of common schools evidenced the willingness of the Mormon Church to withdraw from its political and educational roles. In return,

Presidents Harrison and Cleveland granted amnesty to polygamists and returned Church properties.

The focus of women's political activities then turned from a religious patriotism to a more specific interest in defending women's rights and in particular their right to suffrage. Though this right had been readily granted by the Mormon establishment when women's political support was needed, female suffrage was the most controversial issue in the final constitutional convention in 1894. The political expertise gleaned from their participation in the struggle for statehood served Mormon women well; women's suffrage was upheld and Utah entered the union as the third state with female suffrage, twenty-four years before the passage of the Nineteenth Amendment extended women's suffrage throughout the nation.

In the first state elections women served on the Republican State Central Committee as vice-chairman and secretary. Dr. Martha Hughes Cannon became the first woman in the United States to serve as a state senator and Eurithe K. LeBarthe and Sarah E. Anderson won house seats.

Women's participation in the political struggle for statehood and their continued political activism were unusual at a time when other American women were just beginning to voice themselves politically. Initially, national issues such as the extension of United States sovereignty across the continent and the demand for Mormon conformity with national norms determined Utah's fate. Because Utah's theocratic autonomy conflicted sharply with the rapid unification and homogenization taking place nationally, the struggle for Utah's statehood was unusually protracted. The publication of the Manifesto and later Church acts abandoning Mormon claims to temporal power ended the conflict. Utah had acceded to the national demand for a monogamic, non-theocratic, capitalistic state.

However, women did have some influence on the course of the struggle. Women are sometimes credited with delaying the stringent provisions of the Cullom Bill for twelve years.[27] At the very least they succeeded in convincing the opposition of their virtue. The *New York Herald*, in reporting the 1870 mass meeting, conceded:

We venture to say that whatever may be the individual reader's opinion of merits or demerits of Mormon institutions, it will not be denied that Mormon women have both brains and tongues. Some of the speeches give evidence that in general knowledge in logic and rhetoric the so-called degraded ladies of Mormondom are quite equal to the Women's Rights Women of the East.[28]

The "Women's Rights Women" of the National Women's Suffrage Association not only recognized Mormon women's intellectual equality, but defended in Congress Utah women's right to suffrage during the Edmunds and Edmunds-Tucker debates. In addition, the Mormon women's petitions for protection of legitimacy and inheritance rights bore fruit; polygamous children conceived before the Manifesto were granted legitimacy, and previously contracted marriages were effectively honored.

But the greatest benefit the women gained from their participation in the statehood struggle was their political expertise. As Mrs. Isabella Horne in her introductory remarks to the 1886 mass meeting had stated:

It has been said by some, "What good will it do to hold a mass meeting?" If it does no other good, it will be a matter of history, to be handed down to our posterity, that their Mothers rose up in the dignity of their womanhood to protest against the insults and indignities heaped upon them.[29]

Furthermore, participation in the statehood struggle led to the franchise and the right to hold public office. The potential of these precocious victories was emphasized in an *Exponent* editorial in April 1896, which warned:

The women of Utah are being watched as no other women are at the present time, and it should be their laudable ambition to set an example even in political affairs that other states can point to with pride and seek to emulate.[30]

Relief Society leaders Elizabeth Ann Whitney, Emmeline B. Wells, and
Eliza R. Snow. #P892, courtesy of LDS Archives.

Mormon women's experience as victims of and participants in the statehood struggle left them with an interest, progressive in their day, in more general political issues. The nature of this interest is perhaps best exemplified by the following editorial in the *Exponent* in August 1893:

In the present state of affairs in this country, women are and very naturally must be [as] deeply interested as men if not even more. Women will likely be the greatest real sufferers for more men run away from trouble than women. . . . Consequently, women should take an active part in ameliorating the condition if anything can be done, and at any rate to try and become acquainted with the situation and see wherein their efforts may be available.[31]

The experiences of the statehood struggle also created among the women an awareness of their political responsibilities and possibilities. A poem from an *Exponent* of October 1894 illustrated this awareness:

Equal Rights

Now the voice of womankind is startling all the world;
   Woman must have equal rights with man.
Everywhere beneath the sun her banner is unfurled.
   Woman must have equal rights with man.
We but ask for freedom and the right to live and be,
   What we are designed in God's great plan;
And we're sure all thinking men will very shortly see,
   Woman must have equal rights with man.

Come my sister, let us rise and educate our minds,
   Put aside our follies great and small;
Work with heart and soul to help all womankind,
   Gather round our standard one and all.
Do not pause nor falter, but be valiant in the fight,
   And the flame of liberty we'll fan.
Till it spreads o'er all the land, then hail the time of right,
   When woman shall have equal rights with man.[32]

It is doubtful that this strong expression of female independence would have been possible had the statehood struggle not exposed Mormon women to the potentialities of political activism.

Although national developments dominated the early progression of the Utah statehood struggle, later events were largely determined by the resolution of differences between national and Mormon mores. Women's influence and interests were important factors in this reconciliation. Their protests helped delay enactment of the most stringent anti-polygamy legislation; and their influence ensured legitimacy and inheritance protection for polygamous children. These women exhibited massive unified political activism far in advance of their sisters in the rest of the country. This experience gained them the privileges of being the third state with female suffrage and the first to have a female state senator. Ironically, a result of the national campaign to free Mormon women from the bonds of polygamy was an unprecedented political activism.

Notes

1. Edward W. Tullidge, *Women of Mormondom* (New York, 1877), p. 389.
2. Leonard J. Arrington, *Great Basin Kingdom* (Lincoln: University of Nebraska Press, 1958), p. 352.
3. Horace Greeley, *An Overland Journey* (New York: Alfred A. Knopf, 1964), pp. 193, 211.
4. Gustive O. Larson, *The Americanization of Utah for Statehood* (San Marino, Calif.: The Huntington Library, 1971), pp. 27–28.
5. Ibid., p. 6.
6. Ibid., p. 59.
7. Howard Roberts Lamar, *The Far Southwest 1846–1912, A Territorial History* (New Haven: Yale University Press, 1966), p. 340.
8. Larson, p. 29.
9. Tullidge, *Women of Mormondom*, p. 380.
10. Ibid., p. 384.

11. *Mormon Women's Protest . . . An Appeal for Freedom, Justice and Equal Rights. A full account of proceedings at the Great Mass Meeting held in the theatre*, Salt Lake City, 6 March 1886, p. 28.

12. Emily Dow Partridge Young journal, Harold B. Lee Library, Brigham Young University, p. 42.

13. Tullidge, *Women of Mormondom*, p. 392.

14. Larson, p. 72 and Tullidge, *Women of Mormondom*, p. 452.

15. Edward W. Tullidge, *History of Salt Lake City* (Salt Lake City: Star Printing Co., 1886), pp. 435–37.

16. Tullidge, *Women of Mormondom*, p. 381.

17. Ibid., p. 385.

18. Ibid.

19. Tullidge, *History of Salt Lake City*, pp. 557–58.

20. Larson, p. 88.

21. *Salt Lake Tribune*, 17 November 1878, p. 1.

22. *Deseret News*, 10 November 1878, p. 66.

23. Kimball Young, *Isn't One Wife Enough?* (New York: Henry Holt and Co., 1954), p. 47.

24. Tullidge, *History of Salt Lake City*, pp. 824–25.

25. *Mormon Women's Protest*, p. 80.

26. Ibid.

27. Tullidge, *Women of Mormondom*, p. 452.

28. Larson, p. 68.

29. *Mormon Women's Protest*, p. 8.

30. *Woman's Exponent*, 22 (15 March, 1 April 1896), 132.

31. Ibid., 22 (15 August 1893), 20.

32. S. C. M., "Equal Rights," *Woman's Exponent*, 23 (15 October 1894), 195.

Suffrage leaders Emily Richards, Sarah M. Kimball, and Phoebe Beatie in 1875. #C-95, Box 2, Fol. 4, used by permission, Utah State Historical Society; all rights reserved.

Feminists
Judith Rasmussen Dushku

In a letter to the editor dated August 1877, a Philadelphia woman confessed that until she read the *Woman's Exponent* she had not looked upon "woman suffrage in Utah as worth a fillip." Under polygamy, she had assumed, "each man has not merely his own vote, but just as many votes as he owns wives, and that each woman is either an oriental doll or a domestic drudge, with neither impulse nor impetus towards an individualized existence." The outspoken feminism of the *Exponent* changed her mind and she acknowledged that "the women of the States have jumped at very unjust conclusions in regard to their sisters in Utah."[1]

In the 1870s Utah's women were indeed misunderstood. In important respects, they still are. In most histories of the movement, female suffrage in Utah has been treated as a curiosity strangely unrelated to feminist agitation elsewhere. Historians have been unable to explain why the "last outpost of barbarism" should have extended the vote to women in 1870, fifty years before the nation adopted the Nineteenth Amendment and decades before women's suffrage had acquired respectability elsewhere. Some writers have suggested that the male hierarchy simply saw a chance to enlist the help of women against threats from anti-polygamists in Washington and at home.[2] Mormon writers have more often seen the suffrage act as a logical extension of the law of common consent, which had included both sexes from the earliest years of the Church.[3] But neither group has paid enough attention to the women themselves and to their relationship with the wider equal rights movement of the nineteenth century.

While Utah women first received the vote without petitions or demonstrations, they still spoke out, freely and frequently, in behalf of the extension of that right to women elsewhere. They campaigned in favor of the other causes motivating eastern feminists—wages, educational opportunities, and legal status. In 1887, when Congress took away their right to vote with the passage of the Edmunds-Tucker Act, their feminism acquired a new urgency. By 1895 they were prepared, organizationally and ideologically, for victory in the suffrage controversy which erupted in Utah's statehood convention. For twenty-five years Utah's independent women showed their dedication to the cause. They demonstrated their feminism in three major areas—in publishing, in grass-roots organizing, and in personal association with national women's rights leaders.

I

The *Woman's Exponent*, a bi-monthly paper produced in Salt Lake City from 1872 until 1914, did not significantly alter its focus on women's issues through more than forty years of publication. Its tone was neither self-conscious nor cautious, and it firmly and directly discussed feminist ideas and explained how they enhanced gospel ideals. Modern readers are often surprised at its forthrightness. "Woman feels her servitude, her degradation, and she is determined to assert her rights," said an editorial of the 1870s.[4] For more than twenty years the subtitle of the paper was, "The Rights of Women of Zion and the

Rights of Women of all Nations."[5] The history of the *Exponent* testifies both to the vigor with which Mormon women agitated for the goals of the national movement and to the widespread official support which made such agitation possible.

Significantly, the *Exponent* was first published on Brigham Young's birthday, 2 June 1872, and every June thereafter tribute was paid to him. The anniversary issue for 1881, for example, praised his efforts in behalf of the Relief Society and of women's suffrage and went on to explain his role in the founding of the paper:

President Young was also desirous the women of Zion should publish a paper in their own interest, and was solicitous that it should be extensively circulated, and that the sisters should preserve their volumes and have them bound, for, he said, "It will contain a portion of Church history, the record of the works and experiences of women," and in honor of him this paper was first issued on his birthday the first of June, 1872.[6]

It is not surprising that passages from Brigham Young's speeches were often printed. He had been the paper's first advocate. But other authorities were equally generous in their support. In a discourse given 10 May 1874, President George A. Smith said:

The Woman's Relief Society are publishing a paper called the *WOMAN'S EXPONENT*, which is a very ably edited sheet, and one containing a great deal of information. I am surprised that the gentlemen in the Territory do not take it. I invite all the elders, bishops, and presiding officers in the stakes of Zion, on their return home, setting the example themselves, to solicit all their brethren, and especially the sisters, to become subscribers of this little sheet. . . . I will say that we expect in a short time, through the patronage of the brethren and sisters, that the ladies will be able to enlarge this paper, and to extend its influence far and wide.[7]

From its inception then, the *Exponent* had the good wishes of the brethren. Yet the *Exponent* was neither owned nor directly controlled by the Church, and it was financed by subscriptions. It did, however, publicize activities of the Relief Society and was widely regarded as the Society's voice. It regularly solicited reports from local branches, as in this announcement from an early issue:

Utah, in its Female Relief Societies, has the best organized benevolent institution of the age; yet, but little is known of the self-sacrificing labors of these Societies. In WOMAN'S EXPONENT a department will be devoted to reports of their meetings and other matters of interest connected with their workings; and to this end the Presidents and Secretaries of the various Societies throughout the Territory are requested to furnish communications which will receive due attention.

Miss Eliza R. Snow, President of the entire Female Relief Societies, cordially approves of the journal, and will be a contributor to it as she has leisure from her numerous duties.[8]

The close association of the *Exponent* with the Relief Society is further evidenced in the careers of the editors. Lula Greene Richards, the founding editor, and a grandniece of Eliza R. Snow, was apparently given the blessing of Brigham Young when she expressed doubt about her abilities to fulfill the assignment. After five years she was succeeded by Emmeline B. Wells, a close friend and counselor of Zina D. H. Young, one of Brigham's wives, who was then Relief Society President. When Sister Wells was herself made president in 1910, she continued to edit the *Exponent*, which survived until 1914, when it was replaced by a Church-controlled *Relief Society Magazine* edited by Susa Young Gates.

The *Woman's Exponent* was an independent paper published with the encouragement and goodwill of Church leaders. Just as the distinction between secular and sacred remained fluid in early Utah, the line between "official" and "unofficial" enterprises had not yet formed. An editorial in the 15 November 1889 issue claimed that for over seventeen years the *Exponent* had been "the official organ of the women of Zion." It was entitled to this distinction, the author went on to say, because it had published reports from all women's organizations: the Relief Society, the Young Ladies' Associations, and the Primary Associations; because it had "always given information on the suffrage question"; because it had advocated the "woman's side of all vexed questions"; because it had published biographical sketches of the leading women of the Church; and because it had publicized the activities of the Woman's Suffrage Association in Utah. "It is certainly in the strict sense of the word a representative woman's paper, and it is more desirable that *every* President of a Relief Society should have a copy, and as many others as can, because it gives them the idea of their own work and that of others, besides general information," she concluded.[9]

As the voice of Utah's women, the *Exponent* exemplified the three defining qualities of feminism in any age: a desire to encourage women to speak for and to women, a sense of injustice and inequality of opportunity, a conviction of the absolute equality of the sexes. These three qualities can be seen not only in the vigorous editorials of Emmeline Wells, but in letters from correspondents in remote places.

Women must stand up and speak for themselves. This had been the conviction of Elizabeth Cady Stanton when she gathered her neighbors together at Seneca Falls. It was the conviction of the editors and authors of the *Woman's Exponent*. An editorial in the 1 March 1878 issue defended women against the charges of "an eminently popular and learned man" who had written that "the greatest nuisance in society . . . is a woman who thinks she has a special mission." Women do have a special mission, the author asserted, a mission that cannot be fulfilled through her influence on her family alone:

If woman has so much wisdom to counsel others, if her advice is judicious and her influence salutary, then why may she not be capable of acting out her own nature, expressing her own views, instead of doing so by proxy through her husband, her brother, or some friend?[10]

Neither vicarious influence nor coat-tail salvation was sufficient for the Latter-day Saint woman. "Girls don't be afraid of the term 'strong-minded,'" another column had cautioned, "for of such there is certainly a necessity; the stronger you are in mind and body the better for you . . . do not wait for any other person to bring you forward."[11]

A correspondent from Manti North Ward noted that it was customary for "the lords of creation" to quote the Apostle Paul in denying women the right to speak. While acknowledging the many good things in the writings of Paul, this sister questioned whether he was qualified to define the position of women:

Now let us ask, Who was Paul? In the first place Paul was a Roman, second an educated lawyer, third he was a bachelor as we learn from reading, 1st. Cor., 7th Chap, 7th and 8th verses, fourth he tells us in his defense before Agrippa that he was "raised a Pharisee" in the strictest sense of the word, and last we know, he did not enjoy that constant and elevating association with Jesus, which the other apostles were privileged to enjoy, and, which might have softened, or slightly ameliorated his views toward women.[12]

After this venture into higher criticism, the writer went on to testify of the coming role of women in Christ's plan, urging her sisters to become Marys, not Marthas. Neither the Pauline epistles nor the contemporary ridicule of witty men altered the desire of Utah's women to speak for themselves.

Zion's women had good reason to complain of injustice. They were held in derision by most of the world. But the *Woman's Exponent* was as ready to expound the common grievances of women everywhere as to defend their own cause. There are examples in every issue. A letter from Grantsville in the 1870s, for instance, decried the sexual exploitation of young women and the double standard of judgment applied to seducer and seduced.[13] A long article in an 1890 paper documented the need for equal pay for equal work,[14] while a poem from the 1880s vowed to "strike" for better working conditions in the home:

> In the daylight shall be crowded all the work
> that I will do:
> When the evening lamps are lighted, I will
> read the papers too.[15]

Emmeline Wells was particularly concerned with the constraints of the pedestal:

See the manner in which ladies—a term for which I have little reverence or respect—are treated in all public places! . . . She must be preserved from the slightest blast of trouble, petted, carressed, dressed to attract attention, taught accomplishments that minister to man's gratification; in other words, she must be treated as a glittering and fragile toy, a thing without brains or soul, placed on a tinselled and unsubstantial pedestal by man, as her worshipper.[16]

Like feminists in the eastern states, authors in the *Woman's Exponent* urged exercise, sensible clothing, and general improvement of health as part of a total platform for the improvement of women's position.[17] They were concerned with the same grievances—sexual, economic, and legal; and they frequently reprinted pertinent articles from women's publications in other parts of the country.

Utah's feminists shared not only a desire to speak for themselves and a sense of injustice, but a conviction of the equality of men and women. "Woman was designed to be something more than a domestic drudge,"[18] wrote an early author. Education and professional advancement were promoted in every issue.

In the "Notes and News" column and in a section called "Woman's Record," the *Exponent* reported on the triumphs of women around the globe in achieving special awards or recognition. One entry told of four women in Boston who "were successful applicants at the preliminary examination at Harvard College." These columns also carried notes on Anna Dickinson, a female lecturer;

Charlotte Cushman, a New York actress; "Four ladies of position in London" who had become home decorating artists; Sarah Woolsey, a writer of children's literature; Rose Lathrop, an artist and illustrator; Matilda Fletcher, a lecturer and writer on the subject of ethics in marriage; and Jenny Lind, the singer.[19] One note on a little girl in San Francisco who had just won a school prize of a trip to Paris said, "This is quite a victory for the girls, and proves the oft repeated assertion that the brains of girls are not inferior to the brains of boys!"[20]

Several columns of each issue were devoted to progress made in the area of women's rights around the country and around the world. The paper often reprinted speeches presented at women's conferences held outside Utah. Emmeline B. Wells, writing later about the *Exponent*, said, "From its first issue it was the champion of the suffrage cause, and by exchanging with women's papers of the United States and England it brought news of women in all parts of the world to those of Utah."[21]

In recording the achievements of women in other places, Utah's women did not forget their own. In fact, they occasionally had cause to gloat. "It was in Utah that the right of women to support themselves as clerks, telegraph operators, and so on, was first publicly and practically acknowledged," claimed an editorial note of 1873.[22] They could also note their own right to vote. No reader of the *Exponent* could mistake the pride of these Mormon women in their own achievements. Said an early issue:

It was telegraphed east and west that two ladies had been admitted to the bar of Utah as practicing lawyers, and the local press has had considerable to say in regard to it; yet it might with equal justness and more force have been telegraphed that here in Utah, decried, abused and maligned as it has been, women enjoy more of what is contended for as woman's rights than they do in any State in the Federal Union; and that they appreciate their position and are seeking to qualify themselves for spheres of usefulness to which their sisters in other parts of the country can only yet look in prospective.[23]

Emmeline B. Wells, editor of the *Woman's Exponent* for thirty-seven years and president of the Relief Society for twenty-one, was photographed in Washington, D. C., possibly in 1879 when she attended her first NWSA convention. #P1700/2882, courtesy of LDS Archives.

Other Utah journals showed an interest in women's rights during these same years. In 1869, for example, the *Utah Magazine* had printed an unsigned article on the economic status of women. "Emancipate wives and give them the same motives for industry and economy that are given to men," it had said.[24] Twenty years later, another popular Utah journal, *Zion's Home Monthly*, ran an article urging the same quality of education for young girls as for boys.[25] But as a vehicle for the expression of feminist ideals, the *Woman's Exponent* stands apart. Written and published by Mormon women, it shows them to have been no passive recipients of a franchise inexplicably offered by the brethren. From 1872 to the end of the century, the paper demonstrated their desire to speak for themselves, to expose injustice, and to publicize and promote equality of opportunity for the sexes.

II

While the citizens of Utah Territory were aware of a wide variety of women's issues, political equality seems to have been the goal which attracted the broadest support. This was particularly true after the female suffrage law of 1870 came under attack from Washington. Initially critics of polygamy had hoped that Utah women would use their vote to change the marital system. When they did not, eastern reformers began pressuring Congress to take the vote away. Zion's feminists soon learned that publishing was not enough. If they were to defend their rights, they had to become involved in organizing and educating their sisters at the local level.

At first this was done through the Relief Society, probably on a semi-official basis. Susa Young Gates wrote that:

The captain of Utah's woman-host, Eliza R. Snow, was foremost in all this labor as in every other during her period of public activity; yet she turned over the active direction of this suffrage movement to that champion of equal rights, Sarah M. Kimball. For many years Mrs. Kimball was the "Mormon" suffrage standard bearer. It would be less than justice if it were not here recorded that her active brain, her unselfish devotion to the work of God, and her magnificent organizing powers bore rich fruit during this vital period (1868–1893) in the history of woman's development in the Church. Following her leadership of the suffrage forces was that other indomitable pioneer, President Emmeline B. Wells. Then in later years came that no less splendid patriot, Mrs. Emily S. Richards, who ably conducted suffrage affairs in this state in the later years.[26]

Incorporating suffrage goals into the program of the Relief Society turned political work into Church work. Many women pursued suffrage work as diligently as they did their religious callings. Tullidge reported that Relief Society President Eliza R. Snow appointed Bathsheba W. Smith as a missionary to go "all through the South" and preach retrenchment. Sister Snow added that Sister Smith could "preach woman's rights on her mission," if she wished.[27]

Sister Wells recalled that Sarah M. Kimball, "leader in the Relief Society and later a nationally known woman's rights advocate," began programs for civic education for women in Utah. "She helped form clubs, organize classes in history and political science, and directed the work generally."[28] She used the Relief Society to promote activities which increased the knowledge of the sisters in matters of government and law. "Relief Society meetings became . . . mock trials, and symposia on parliamentary law."[29]

Not all the organized suffrage activity was within the Relief Society. In 1889, two years after the Edmunds-Tucker Act disfranchised Utah's women, the Territorial Suffrage Association was organized with one hundred members. The *Woman's Exponent* dealt with news of Woman's Suffrage Association conferences in the same way it reported news of the Relief Society, Primary, and

YLMIA, giving complete accounts of talks given and changes in officers. Reports of regular WSA meetings in Juab County, in Sanpete County, in Ogden City, in Sevier County, and in other smaller towns and counties fill the pages of the *Exponent*, especially between 1875 and 1896, and indicate that there were active chapters all over the territory.[30] Most places that had active Relief Societies in the 1880s and 90s had some kind of WSA organization, or at least were encouraged to do so by Relief Society leaders.[31] A typical *Exponent* report of a Primary-Relief Society-WSA Conference indicated the overlapping of the organizations and suggested that the WSA was not considered an exclusive organization: "At the close of the Relief Society Conference at 4 p.m. a Woman's Suffrage Meeting was held, the greater part of the women remaining."[32] Reports of the meetings indicated that their discussions ranged far beyond the topic of suffrage and touched on many ideas of concern to women, such as family life, women's economic position, and women's relationship to men in marriage.

The Territorial Suffrage Association chapters were officially linked to the NWSA and afforded some Utah women the opportunity to travel to other states and to Washington to lobby Congress for changes in federal legislation that affected them. At a gathering in Washington in 1891, Utah had the second largest number of delegates participating. Although this was probably as much the result of the organizational deterioration of the Association as it was of the high involvement of Mormon women, the distinction inspired further efforts at home.

In the chapter which she contributed to Susan B. Anthony and Ida Harper's massive *History of Woman Suffrage*, Emmeline B. Wells frequently mentioned that while the years under the Edmunds-Tucker Law were oppressive, they did provide opportunities for learning the rules of practical politics which would prove useful later. In 1896, when the opportunity for statehood finally came,

Utah's women were prepared to work for the restoration of their political rights. Knowing there was some fear that a clause guaranteeing female suffrage might be omitted from the proposed constitution in order to make it more acceptable to gentile voters in Utah and to Congress, women became active in drafting committees and in the pre-convention meetings of the two parties. Their efforts paid off. Despite the persuasive oratory of B. H. Roberts, the suffrage clause was adopted. True, the women had the support of the Church hierarchy, from President Wilford Woodruff on down. But as a modern student of this period has concluded:

Support from the top . . . was not enough. The woman suffrage leaders had carried their educational efforts throughout the territory, and there was no question that they had developed broad support. A movement so widespread, so completely dominated by the "respectable" women of the territory, could hardly be laughed off as the pet cause of a few radicals.[33]

In grass roots organization as in publishing, Utah's feminists showed their intelligence and determination.

III

Although territorial branches of the Woman's Suffrage Association were not organized until after the disfranchisement crisis of 1887, influential Mormon women had established ties with the national women's movement long before that. In 1871, a large group of sisters had turned out to greet Elizabeth Cady Stanton and Susan B. Anthony on their first trip west. As Mrs. Stanton recalled the visit some years later, "It was at the time of the Godby secession, when several hundred Mormons abjured that portion of the faith of their fathers which authorized polygamy." Briefed by Judge McKeon, she seized the opportunity to speak to a large assembly of Mormon women on "polyandry, polygamy, monogamy, and prostitution":

After this convocation the doors of the Tabernacle were closed to our ministrations, as we thought they would be, but we had crowded an immense amount of science, philosophy, history, and general reflections into the five hours of such free talk as those women had never heard before. As the seceders had just built a new hall, we held meetings there every day, discussing all the vital issues of the hour; the Mormon men and women taking an active part.[34]

In a time of schism, Mrs. Stanton's flirtation with the seceders might have alienated the Church leadership. Apparently this did not happen, for the long involvement of Emmeline Wells and her associates in the national suffrage movement dated from this period. Mrs. Stanton found much to praise in Mormon life, while Sister Wells found a new calling in the women's movement. In an account written much later for Susan Anthony's history, Sister Wells pointed with pride to the large number of Utah women who became active in the suffrage movement in the 1870s:

The fact that the women of Utah were so progressive in the suffrage question and had sent large petitions asking for the passage of the Sixteenth Amendment to the Federal Constitution to enfranchise all women, resulted in an invitation for [Mrs. Wells] to attend its annual convention at Washington in January, 1879.

She went on to note that the Utah delegates were invited to speak at the convention and selected to go before Congressional committees and the President of the United States "as well as to present important matters to the Lady of the White House."[35]

Since Mormons were regarded as a strange and dishonorable sect by many Americans at this time, and their polygamous marriages were abhorrent to most of those who allied themselves with the cause of women's rights, it is particularly interesting that within one branch of the women's movement a relationship of tolerance, and even respect, developed between Mormon and gentile women. Susan B. Anthony's letters home during her first visit to

Utah show her own initial repugnance. "The system of the subjection of woman here finds its limit, and she touches the lowest depths of her degradation," she wrote. Still, she could see polygamy as only a more advanced form of the abuses of monogamy:

When I look back into the States, what sorrow, what broken hearts are there because of husbands taking to themselves new friendships, just as really wives as are these, and the legal wife feeling even more wrong and neglected.[36]

If Utah's women did not convince her of the values of polygamy, they at least demonstrated their own interest in female rights. According to one biographer, Miss Anthony "formed several friendships with Mormon women and decided to regard them as she regarded her conventionally married friends. There were no obvious signs of difference between them and these intelligent Mormon ladies."[37]

Actually, Mrs. Stanton and Miss Anthony had already shown an ability to get along with almost anyone who advocated women's rights. Their friendship with the notorious Victoria Woodhull during this period had scandalized their more respectable associates.[38] Having demonstrated a willingness to overlook free love, spiritualism, and quack healing, they could learn to like polygamists as well. Perhaps equally remarkable is the fact that the Mormon women unequivocally embraced them, for in the 1870s their indiscriminate friendships and willingness to embrace unpopular causes had brought them under repeated attack from more moderate participants in the suffrage movement. Although two columns in the *Exponent* in June of 1872 attacked "dangerous excesses" in the women's movement, citing attacks upon "the family circle, filial love, parental care, and fraternal affection" by unnamed radicals,[39] it did not attack Woodhull or her sister Tennie Clafin directly. Throughout this period, the paper reported on the activities of these notorious women

rather objectively and with no editorial comment.[40] It remained solidly behind the activities of Elizabeth Cady
Stanton and Susan Anthony regardless of their difficulties
in the East. Perhaps this is a case of two equally unpopular groups finding strength in each other.

In 1890, the participation of Mormon women in the
national women's movement became a divisive issue in
the East. The National Woman's Suffrage Association,
under the leadership of Miss Anthony and Mrs. Stanton,
had always been considered too radical by the more conservative American Woman's Suffrage Association led by
Lucy Stone and Julia Ward Howe. In the 1880s, great efforts had been made to unite the two groups, but the latter faction had refused to join an organization to which
Mormon women belonged and which endorsed women's
trade unions, both acceptable to the NWSA. In 1889, a
conference was held in Washington and the groups tried
to work out their differences. Pressure was put upon Elizabeth Cady Stanton, president of the National group, to
compromise her position. She did not. She would not be a
part of any organization that did not make *all* women feel
welcome if they shared common goals.[41] She made it particularly clear that "Mormon women, black women, and
Indian women" must not be excluded from the Association or she would sever her connection with it. With Susan B. Anthony's support, she prevailed, and the two
groups were joined.[42]

Soon after, Elizabeth Cady Stanton, then seventy-
seven years old, stepped down from the leadership of the
organization and Susan B. Anthony became president.
Miss Anthony traveled to Utah to meet with Mormon
women on several occasions, and she became an important link with the women there. To the Latter-day Saint
women, her visits to Utah were special events, and her
statements were widely discussed in the press. In 1896,
when Utah became a state and women's suffrage was restored, she joined her friends in Utah in the celebrations

honoring their victory. As she traveled through the state, she was "honored in every possible way."[43] Miss Anthony wrote that she felt a spirit of warmth and openness when she was with the Mormon women, and that she counted some of them among her close friends.[44] In 1900, Mrs. Wells and several other Mormon women traveled to Atlanta, Georgia, to attend the Susan B. Anthony eightieth birthday celebration. Miss Anthony was given a length of silk produced in the Utah sericulture project. In a letter of thank-you she wrote:

> My pleasure in the rich brocaded silk is quadrupled because it was made by women politically equal with men. The fact that the mulberry trees grew in Utah, that the silk worms made their cocoons there, that women reeled and spun and colored and wove the silk in a free State, greatly enhances its value. My dressmaker in the near future will make it into the most beautiful gown that your octogenarian friend ever possessed.[45]

Susan B. Anthony had come a long way since her first trip to Salt Lake City, but then so had Utah.

In the long controversy between Utah and the federal government, Utah women had gained and then lost the vote. In the quarter century between the suffrage law of 1870 and the state constitutional convention of 1896, they demonstrated a consistent and articulate feminism. Ironically, the marital system which Susan B. Anthony had so deplored in her early visit was considered by Utah's feminists as one of the keys to their liberation.

As early as 1869, the editor of *Utah Magazine*, E. L. T. Harrison, commented on a remark made by a visitor from the East suggesting that Mormonism might lead the way in asserting the rights of women. Said he, "A very suggestive remark, anyway, and one which, we believe, despite present appearance to the outside world, will be found in due time to have contained the germ of a correct prophecy."[46] This theme was echoed in many places and it usually related to polygamy.

Mormon women were aware that most outside observers did not take their feminism seriously because of their participation in plural marriage. They often wrote and spoke of how misunderstood they were by the gentile world. While women's rights advocates outside Utah saw polygamy as a severe oppressor of women, Mormon women felt that plural marriage actually freed them and expanded their opportunities for development. Many Latter-day Saint women saw themselves as not only part of the women's emancipation movement, but beyond or ahead of it. Today's radical feminists might not endorse plural marriage as the solution to some of these problems, but Mormon women did. Polygamy, they said, relieved women of the loneliness and drudgery of monogamous, single-family living, offering opportunities for a variety of intimate friendships, and for shared household and child-care responsibilties. It also emancipated them from other marital duties, if Mrs. Stanton's report is correct: "The women who believed in polygamy had much to say in its favor, especially in regard to the sacredness of motherhood during the period of pregnancy and lactation; a lesson of respect for that period being religiously taught all Mormons."[47] In a day when even the outspoken Mrs. Stanton dared speak of no other form of birth control than abstinence,[48] the Mormon system had its appeal.

But feminist advocacy of polygamy went beyond these issues to a more fundamental problem. An article in an 1874 issue of the *Woman's Exponent* had defended the virtue and integrity of plural wives and had gone on to ask:

Is there then nothing worth living for, but to be petted, humored and caressed, by a man? That is all very well as far as it goes, but that man is the only thing in existence worth living for I fail to see. All honor and reverence to good men; but they and their attentions are not the only sources of happiness on the earth, and need not fill up every thought of woman. And when men see that women can exist without their being constantly at hand, that they can learn to be self-reliant or depend upon each other for more or less happiness, it will perhaps take a little of the conceit out of some of them.[49]

The "ultimate degradation" became the path of liberation. Plural marriage showed women they could live their lives without the continual attention and adulation of a spouse. Or at least so it seemed from the editorial offices of the *Woman's Exponent*.

Obviously, Mormon feminists made few converts to their peculiar social system. With statehood they regained the franchise, yet they lost the marital plank of their platform. American society was not ready to allow them both.

In publishing, in grass-roots organization, and in personal association with women's rights leaders, Utah feminists accomplished much in the years from 1870 to 1896. They encouraged thoughtful discussion in their own society of issues regarding the worth and responsibilities of the sexes, they demonstrated that feminist ideals could be compatible with Mormon doctrine, and they forged a direct and active link with the wider movement for equal rights.

Notes

1. *Woman's Exponent*, 6 (1 September 1877), 49.
2. Eleanor Flexner, *A Century of Struggle* (New York: Atheneum, 1972), p. 163.
3. Thomas G. Alexander, "An Experiment in Progressive Legislation: Woman Suffrage in Utah in 1870," *Utah Historical Quarterly*, 38 (Winter, 1970), 21, 29–30.
4. *Woman's Exponent*, 6 (1 July 1877), 20.
5. This slogan appeared on the masthead of the *Woman's Exponent* from 1 November 1879 to 15 December 1896.
6. *Woman's Exponent*, 10 (1 June 1881), 4.
7. Ibid., 3 (12 June 1874), 11.
8. Ibid., 1 (1 June 1872), 1.

9. Ibid., 18 (15 November 1889), 92.

10. Ibid., 6 (1 March 1878), 148.

11. Ibid., 3 (15 January 1875), 123.

12. Ibid., 18 (1 June 1889), 1.

13. Ibid., 1 (1 August 1872) 13.

14. Ibid., 18 (15 February 1890), 136.

15. Ibid., 18 (15 August 1889), 43.

16. Ibid., 1 (15 July 1872), 29.

17. Ibid., 1 (31 January 1873), 131; also 1 (15 August 1872), 46; 6 (1 February 1878), 132.

18. Ibid., 1 (1 October 1872), 69.

19. Ibid., 3 (1 December 1874), 97.

20. Ibid., 18 (1 July 1889), 18.

21. Susan B. Anthony and Ida Husted Harper, eds., *The History of Woman Suffrage*, 6 vols., (Rochester, New York: Susan B. Anthony, 1902) 4:936–37.

22. *Woman's Exponent*, 1 (1 April 1873), 161.

23. Ibid., 1 (1 October 1872), 68.

24. E. L. T. Harrison, "Talk About Woman's Wages," *Utah Magazine*, 3 (31 July 1869), 203.

25. "Girls Who Make Their Own Way," *Zion's Home Monthly*, 1 (15 May 1889), 338.

26. The General Board of the Relief Society, *A Centenary of Relief Society: 1842–1942* (Salt Lake City: The Deseret News Press, 1942), p. 67.

27. Edward W. Tullidge, *The Women of Mormondom* (Salt Lake City: n.p., 1965), p. 505.

28. Anthony and Harper, 4:947.

29. Alexander, p. 28.

30. *Woman's Exponent*, see especially issues from 1887–89.

31. *A Centenary of Relief Society*, pp. 65–67.

32. *Woman's Exponent*, 18 (15 June 1889), 12.

33. Jean Bickmore White, "Woman's Place Is in the Constitution: The Struggle for Equal Rights in Utah in 1895," *Utah Historical Quarterly*, 42 (Fall 1974), 367.

34. Elizabeth Cady Stanton, *Eighty Years or More: Reminiscences 1815–1897* (New York: Schocken Books, 1971), pp. 283–84.

35. Anthony and Harper, 4:937–38.

36. Ida Husted Harper, *Life and Work of Susan B. Anthony*, 3 vols., (Indianapolis: The Hollenback Press, 1908), 1:390.

37. Katherine Anthony, *Susan B. Anthony: Her Personal History and Her Era* (Garden City, N.Y.: Doubleday & Co., Inc., 1954), p. 262.

38. Flexner, p. 153.

39. *Woman's Exponent*, 1 (15 June 1872), 10.

40. Ibid., 1 (15 September 1872), 62; also 1 (1 July 1872), 22.

41. Alma Lutz, *Created Equal: A Biography of Elizabeth Cady Stanton* (New York: The John Day Co., 1940), p. 271.

42. Ibid., pp. 281–82.

43. Anthony and Harper, 4:944.

44. Theodore Stanton and Harriet Stanton Blatch, eds., *Elizabeth Cady Stanton: As Revealed in Her Letters, Diary and Reminiscences*, 2 vols., (New York: Harper & Brothers, 1922), 1:66.

45. Harper, 2:1,202.

46. "Our Women's Platform," *Utah Magazine*, 3 (8 May 1869), 6.

47. Stanton, *Eighty Years*, p. 283.

48. Louise Noun, *Strong-Minded Women* (Iowa City: The Iowa State University Press, 1969), p. 184.

49. *Woman's Exponent*, 3 (30 September 1874), 67.

Susa Young Gates, daughter of Brigham Young, suffragist, journalist, genealogist, and mother of thirteen. #P1700/523, courtesy of LDS Archives.

Susa Young Gates
Carolyn W. D. Person

Susa Young Gates was born 18 March 1856 to Brigham Young and his twenty-second wife, Lucy Bigelow Young, in Salt Lake City. She was their second daughter, called Susa or Susannah or Susan, and was the first child to be born in the Lion House, the communal home Brigham Young had built for ten of his wives in the new Zion. It was an auspicious beginning for this lion's cub, who would one day be called "the most talented child of Brigham Young."[1]

During her lifetime of seventy-seven years, she was a prolific writer, musician, genealogist, teacher, organizer, administrator, home economist, public speaker, researcher, traveler, suffragist, and Church worker as well as a wife and the mother of thirteen children. Called "the most versatile and prolific Mormon writer ever to take up the pen in defense of her religion,"[2] she also earned for herself a number of unofficial titles, including "the mother of physical education in Utah."[3] She corresponded with Tolstoy and took tea with Queen Victoria. Susan B. Anthony once offered her the post of secretary of the National Council of Women if she would give up her militant Mormonism; Susa declined.

Yet for all her triumphs, she knew inadequacy, disappointment, and failure. Married at sixteen, she was divorced at twenty-one. Only five of her thirteen children survived to adulthood. Despite a lifelong commitment to

the Church, she underwent a spiritual crisis in middle
age, and as an old woman, though she had personally cat-
alogued over 16,000 Young family names, she lamented
her inability to have the beloved daughter of her first
marriage sealed to her in the temple. Susa Young Gates
could no more be called a "typical Mormon woman" than
her father could be called an "average Latter-day Saint."
Still, in her brilliant and independent way she epitomized
many of the tendencies of her age. Her conflicts as well as
her successes tell us much about the role of women in late
nineteenth century Utah.

I

A child of the Lion House was a privileged child. As a
daughter of Brigham Young, Susa had the best early education available in the Valley. She attended her father's
private school, had music lessons and ballet study with
Sarah Alexander, and had the opportunity to advance to
higher grades at a time when only a few children were
able to do so. Her quick mind and self-described passion
for music and books repaid the investment.

At the age of thirteen she entered the University of
Deseret. In 1870 she was appointed co-editor of the *College Lantern*, said to be the first western college newspaper.[4]

In agreement with her father's principles, Susa's education was practical as well as theoretical. She completed a
course in telegraphy and graduated as the "star pupil"
from Church recorder David W. Evans' class in stenogra-
phy. She was an official reporter for the first Retrenchment Society,[5] and prior to moving to St. George with her
mother and sister to make a winter home for Brigham
Young, she completed a course in bread, cake, and candy-
making from the Golightly Bakery[6] When she was established in St. George, she taught piano and voice and enjoyed success as an actress. She also organized the "Union

Club," a social group of both sexes. But this teenage whirl of activity soon came to an end.

At the age of sixteen, half-way into adolescence, Susa assumed the responsibilities of an adult. In 1872 Susa married twenty-one year old Alma Bailey Dunford, an English convert and dentist. In this same year, as a married woman, Susa voted in her first election. The marriage was not destined for success. In her own words, it "was a most unfortunate one" and ended in divorce in 1877, the same year Brigham Young died. Two children had been born, Leah Eudora Dunford (1874–1965) and Alma Bailey Dunford (1875–1895). Dr. Dunford is said to have been kindly, talented, educated, and respected. One biographer has speculated that the marriage failed because of Susa's youthful ignorance and unpreparedness for sexual intimacies and because of Dunford's drinking habit.

This early failure seemed to have moved Susa to an unexpected frankness in her later discussion of sexual matters, an attitude uncommon in the milieu of her Church and times. In her novel, *John Stevens' Courtship* (1894) she wrote, "Married people should be mated on the three planes upon which human beings meet and mingle—the physical, the mental, and the spiritual."[7] In what has been called her best novel, *The Prince of Ur* (1915), her realistic scenes of human love were shocking in their day. At age sixty-five she wrote of sex:

Be sure to picture the normal and beautiful results of such appetites, when legally awakened and domestically satisfied. Let your information contain many "do's!" as well as a few disciplinary "don'ts!" Teach [a young girl] that repression is as unnatural as lewdness.[8]

That she carried the burden of her unsuccessful marriage, about which she seldom spoke, is indicated by a remark she made while on her death bed: "May the Lord forgive me for any wrong I may have done Dr. Dunford—unknowing."[9]

Dr. Dunford remarried in 1882 and fathered a large, distinguished family. He became well known in the west, instituting a state-wide health program to train young dentists. Five years before his death he broke his drinking habit. His civil divorce with Susa was made final in the temple 6 August 1890 by President Wilford Woodruff.[10]

In 1878, following the advice of Erastus Snow, the divorced Susa arrived at the Brigham Young Academy in Provo, on a scholarship given by President John Taylor. There she organized the music department and conducted two choral bodies and a choir. She planned to travel to London to continue her studies, but her friend Joseph F. Smith advised her to go instead to the Sandwich Islands (Hawaii). She did so, and while traveling with "Aunt" Zina Young, became reacquainted with Jacob F. Gates, a released missionary whom she had met previously in St. George. On 5 January 1880 they were married in the St. George Temple.

Susa often quoted a statement her father had made to her once in conversation:

Daughter, use all your gifts to build up righteousness in the earth. Never use them to acquire name or fame. Never rob your home, nor your children. If you were to become the greatest woman in this world, and your name should be known in every land and clime, and you would fail in your duty as wife and mother, you would wake up on the morning of the first resurrection and find you had failed in everything; but anything you can do after you have satisfied the claims of husband and family will redound to your own honor and to the glory of God.[11]

When she married Jacob Gates, this counsel became her creed. Gates was an exceptional husband, and Susa considered him an ideal mate. Their life together was mutually rewarding.

The Gates began married life in St. George. Susa made some attempt to enlarge her domestic horizon with outside endeavors. In the year of her marriage she accepted the commission of Eliza R. Snow and Edward W. Tullidge to lecture and sell *Women of Mormondom*. Two years later she represented St. George at the State Constitutional Convention. But for most of the next ten years she was absorbed in the births and deaths of children. Emma Lucy was born in December of 1880, Jacob Young in 1882, and Karl Nahum in 1883, the year that the Gates moved to Provo. In 1885, Susa lost the first child of the eight she would bury. Mark was born on 20 January and died 21 April. Susa's mother, Lucy B. Young, recorded this sad period in a letter to her own mother, Mary G. Bigelow:

The folks [are] all well, however I think our Darling Susa is far from it. She is in a delicate situation [pregnant] and what makes it so much worse, she is in a very low state of nervous prostration, and has been very sick since her darling Mark was taken away, and in hopes that a change would do her good, they had arranged to take a trip up in the canyon. [12]

When, soon afterward, the Gates were again called to the Sandwich Islands Mission, Susa's mother accompanied them. She served as midwife when Joseph Sterling was born in 1886. Two other sons followed, Brigham Cecil in 1887 and Harvey Harris in 1889. In the spring of 1887, the two eldest Gates boys died one month apart of "diptheriatric croup." They were four and three years old. Susa had the bodies sealed in metal coffins so they could be transported to Provo for burial beside their brother Mark. [13]

The Hawaii years were unusually busy for the young wife, who had to produce all the clothing worn by her growing family except for men's coats and breeches. In 1888, she wrote her mother:

I want to whitewash and clean my old house here before Conference. In fact I've got so much to do I don't know what to do first. My little baby-dresses are all worn out so I must make a new supply.

Then Lule's clothes are all worn out, and Cecil is wearing Violet's and Freddies, and Joe's old clothes. I shall have to make up a supply for him. Then, of course our clothes to travel in will have to be made before I am sick [confined in childbirth] as I shall be hardly able to do anything after. [14]

While she did find time to manage a correspondence with the Russian writer Leo Tolstoy during this period, she recorded these years as a "time I did not continue my public work or writing, thinking my husband did not want me in the limelight. There came a time, however, when he took the initiative and said, 'Susa why don't you write?' That was all I needed and I started again."[15]

As the mission in Hawaii drew to a close, Susa began planning a new direction for her life. With the advice and consent of her husband and the support of her friend Joseph F. Smith and his wife Julina, she decided to start a magazine of her own. Originally she had thought of associating herself as a subordinate editor of the *Woman's Exponent*, but after consultation with Dr. Romania B. Penrose, who advised her that Emmeline B. Wells "virtually owns the whole thing," she diverted her interest to the founding of a new journal directed to young women.[16] Dr. Penrose further advised Susa that a new magazine would "pay you handsomely if well canvassed and enable you to hire all your wood cut and your water drawn and babies well tended by those not having the ability—or wish to do greater things."[17] (Later Susa earned $35 a month as editor.) Her husband fully supported the plan, insisting that she devote her literary labors to building an original magazine rather than giving her time and talent entirely to other Utah periodicals.

So it was that in 1889 Susa Young Gates gave birth to her ninth child and seventh son, returned from Hawaii and set up housekeeping in Provo, received permission from the authorities to proceed with her magazine, and produced the first issue of the *Young Woman's Journal*. At thirty-three Brigham Young's daughter had found a way to use all her gifts.

II

As the *Woman's Exponent* had been the organ to the Relief Society, Susa's proposed publication, the *Young*

Woman's Journal, would be the organ of the Young Ladies' Mutual Improvement Association.

The entire editorial and financial responsibility for the *Journal* was hers, although the official head of the enterprise was YLMIA General President Elmina S. Taylor. Susa had to sell the magazine. She enlisted the aid of her mother, who became the traveling representative. Canvassing subscriptions, Lucy traveled back and forth between St. George and Salt Lake City, sometimes driving her own buggy. She did this for about nine months, the first time that any woman in the Church canvassed for a publication of any sort.

The venture was successful, and Susa was able to present the financially secure magazine to the General Board of the YLMIA in its eighth year (1897).

The *Young Woman's Journal* encouraged the young women of the Church to write. Susa set the *Journal's* goals:

First . . . the genuineness of the thought, and the indirect as well as the direct teaching must never be doubtful; second, from the first number the regular contributors must be home writers . . . and, too, they should receive something, if ever so little, for their work. The writer's brains were as worthy of hire as the type-setter's hands.[18]

Her own ten years as a "home writer" must have strengthened her feelings in this matter.

The decade in which Susa edited the *Journal* was packed with additional responsibility, travel, and activity. The *Journal* alone demanded full-time involvement, and more, since it was published in Salt Lake City, and Susa's home was in Provo. Though she had a family of little children, for eleven years she journeyed to and fro, meeting the public and doing editorial work. Her dedication to the *Journal* entailed many personal sacrifices, but she gave it a firm beginning.

The magazine lasted well beyond her tenure, surviving until 1929, when it was merged with the *Improvement*

Era. Susa was recorded as having mixed feelings at this juncture, fearing that her "girl writers" might not find as adequate a reception for their efforts in the next format, yet faithfully she conceded that the consolidation was inspired, "there is no doubt of that."[19] At the *Journal's* demise she wrote:

Into the web and woof of life are woven many strands of drama, bright comedy, and solemn tragedy. The genesis of life, animate or inanimate, is always accompanied with pain, yet it is also tempered with the joy of creation. Dissolution involves both the agony of parting and surcease of struggles. Conceived in faith and hope, nourished with tender sympathy, matured into a fruitful literary entity, the *Young Woman's Journal* now fades into the pages of history as a past achievement. Who may sound its death knell? Not I! Life is my concern, not death![20]

She might have been commenting on her own life, for the years which followed her return from Hawaii had their share of pain as well as faith and hope.

In 1890 Susa agreed to accompany her mother to Worcester, Massachusetts, to attend a Bigelow family reunion. Their train had just reached Weber Canyon when it was wrecked. Lucy dragged her injured, unconscious daughter out a car window and carried her on to the next train going east:

Susa lay unconscious for eight hours, and a German physician on board, eloquently tried to reassure [Lucy] by telling her the injured girl might awaken with her brain-power impaired for life while her hand would be of no possible use to her as long as she lived. [Lucy] knew better. She got out her little bottle of oil, and annointed the hand before the splinters and bandages were placed on Susa's hand and arm, and prayed mightily.[21]

It was a painful trip for Susa, who was obliged to keep her arm in a sling for months following the accident. The bruises her mother sustained gradually healed, and both women were grateful that Lucy B. Young's "prayers were effectual" and that they had continued the journey. While in Massachusetts they stopped in Boston and spent some time in the New England Genealogical Library, and then continued homeward via New York City and St. Louis, where they stopped to visit the Hygienic College presided over by Dr. Susanna W. Dodds with whom Susa had been in correspondence for years.

In 1891 Susa journeyed to Denver to attend a convention of the Women's Council. She also traveled to Washington, D. C., to attend a National Council of Women congress. She founded the Utah Woman's Press Club, and had a baby, Sarah Beulah, born June 21. In 1892 she spent the summer in Massachusetts, attending the summer school of Harvard University, and doing Young family research at the genealogical library. It was during her Cambridge sojourn that she became acquainted with a young Harvard student, John A. Widtsoe, who later married her eldest daughter, Leah Dunford. Dr. Widtsoe later recalled that summer of 1892 and described Susa as "a woman of superb intelligence and magnificent power. . . . We became good friends and spent much time together."[22] They remained lifelong friends and confidantes. Back home again, Susa was appointed to the Board of Trustees of Brigham Young University, in which capacity she served until 1925.

In 1893 she was the stenographer for the Salt Lake Temple dedication, and took the official minutes for each one of the forty-one dedicatory services which were held between April 6 and April 24. She also published a book, *Lydia Knight's History*; attended a Women's Congress in Washington, D. C., as well as the World's Fair; was a charter member of the National Household Economic Association; and had a baby, Franklin Young, born May 17. Susa lost her breast milk for this baby, and was obliged to find a wet-nurse.[23] In addition to meeting the many other demands made upon her time, she had managed to nurse her babies.

The following year Susa organized the Domestic Science Department at BYU, published another book, and had another baby, Heber, who was born and died on 22 November 1894. In 1895 she organized Parents' Classes at

BYU; in 1896, the year of Utah statehood, she was appointed Press Chairman of the National Council of Women, and had another baby, Brigham Young Gates, born April 19. In 1897 she organized the Sons and Daughters of the Utah Pioneers. She also wrote a series of lessons for the Young Ladies' Mutual Improvement Association.

In 1898 her travels took her to Toronto, Canada, where she was a delegate and speaker to the International Congress of the Household Economics Organization, and to Omaha, Nebraska, where she was personally honored by the same organization. In June President Joseph F. Smith presided over the Salt Lake Temple wedding of her daughter Leah and the *summa cum laude* Harvard graduate, John A. Widtsoe. In July her youngest daughter, Beulah, died at the age of seven. In November Susa founded the Utah Daughters of the American Revolution. One of her favorite sayings was "Keep busy in the face of discouragement."

Travel was no simple matter in the 1890s, but it brought particular problems for the Mormon woman, who was "even more unpopular in the outside world than the Mormon man," Susa wrote. "They were actually thought of as debased slaves, ignorant beyond description, and utterly immoral and unchaste."[24] Whatever personal pleasure her travels may have given her, Susa thought of them as part of her calling as a daughter of Zion. In a letter to "Aunt" Emmeline B. Wells written in the spring of 1899, she revealed that *modus operandi* of her decisions to travel or not to travel. Speaking of the forthcoming International Women's Congress to be held in London she wrote:

I don't know at all whether I will go or not. I am leaving it all with God. If the way opens up, I shall feel that it is right for me to go; if not I shall feel that it is right for me to get some of the sisters to read my paper, and shall stay at home cheerfully.[25]

The way opened up, and the month of June found Susa and her mother in London. Lucy was an official "Patron" of the congress; Susa was a delegate and an invited speaker. She had also been appointed delegate to the meeting of the Woman's Christian Temperance Union held in England at the same time. The fact that she had been asked by Dr. May Wood-Allen to represent the women of America at a meeting to discuss "Equal Moral Standards for Men and Women" suggests that the international travels of Utah's women had done much to dispel the prejudice against them. Still, Susa is said to have caused a sensation upon presenting herself not only as a Mormon woman, but also as the daughter of Brigham Young, there to represent American women on this "delicate moral question."[26]

Susa and her mother enjoyed the many festivities associated with the International Council of Women during their London stay. They attended receptions hosted by the Duke and Duchess of Sutherland and the Countess of Aberdeen. They enjoyed particularly the private art collection of Lady Battersea at Surrey House, Marble Arch. Susa observed the works of Rubens, Tintoretto, and Burne-Jones. The women also took refreshments as guests of the Rothschilds, had luncheon with Lord and Lady Aberdeen, walked the gardens of the Lord Bishop of London, and took tea with Her Majesty, Queen Victoria, who had invited the women of the International Council to Windsor Castle. Susa felt there was deep significance in the Queen's invitation:

There was much to encourage the earnest heart in this public recognition of royalty given to the women all over the world who are struggling to make woman and humanity as free and as forceful a factor in the world as man and war now is.[27]

They went by special train, two hundred women, and were duly greeted by that "noble, pure, beautiful" and aged Queen. Susa relinquished her place in line to "our revered American Queen, Susan B. Anthony," and following the Queens' mutual inspections, tea was announced in St. George's Hall. Susa wrote:

We all hastened into the great hall, where delicious tea in the loveliest blue china cups, with massive silver teaspoons, was served to everyone. Yes, everyone! We do not drink tea, as you know, but we knew "our manners" too well to refuse such a lovely invitation from such a lovely lady. . . . Who shall gainsay the truth of a remark that "never had there been such a good cup of tea as that drunk out of the Queen's Sevres China."[28]

The first-born daughter of the Lion House had come far.

More interesting than her glittering social calendar, however, is the paper which Susa presented to the International Women's Congress in London. Entitled "Scientific Treatment of Domestic Service," it proposed the empirical, rational and ethical training of domestics. Thorough education in home economics and in home situations, Susa thought, would lead to a skilled trade or profession in the domestic arts. This paper allowed insight as to how Susa herself managed to accomplish so much at a time when she had a household of young children. She enjoyed the encouragement and support of her husband as well as the dedication of her mother, and she also had access to "servant girls," who were young women of the community. The rationale was that "the maid of today is the mistress of tomorrow."[29] By rallying these supporters around her, Susa was able to lead a taxing public life through efficient organization and administration of her household responsibilities.

Her superior management skills did not, however, dull her perception of the general plight of women. It was during this decade that she wrote:

To bake, to churn, to wash, to scrub, and to attend to the many wants of a large family kept the hands of the mother and eldest girls busy.

So it ever is with women. Or rather let me say so it has ever been. Nations and kingdoms rise and fall, men arise and go out to battle, or standing in the midst of power and strife, ascend to the clouds or sink into obscurity or disgrace; but the woman— she sits in her house weaving and toiling, the dinner must be cooked and set out though no one eat thereof; the cloth must be fashioned though the form for which it is designed sleep in the grey dust before it shall have been completed—all the hum-drum of life holds her down, while the earth itself may be tot-tering on its axis.[30]

The hum-drum had not held Susa down. In the eleven years between her return from the Sandwich Islands and the end of the century, she had founded and financed a new periodical for women, traveled extensively in the eastern United States and Europe, established a new de-partment at Brigham Young University, organized two statewide associations, held a responsible position in an international organization of women, published a work of history, and given birth to four children. "Growth, activ-ity, development, progress—all these are the ruling forces of a busy and conscientious life," she had written.[31] Yet for Susa, such achievement had its price.

In a letter dated 1897, Lucy Bigelow Young wrote her daughter:

You know, well, do you not, that you have been willing to work, yes indeed, and work hard too, both physically and men-tally. Yes, verily yes! I can testify before my God and His holy angels and all good men, both in Heaven and on the earth that I know that you have worked in manual labor until you have al-most fainted with exhaustion, and in fact, lost the lives of the little ones in embryo which God had committed to your care for this earth, or for this life. And also, on many occasions, came very nearly losing your own life as the result of overwork, and further more, I have also seen you work in your literary labors until it seemed as though your head and brain would almost burst. And your mind was just perfectly exhausted.[32]

Susa entered the twentieth century with a nervous break-down. One biographer has suggested that "she had over-taxed her strength in defense of women's rights; it was one of the few occasions when she lost sight of her phys-ical limitations."[33] Perhaps her own brilliance was as much to blame. Success brought its own conflicts and de-manded resolution of some difficult problems, as her later activities and writing reveal. For three years she was ill. Sometimes the doctors thought she had cancer and other times a liver ailment. Some of them faulted her vegetarianism. Her weight dropped to eighty-five pounds and she wrote, "My life was despaired of but Patriarch White promised I should live to do Temple work, and I have ever since."[34] She was carried to the Salt Lake Temple in a chair, and from that time forward became one of the most devoted temple workers in Church history.

From an external record of her activity, it would be impossible to say that Susa Young Gates had ever been anything but fully committed to Mormonism, but by her own account a profound inner change had occurred in the last years of the nineteenth century, interestingly enough at the very time she had been intensely involved in establishing her own career and in promoting the cause of women in national and international councils. In later life she admitted to not having received a spiritual conviction of the gospel until her fortieth year.

While she had been a rational convert, and obedient to the precepts taught by her father, her spiritual conversion came only after a year of intense fasting and prayer. She wrote, "I disciplined my taste, my desires and my impulses—severely disciplining my appetite, my tongue, my acts . . . and how I prayed!" She received her testimony, and from that time forward, as before, but with renewed vigor, she measured all truths, facts, and philosophies which came to her attention "By one standard only: Does this or that idea or theory agree or does it conflict with the truths of the Gospel as taught in the ancient and modern scriptures—if it agrees, it is mine! If it does not, I cast it out, or lay it upon the altar of prayer till God reveals the truth to His Prophet at the head of His Church."[35]

Patriarch White's blessing seemed to have reinforced the primacy of the spiritual dimension in her life. Susa's recovery was complete, but not immediate. Although she was well enough to attend the International Council of Women meetings in Copenhagen in 1901, she was unable to fulfill a mission call accepted with her husband in 1902. Shortly after their arrival in New York, her health broke completely, and they were obliged to return home. But by 1903 she was traveling again, this time to attend a National Council of Women Executives session in Washington, D. C.

Susa was by her own description an excellent cook, and she enjoyed entertaining. At one time or another she entertained in her home May Wright Sewell and Charlotte Perkins Gilman, leading feminists, as well as F. Marion Crawford, a popular novelist, and Ella Wheeler Wilcox, a writer of popular verse. She had many famous guests in these years including Susan B. Anthony, Dr. Anna Howard Shaw, Ida Husted Harper, Dr. Geisel of the Women's Christian Temperance Union, and Clara Barton. Susa apparently found association with non-Mormon feminists and reformers and continued participation in the women's suffrage movement compatible with gospel truths. But as her health improved she began to direct her energies toward more esoteric aspects of Mormonism.

Susa had always been interested in temple work. She had been the first person baptized in the St. George Temple after its dedication by Brigham Young in 1877 and had been the official stenographer not only at the dedication of that temple but of those at Logan, Salt Lake City, and Cardston, Canada. In the early years of the twentieth century this devotion to temple work intensified. In 1906 she organized the genealogical departments in the *Inter Mountain Republican* and the *Deseret News*. She edited columns for these papers for the following ten years. In 1907 she organized the first genealogical class work and published the first elementary treatise on genealogy. She devised a systematic index of names for the Church and wrote genealogical guides in 1909, 1911, and 1924. In 1914 she published the *Surname Book and Racial History*, which became a widely used tool in the field. In 1915 she introduced genealogical classwork at the International Genealogical Conference held in San Francisco.

Daughters of prominent Salt Lakers in their mother's dresses, c. 1896. The girls, many related to Brigham Young and Hiram Clawson, are attending a social reunion at the Beehive House. *Back row, left to right:* Anna Sears Young, Teresa (Tessie) Clawson Groesbeck, Alice Clawson Campbell, Miriam (Minnie) Hardy Hawkins, Mary (Mame) Clawson Beatie. *Front row, left to right:* Ivie Clawson Greene, Carlie Louine (Lulu) Clawson Young, Lutie Young Brockbank, Kate Clawson Lambert, and Henrietta (Hettie) Young Swenson. The picture was published in *Deseret Evening News,* 19 December 1914. #P3172, courtesy of LDS Archives.

In 1922 she resigned as editor of the *Relief Society Magazine*, which she had founded in 1913, in order to accept more genealogical assignments. In 1923 she was appointed head of the Research Department and Library of the Genealogical Society of Utah. Susa spent the last years of her life doing ordinance work with her husband, Jacob, who was an official of the Salt Lake Temple. Outside her home life, she considered her efforts on behalf of the dead her greatest work.

In 1922 Susa published a pamphlet entitled the "Teachings of Brigham Young." That same year she was asked by the general authorities to begin a history of women's activities in the Church. These two themes—the greatness of her father and the achievements of women—had been central to her own life. The way in which she elaborated them in her mature years is as revealing of her character and personality as anything she ever did.

To facilitate her work on the women's history, Susa was given an office in the Church office building. She collected and organized much data on the subject and listed twenty-nine chapters with titles from "Women in the Plan of Salvation" to "The Future and Women." The book, entitled "Women in Mormon History," was not completed, though she worked on the manuscript until a few days before her death. Compiled mainly in the seventh decade of her life, her manuscript supported a conservative theological position:

God did not send woman in the world to begin the creation of His children, until man had led the way; nor did He send woman to bring salvation to the crushed millions who have and who do live on earth. Men should lead in life.[36]

This may seem surprising from one who had spent so many years advancing the rights of women, but in an essay written a few years later she told how in the early years of her marriage to Jacob Gates she had confronted and resolved the dilemma of the talented woman in a patriarchal church:

My husband and I were on the Sandwich Islands on a mission in 1888 and Prest. Joseph F. Smith was also there. Regular priesthood meetings were held in the mission house, and I said to Prest. Smith one day: "How is it that you call in all these boy elders and leave me out of your council meetings? Don't you realize that I know more about the Gospel and human problems than those boys do? Why, there are only two men here—yourself and my husband—who I acknowledge as my superiors in wisdom, intelligence, and leadership. Then why shut me out?" He replied—"You admit that your husband, Jacob, and myself are your superiors? Well, that's the whole question in a nutshell. Who is the greatest woman of modern times?" Eliza R. Snow, I answered. "Admitted! But do you consider her the superior or even the equal in intelligence or leadership to the Prophet Joseph Smith, or to your father, Brigham Young?" No, no! Decidedly not! I hastened to reply. "Then, that is the key. Wherever you'll find a superior woman, you'll find a man just one step ahead of her, who will be her leader and guide, as Christ is the head of all men holding the priesthood." . . . After I had my key from President Smith in regard to woman's relationship to the priesthood I was perfectly satisfied—nay, more—womanhood was glorified for me. . . . No normal woman cares to take the responsibility of deciding crucial points— either in domestic, spiritual, or even civic life.[37]

Written in 1932, at the age of seventy-six, these passages indicate some rationalization was necessary for this intelligent and powerful woman to function obediently and gladly in the male hierarchy of the Church to which her life was committed.

Her interest as reflected in the manuscript of "Women in Mormon History" remained with the Church model of women. Her thoughts ranged from the notion that "The use of the ballot tends to increase woman's poise, for she has nothing left to ask for, and so turns with delight to giving her best self, her fuller attention in the usual channels of domestic and social life, with the added zest of an occasional vital interest in civic affairs" to the more skeptical statement that "Women will do as much good, no more, than men will. Her virtues and her faults will be the same civilly as they are socially and commercially. Women themselves have made the mistake of urging that the vote will enable them to purify politics, and to reform the world. What nonsense!"[38] Her manuscript further revealed her distress that some women had already abused their hard-won suffrage:

With the coming of equal franchise all over the world, achieved through relentless pressure of dissatisfied women, we may well look with apprehension into the future of the world if they are left to themselves. Women in New York State are today clamoring for the birth-control law which will make it obligatory [to give] all women information as to controlling child-birth possibilities. This vicious legislation is but the companion of laws which make vice easy for men, with the punishment for all women.[39]

Susa was obviously not an advocate of birth control. One of fifty-six children of her father, she had borne thirteen children and had suffered six "terrible" miscarriages. None of this changed her positive view of the value of children. In fact, she retreated from her feminist attitudes as she grew older. Her views towards female involvement in public life seemed to have tempered. She wrote, "Women who have tasted public life realize more keenly perhaps than any others the need of shelter and protection for their sex through some of the old-fashioned customs and ideals."[40] Susa gave her most profound attention to these old-fashioned customs and ideals, the home and family. Her husband and children were devoted to her, and she described them as "her fondest lovers and fastest friends."[41]

Of the five children who survived to adulthood, Susa's eldest daughter Leah Dunford Widtsoe (1874) was her mother's literary collaborator, confidante, and close friend. She graduated as valedictorian of her class from the University of Utah in 1896, receiving a Normal Diploma. She continued her study in home economics at the Pratt Institute in Brooklyn, New York, the foremost school in the United States at this time for home economics. She was the first western graduate of the school. In 1897 she returned to Utah to accept an appointment at BYU. Like her mother she was a lecturer and writer, collaborating not only with her mother, but also with her husband who had a distinguished career as scientist, writer, and administrator before being appointed a member of the Council of the Twelve Apostles.[42]

Emma Lucy Gates Bowen (1880) has been called Utah's greatest operatic singer. Her coloratura soprano was famous in German opera houses. She was variously called the "Utah Nightingale" and "Utah's first lady of music." As far as she knew, she was the first American girl to debut at the Royal Opera House in a role that demanded dialogue in a foreign tongue. During her four years in Germany as prima donna she sang more than fifty roles, ranging from the highest role written for a coloratura soprano (*Queen of the Night*) to mezzo-soprano (*Carmen*). World War I brought her international career to a close.[43] She returned to Utah and gave her energy to music in her own community. She married attorney and member of the Council of the Twelve Apostles, Albert E. Bowen, and reared his twin sons, Albert and Robert. She was quoted as saying "looking back on my life now, if I had to choose between home and children and a career, I'd take the home and children."[44] Lucy Gates, prima donna to the end, died in 1951.

B. Cecil Gates (1887) was a musician and composer. He was a graduate of the Schrwenka Conservatory of Berlin, Germany. With his sister Lucy as impresario, he founded the Lucy Gates Opera Company in 1915 to bring grand opera to the intermountain west. He was also the director of the LDS School of Music, and the conductor of the Mormon Tabernacle Choir. He married Gweneth Gibbs, with whom he collaborated on "The Gates Story Music," published in 1924.

Harvey Harris (Hal) Gates (1889) was a Hollywood motion-picture writer. Some of his better known films

were "Hell Divers," "Hurricane's Gal," "Legally Dead,"
"Merry-go-round," and "My Mamie Rose." Hal's early
return from his second mission and his subsequent marriage to a Catholic girl almost broke his mother's heart.
Susa felt she had somehow failed as a mother and was
quoted as saying that "I could die happy if Hal were to
come back into the Church and if Leah were sealed to me
in the Temple."[45]

Franklin Young Gates (1893) was a pioneer in the early days of radio. He was a graduate of the University of
Utah, and spent a year at Harvard University. He taught
at BYU. By any standard Susa reared an outstanding family.

Susa wrote that "Being a woman I love power,
strength, and right leadership in men."[46] She loved Jacob
F. Gates, who has been described as "A man of good
judgment and sterling character . . . that uncommon type
generally spoken of as well-balanced."[47] His generosity in
allowing his wife's time and strength to be given to much
public labor was more than repaid by the devotion and
loyalty accorded the husband and father in his home-life.
In 1899 Susa's son-in-law, John A. Widtsoe, wrote her:

I admire Brother Gates. Without his willingness you could not
do so much. So few men are willing to undergo a little personal
inconvenience to let their wives do anything. The exceptions
are loved so much the more. A man's life is not measured alone
by what he accomplishes. More than that, is what he enables
others to do.[48]

Susa and Jacob Gates seem to have been ideally mated.
She gave him the credit for her successes. She said, "I
think a woman should respect and obey her husband in
righteousness, and I think what little success I have made
is because I have never disobeyed my husband or the
counsel of those over me."[49] But the supreme model of
"power, strength, and right leadership" in her life remained her father.

The magnum opus of her eighth decade was the *Life
Story of Brigham Young*, which was published in London

in 1930 and was said to be "probably the first book, frankly pro-Mormon, to be published in England by others than the Church."[50] The Jarrolds edition is liberally laced with personal recollections and not-so-subliminal doctrine. The book received good reviews and was published later in the United States.

In defense of the criticism that Susa was too subjective, "too much of a missionary writing a tract . . . too bent on justifying, not to say whitewashing the 'old billy goat,'" Paul Cracroft has written:

Mrs. Gates knew Brigham Young as only a talented, artistic woman can know a forceful, dynamic father; she drew much of her ability, much of her personality from him and attributed her success to the training he had given her. And with what he gave her, and with what she acquired herself by writing constantly, developing her ideas, creating again the man who had determined and encouraged her own outlook on life—with all these endowments she was able to capture a fair share of the spirit and motivation of a great and misunderstood man.[51]

Susa Young Gates understood her father because she was so much like him. She had obviously inherited much of his initiative, organizing ability, sociability, and capacity for leadership. But she was the daughter, not the son, of a great man, and she was profoundly aware of the difference this made in her life.

While Susa was generally well-liked and respected, there were those who were threatened by her self-confidence. She herself was aware of being frank, outspoken, impatient, somewhat impetuous, jealous of her time, and perhaps vain. Her directness was at times perceived as a lack of tact. Cracroft suggested that her use of pseudonyms in her writing may have been her attempt to counter such resentment, perhaps to cover what she feared might be a growing pride in her work.[52] Susa's achievements gave her a right to pride. Yet her heritage as a Saint, as a descendant of a Prophet, and as a woman taught her to fear it:

Daughter, use all your gifts to build up righteousness in the earth. Never use them to acquire name or fame. Never rob your home, nor your children.

Susa used these words of her father as a guide for her life. Her devotion to family, faith, and Church were developed with the same remarkable vigor as her many other gifts.

Notes

1. Leland A. Fetzer, "Tolstoy and Mormonism," *Dialogue*, 6 (Spring 1971), 17.
2. R. Paul Cracroft, "Susa Young Gates: Her Life and Literary Work" (master's thesis, University of Utah, 1951), p. 73.
3. Susa Young Gates, *History of the Young Ladies' Mutual Improvement Association* (Salt Lake City: General Board of the YLMIA, 1911), p. 126.
4. Leonard J. Arrington, "Blessed Damozels: Women in Mormon History," *Dialogue*, 6 (Summer 1971), 26.
5. John A. Widtsoe, "Sketch of Susa Young Gates," manuscript annotated by Susa Young Gates, c. 1924, p. 3, LDS Church Archives.
6. Susa Young Gates, "Lucy Bigelow Young," 1931, p. 72, in author's collection.
7. Susa Young Gates, *John Stevens' Courtship* (Salt Lake City: The Deseret News, 1909), p. 87.
8. Cracroft, p. 143.
9. Ibid., p. 38.
10. Ibid., pp. 8, 9.
11. Susa Young Gates, *The Life Story of Brigham Young* (London: Jarrolds, 1930), p. 232.
12. Gates, "Lucy Bigelow Young," p. 103.
13. Ibid., p. 134.
14. Ibid., p. 131.

15. Harold H. Jenson, "Susa Young Gates," *The Juvenile Instructor*, 64 (March 1929), 137.

16. Dr. Romania B. Penrose to Susa Young Gates, 26 June 1888, Joseph F. Smith papers, LDS Church Archives.

17. Ibid.

18. Gates, *History of the YLMIA*, p. 107.

19. Cracroft, p. 29.

20. Ibid.

21. Gates, "Lucy Bigelow Young," pp. 143–44.

22. John A. Widtsoe, *In A Sunlit Land* (Salt Lake City: Milton R. Hunter and G. Homer Durham, 1952), p. 38.

23. Gates, "Lucy Bigelow Young," p. 156.

24. Ibid., p. 177.

25. Ibid., p. 191.

26. Ibid., p. 212.

27. Ibid., p. 206.

28. Ibid., pp. 207–215.

29. Susa Young Gates, "Scientific Treatment of Domestic Service," *Young Woman's Journal*, 10 (October, 1899), 403.

30. Gates, "Lucy Bigelow Young," pp. 13–14.

31. Susa Young Gates, "Mrs. Susa Young Gates," p. 3, LDS Church Archives.

32. Gates, "Lucy Bigelow Young," p. 166.

33. Cracroft, p. 16.

34. Jenson, p. 137.

35. Susa Young Gates, *Why I Believe the Gospel of Jesus Christ*, pamphlet (Independence, Mo.: Zion's Printing & Publishing Co., c. 1931), p. 27.

36. Susa Young Gates, "Women in Mormon History," 1918–33, pp. 3–4, LDS Church Archives.

37. Gates, *Why I Believe the Gospel of Jesus Christ*, pp. 13–14.

38. Gates, "Women in Mormon History," pp. 3–5.

39. Ibid., p. 15.

40. Ibid., p. 16.

41. Gates, "Mrs. Susa Young Gates," p. 3.

42. The distaff determination was disseminated into succeeding generations by the two Widtsoe daughters. The eldest "liberated" Zion's Canyon in 1920 with six other "daring female explorers." The younger daughter Eudora Widtsoe Durham studied at the Sorbonne in Paris 1930–31, and at the University of London, 1931–33.

43. Raye Price, "Utah's Leading Ladies of the Arts," *Utah Historical Quarterly*, 38 (Winter 1970), 73–74.

44. Ibid., p. 74.

45. Cracroft, p. 38.

46. Gates, *Why I Believe the Gospel of Jesus Christ*, p. 12.

47. Widtsoe, "Sketch of Susa Young Gates," p. 1.

48. Gates, "Lucy Bigelow Young," p. 188.

49. Jenson, p. 135.

50. Widtsoe, *In A Sunlit Land*, p. 201.

51. Cracroft, pp. 136–37.

52. Ibid., p. 34.

The first Relief Society Hall, the Fifteenth Ward, Salt Lake City. Negative #6776, used by permission, Utah State Historical Society; all rights reserved.

Charitable Sisters
Cheryll Lynn May

Nineteenth century accounts agree that Mormon women possessed a degree of vigor, initiative, and out-spoken advocacy of various causes unparalleled anywhere in the American West, and seldom matched by their eastern sisters. Nowhere can a more impressive example of this wide-ranging initiative be found than in the chronicles of the major women's organization of the Church, the Relief Society. A review of the major activities of this remarkable organization in the nineteenth century clearly reveals this initiative, yet the brilliant record seems to obscure rather than illuminate reasons for the great changes that have taken place in the scope and viewpoint of the Society since that time.

This extraordinary society came into being 17 March 1842 in Nauvoo, Illinois. Joseph Smith organized the group of ladies "under the priesthood and after the pattern of the priesthood," after dismissing the constitution Eliza R. Snow had prepared as *not* being what the ladies wanted, though it was "the best he had ever seen." Emma Smith was elected president, choosing Sarah M. Cleveland and Elizabeth Ann Whitney as her counselors. Sister Snow was elected secretary.[1]

Joseph Smith reported the formation of the "Ladies Relief Society of the City of Nauvoo" in the 1 April 1842 issue of the *Times and Seasons*:

There was a very numerous attendance . . . of some of our most intelligent, humane philanthropic, and respectable ladies; we are well assured from a knowledge of those pure principles of benevolence that flow spontaneously from their . . . bosoms, that with the resources they have at command they will fly to the relief of the stranger, they will pour in oil and wine to the wounded heart of the distressed; they will dry up the tear of the orphan, and make the widow's heart rejoice.[2]

According to reports of Sarah M. Kimball and other contemporaries, the initiative for the formation of the Relief Society came from the ladies of Nauvoo, who felt that through such an organization they could respond more effectively to the needs of the poor and ailing, particularly those who had been subjected to various deprivations as a result of the Missouri persecutions. In August of 1843, four Relief Society members from each Nauvoo ward were appointed to "search out the poor, and suffering, and to call on the rich for aid and thus as far as possible relieve the wants of all." This practice of sending out visiting teachers has been an abiding legacy of the early Relief Society. Members were also interested in collecting money to speed the completion of the Nauvoo Temple.[3]

Joseph Smith displayed active interest and support for the society from its earliest formative stages. He attended many of the early meetings, preaching often to the women about the special roles of wives, mothers, and daughters in promoting the gospel. From March of 1842 until March of 1844, when the pressures of renewed persecutions forced a suspension of the group's formal activities, the members of the Society contributed immeasurably to the welfare and comfort of the unfortunate, as well as to the temple-building effort.

During the first two decades in the Salt Lake Valley, a number of local Relief Societies functioned sporadically on the ward level, but it was not until 1867 that Brigham Young appointed Eliza R. Snow to reestablish the organization in all the wards and branches under centralized Church leadership. By the end of 1868, Relief Society organizations were functioning in the twenty wards in Salt Lake City, in nearly every county in Utah, and in other nearby communities.[4]

The six decades from 1870 to 1930 were, for the Relief Society, years of vigorous activity on a remarkably wide range of projects. During this period the influence of the organization as a semi-independent "power" within the Church, and within the national women's movement, reached its peak. A detailed description of the many Relief Society programs initiated in the late nineteenth and early twentieth centuries can be found in the various official histories,[5] but a brief overview will indicate the breadth and variety of the organization's concerns.

A constant objective of Relief Society members, as the name of the group implies, has been to provide welfare and charity services for those in need. A few lines from Emmeline B. Wells' history of the Relief Society, written in 1895 when she was General Secretary, illuminate both the nature and the spirit of these charitable services:

The main objective of the Society is the care of the needy, the sick, the helpless and the unfortunate, to visit the widow and the fatherless, to administer comfort and consolation as well as temporal relief of physical wants, to see that none are left to suffer . . . also to care for the dying and the dead, to be at the bedside of the lonely ones when death is near, to robe the body neatly and properly for burial when all is over, and to perform those kindly deeds with tenderness and grace.[6]

The Society, in performing these compassionate services, was fulfilling the original purposes for which it had been organized in Nauvoo. After 1866, however, the activities of the group went far beyond these simple acts of kindness. Various "welfare services" became increasingly specialized, and often institutionalized, and many Relief Society programs became only remotely related to the original charitable functions of the organization.

While the Relief Society had always been deeply concerned with caring for the sick, it was not until the Utah period that this concern was translated into well-defined institutional forms. In 1873 President Brigham Young asked Relief Society presidents throughout the Church to appoint three women from each Salt Lake City ward and one from each settlement to study physiology and nursing. Classes in these subjects were initiated in the fall of that year. Over the next several decades hundreds of Relief Society women entered the program, attending private classes in nursing and obstetrics conducted by Mormon women physicians.[7] In the spring of 1898, the Relief Society Nurse School was organized by the Salt Lake Stake Relief Society, and it continued to train Mormon women in nursing for over two decades. In 1920 the school was replaced by a one-year "Nurse Aid" training course at the Salt Lake LDS Hospital. This course, although discontinued in 1924 due to objections by the National Hospital Training School Rating Bureau, provided an early model for the one-year courses in practical nursing offered today in every major community in the country.[8] The Society continued for many years after the discontinuance of its own nursing courses to provide scholarship and loan support for those interested in nursing careers.[9]

In addition to the training of nurses, efforts were made to improve the general quality of hospital care. Special attention was given to child and maternal health. The Deseret Hospital was established by the Society in 1882 and administered by the Society during its twelve years of life.[10] A number of maternity hospitals were established and run by various stake Relief Societies. Those in Snowflake, Arizona, and Cottonwood Stake, Utah, were still operating in 1960. Other Society activities in this field included operating milk depots for children during the summer, sponsoring summer trips for malnourished children, conducting clinics for preschoolers; supplying layette kits to new mothers; providing payment, when necessary, for general medical and dental care, and organizing an extensive program of health and child care education.[11]

Many other demands were made on the time and talents of Relief Society women during this period. In 1876 Relief Society members were called by Brigham Young to carry out a systematic program of saving grain against a time of need. The sisters of the Society set out to fulfill the call with their typical vigor and energy:

They raised wheat, gleaned in the fields, and bought wheat with funds raised through sale of such items as quilts, carpets, rugs, jam, and Sunday eggs. Sometimes they would follow the threshing machine with a team and wagon to gather in the wheat. They also solicited wheat from door to door.[12]

Scores of Relief Society granaries were constructed throughout Utah and in other Mormon settlements to store the wheat. Relief supplies of wheat were sent from Relief Society stores to the victims of the 1906 San Francisco earthquake and to Chinese famine victims the next year. In 1918 the Society sold its entire wheat inventory, 200,000 bushels, to the United States Government for war relief purposes. The Relief Society grain-saving program continued until the 1930s when it was incorporated into the newly-established general Church Welfare Program.[13]

In 1877 the Relief Societies throughout the Church were assigned by President Young, "to raise silk and do all in their power to clothe themselves and their families."[14] In attempting to fulfill this mission over the next generation, Relief Society members spent countless hours planting and caring for mulberry trees, raising silkworms (usually in their homes since few could afford cocooneries) and establishing a number of primitive silk "factories." Though the Utah sericulture experiment was abandoned in the early twentieth century, it was vigorously supported by Relief Society leaders until the General Authorities decided that it was economically unfeasible.[15]

Silk culture: women are picking cocoons from mulberry branches about 1895. The box in front is full of silk worms. George Edward Anderson, photographer. #P1294/2, courtesy of LDS Archives.

In addition to the multitude of health, welfare, and other service programs operated by the Relief Society in the 1870–1930 period, the Society also sponsored a variety of educational and cultural activities for its members. Prior to 1902, occasional classes on subjects of special interest to pioneer women were sponsored by the Society. These classes most often related to infant and maternal health and hygiene. From 1902 onward, however, "Mother's Classes" were instituted as a regular feature of the Relief Society program.[16] While the precise class content differed in the various wards and stakes, the general subjects were "homemaking skills" and "family relations." In 1914 the Relief Society General Board adopted a "uniform course of study" for use throughout the Church. The scope of the subject matter was at this time significantly expanded to include not only courses on homemaking but also monthly lessons in the fields of "theology," "social science," and "literature." In the year 1930, for example, Relief Society members were receiving regular classes in homemaking, monthly theology lessons on the Book of Mormon, literature lessons on "biography," and social science lessons on "The field of Social work."[17]

The Relief Society during the period under discussion was the most independent of the Church auxiliary organizations. The term "independent" here must be interpreted carefully. The Society was never independent in the sense of challenging priesthood authority or in failing to respond eagerly and willingly to instructions of the First Presidency. Such actions would have been unthinkable to Relief Society leaders and members alike. But the distinctly separate organizational structure and programs of the Relief Society reflected the attitude that while priesthood leaders established the general policy goals, the Relief Society leaders were perfectly capable of initiating and executing programs to achieve these goals.

The separate status of the Relief Society within the Church was underscored by the physical separation of the general ward or branch meeting house from the center of women's activity, the Relief Society Hall. Until the 1920s, when it became general practice for a special room for the use of the Relief Society to be included in every chapel, the great majority of the wards and branches of the Church had their own Relief Society halls, furnished by the sisters with tables, quilting frames, cookstoves, chests for storing sewing materials, and other items needed for Relief Society work.[18]

The Society during this period was also financially independent from other Church organizations. Its operating expenses were not allocated from general Church funds but were raised from members' annual dues. Decisions about disbursement of money raised through sale of Relief Society handiwork and other fund-raising projects were made by the Society leaders themselves, not by the general Church presidency. In 1892 the Society was incorporated as a separate legal entity under the name of the "National Woman's Relief Society," so that, to quote the official Relief Society history, "it could be independent and transact its own business in its own name with trustees and all the rights and privileges belonging to a corporate body."[19] The leaders of the organization were consistently supported by the First Presidency in claiming the right to control the disbursement of their stores of grain, even when their decisions conflicted with those of the local bishop.[20]

Another area of activity in which the Relief Society became increasingly independent during this period was the Society's program of publications. The *Woman's Exponent*, the bi-monthly periodical inaugurated in 1872, was considered first and foremost to be the mouthpiece of the Relief Society.[21] The *Exponent* ceased publication in 1914, and the next year saw the birth of a monthly journal published exclusively by and for the Society—the *Relief Society Magazine*. The *Magazine* continued publication under Relief Society auspices until 1970 when, at the direction of the First Presidency, its publication was suspended. Over the years the Relief Society issued scores of Relief Society handbooks, various lesson books, song books, and several official histories.

In reviewing the activities of the Relief Society during the 1870–1930 period, one is impressed not only with the variety of the organization's concerns, but also with the spirit in which these enterprises were carried out. Though seldom specifically articulated, the attitude conveyed by Relief Society women was one of tremendous confidence in themselves and in their ability to fulfill, and in many respects actually to define, their "callings" in the Great Basin Kingdom. In sharp contradistinction to the passive and protected Victorian ideal of femininity then dominant in the rest of the country, the model Relief Society member was an active and absolutely necessary participant in the building of Zion. Relief Society women acted on the assumption that the challenge of "building the kingdom" would require the full scope of their energies and talents, not merely those considered by the rest of the country to be "ladylike." As a result, a chronicle of Relief Society activities during these years is one replete not only with examples of charity and sacrifice, but also with a multitude of economic, political, and cultural projects that demanded a high level of executive and organizational ability.

From the 1930s onward, the activities of the Society, and their relation to the priesthood authority structure, have undergone a gradual but significant change. The scope of the Society's concerns has narrowed considerably, and the degree of organizational autonomy enjoyed by the group has been greatly reduced. Some of the early functions of the Relief Society were discontinued in the twentieth century simply because other agencies developed, both within and outside the Church, which could do these jobs better. As the Mormon settlements sank

roots and progressed past the frontier stage, more specialized public and private agencies were established to provide a variety of health and welfare services. Relief Society nurse-training courses were no longer necessary when
various universities and hospitals established their own
nursing education programs. Within the Church, the
Welfare Plan was established as a specialized agency to
provide for the physical needs of those unable to provide
for their own. This agency superseded the grain-saving
program of the Relief Society, and also rendered unnecessary the monthly solicitations by the visiting teachers on
behalf of the poor. [22]

But the transfer of many of the Relief Society's early
"callings" to other more specialized agencies has been
only one of the processes through which the scope and independence of the organization have been restricted. The
abandonment of separate Relief Society halls in favor of a
Relief Society room within the general meetinghouse
meant that local priesthood authorities rather than Society
members would have the final word on the basic facilities
available to the women. For many years the Relief Society
sisters assumed the responsiblity of furnishing and decorating the Relief Society room, and as a result this room
was often the most beautiful and comfortable of the entire
chapel complex. By 1952, however, the Relief Society had
also been relieved of this responsibility. And recently
several chapels have been built with no specially-desig-
nated Relief Society room whatsoever.

The independence of the Society has also been greatly diminished in recent years by the 1969 decisions of the
First Presidency to suspend publication of the *Relief Society Magazine* and to eliminate the Society's financial separation from other Church agencies, incorporating budgetary allotments for the organization into the general
Church budget. The numerous fund-raising projects of
the Society, including the annual bazaars held in most
wards where the ladies sold a wide variety of their handiwork and food items, have also been prohibited by the

First Presidency. Thus the group is now totally dependent for its budgetary allocations upon the decisions of priesthood authorities.

The narrowing scope of Relief Society concern and activities is nowhere more clearly reflected than in a comparison of the content of the Society's program of lessons in the twenties and thirties with the content of the same lessons today. While the four lesson categories still exist (homemaking, social relations, cultural refinement, and spiritual living), the real differences among these apparently widely varying fields have been largely erased. As many Relief Society teachers have noted, all lessons today are basically concerned with "Spiritual Living in the Home." A listing of the titles of some of these lessons in the twenties and thirties alongside their more recent counterparts should illustrate the trend:

Subject: Social Relations

Year	*Course Title*	*Year*	*Course Title*
1924–25	"The Field of Social Welfare"	1961–62	"The Place of Woman in the Gospel Plan"
1926–27	"Child Welfare"	1962–65	"Divine Law and Church Government"
1928–29	"Child Study"		
1930	"The Field of Social Work"	1965–66	"Teaching the Gospel in the Home"
1930–32	"Personality Study"		

Subject: Cultural Refinement

Year	*Course Title*	*Year*	*Course Title*
1924	"American Literature, the New England Period"	1964–66	"The Individual and Human Values as Seen Through Literature"
1925	"Later American Poets, Including World War Poets"	1966–67	"Ideals of Womanhood in Relation to Home and Family"[23]
1926–27	"Canadian Poets of World War, & American Novelists & Poets"		

The trend is clearly toward the abandonment of specific academic and cultural topics for a more general approach, where small excerpts from various works are quoted in support of an overriding spiritual point. It appears that during the earlier period it was assumed that Relief Society members could find uplift and inspiration from a wide variety of academic disciplines and artistic fields. By the 1960s, however, this attitude seems to have changed. The relevance of lesson materials to spiritual and domestic concerns is now much more directly and explicitly drawn than it was in the past. Today the value of lesson materials seems to be measured basically in terms of the degree of support and justification these materials give to the primacy of woman's domestic role.

While the range of activities and the organizational independence of the Relief Society have been declining, the intensity with which the Society has pursued its remaining functions—those related to motherhood and promoting a spiritual home life—has steadily increased. The leaders seem to feel that only by strong reassertion of a patriarchal family pattern, and by freeing women from any interests or activities which could possibly divert them from their primary calling as wives and mothers in Zion, can the family be saved.

Today even the staging of an annual bazaar is considered by Church authorities to be an unwarranted diversion from the wifely and motherly duties of Relief Society members. It seems as if in some respects the Victorian female ideal of a century ago, scorned by Relief Society leaders at the time as needlessly wasteful of human potential and as demeaning to women, has been resurrected as a model for the modern Relief Society woman. While differences certainly exist, the similarities between today's "model" Mormon woman and her Victorian counterpart in terms of an exclusive devotion to hearth and home, and the rejection of any executive or professional roles as "unfeminine," are clearly apparent.

Even in this greatly circumscribed role, the Relief Society continues to be a vital and growing organization, warmly supported by the majority of its members. But it must be admitted that there is missing in the modern Relief Society the sense of confidence and exhilaration of reaching out to conquer new frontiers that characterized the group in earlier years. A sense of loss at the Society's decline is naturally felt when one reviews the inspiring achievements animated by the spirit.

The question rises as to whether the Society, in channeling all its efforts toward fulfilling one major need of the women in the Church, might have lost sight of the existence of other needs. One reason for the loss of some of the group's vigor and animation might be the fact that certain very real needs of some Society members are not being met.

Women who find themselves single, divorced, or widowed are automatically out of the mainstream of Relief Society activity and attention. While some effort has been made by the Society to provide lessons for those in the "non-mother" category, the overwhelming dominance of the theme that women gain their only true fulfillment through their relationship to their husbands and children cannot help but make these members feel like second-class citizens. The Relief Society has recently moved to fill this need with a welcome program for single women.

Mature women whose families are essentially grown are also disregarded. Decades of potentially productive life lie ahead of them, and yet official Society policy seems to indicate that their truly "meaningful" life has ended once the most demanding period of childbearing and childrearing is over.

The modern Relief Society has officially chosen to ignore the fact that despite the often-voiced disapproval of its leaders and other Church authorities, many Mormon women do work outside the home. These women have to some degree felt alienated from the organization.

In the nineteenth century Relief Society members were not only expected to care for their families and to render compassionate aid to others in need, they were also expected to develop any other skills they possessed, whether medical, organizational, educational, or whatever, to further the building of the Kingdom. The rigorous demands of a frontier settlement made any other course intolerably wasteful of human resources. One might ask if such waste in human potential is any more tolerable today than it was in 1870.

It is unlikely that any single program could meet the varied circumstances of modern Mormon women. The key to success would seem to lie in employing a flexible approach, tailoring programs to fit the particular needs of each local group. The young people's organizations, for example, have adopted a policy of encouraging local initiative with considerable success.

The Relief Society has the resources for transforming unused talents into solid accomplishments. In the past, Relief Society leaders displayed a striking ability to develop a great variety of innovative programs. When the Society approaches some of the problems of today with the same open and resourceful attitude, it will add yet another page to its impressive list of successes.

Notes

1. Relief Society of the Church of Jesus Christ of Latter-day Saints, *History of the Relief Society, 1842–1966* (Salt Lake City: The Relief Society, 1966), pp. 18–21.
2. Joseph Smith, "Editorial Comment," *Times and Seasons*, April, 1842.
3. *History of the Relief Society, 1842–1966*, p. 18.
4. Ibid., p. 30.
5. The two authorized histories of the Society are *A Centenary of Relief Society* (Salt Lake City: The Relief Society, 1942), and the previously noted *History of the Relief Society, 1842–1966*, published by the Society in 1966.

6. *Woman's Exponent*, 24 (1 October 1895), 59–60.
7. Relief Society, *A Centenary of Relief Society, 1842–1942* (Salt Lake City, 1942), pp. 45–46, hereinafter referred to as *Centenary*.
8. Ibid., p. 46.
9. Ibid., pp. 46–47.
10. Ibid., pp. 47–48.
11. *History of the Relief Society*, pp. 69–79.
12. Ibid., p. 110. Eggs laid on the day of rest were consigned to the Lord's purposes.
13. Ibid., p. 111.
14. *Woman's Exponent*, 6 (15 April 1877), 172.
15. *Centenary*, p. 71.
16. *History of the Relief Society*, pp. 73–74.
17. Ibid., pp. 79–80.
18. Ibid., p. 104.
19. Ibid., p. 36.
20. Leonard Arrington, "The Economic Role of Mormon Women," *Western Humanities Review*, 9 (Spring 1955), 145–64.
21. *History of the Relief Society*, p. 96.
22. Ibid., p. 69.
23. Ibid., pp. 79–80.

The Cannonville Relief Society, Panguitch Stake, Garfield County, about 1880. #P18, courtesy of LDS Archives.

Fictional Sisters

Laurel Thatcher Ulrich

Twentieth century novelists have shown considerable interest in nineteenth century Saints. In the twenty-
five years between Vardis Fisher's *Children of God* (1939)
and Paul Bailey's *For Time And All Eternity* (1964), twenty-
two unmistakably "Mormon" novels were published by
firms like Doubleday and Harpers and reviewed in periodicals like the *New York Times* and *Saturday Review*.[1]
These books, with few exceptions, deal with the pioneer
past. The reader interested in Nauvoo, for example, can
choose in addition to Fisher's wide-screen epic, love stories by Virginia Sorenson and Elinor Pryor, a horseback
adventure by Jonreed Lauritzen, or a Mississippi River
comedy by Joseph Furnas. Other novels explore provin-
cial Utah from Bountiful to the Virgin River, with flashbacks to street meetings in Liverpool or Copenhagen.
Some of these books are bitter, some surprisingly sweet,
most merely dull. Few are familiar to the faithful.

Yet for Mormon women, they have a special interest.
Those of us born in the Church usually come out of Primary
with a picture in our heads of a pioneer grandmother resolutely crossing the plains. In time that image hardens into
bronze, returning to haunt us in vulnerable moments—on
the delivery table, for instance, or while driving through
heavy traffic to yet another meeting. Even converts learn
early to sing the old refrain: "If the pioneers could do it,

why not we?" Church periodicals reinforce our general
sense of flabbiness with stories of faithful wives dying under dripping canvas in the middle of Iowa while reciting
the Biblical "Whither thou goest . . ."[2] Such things surely
happened. Yet most of us have less need for vicarious
grand moments than for an understanding of the everyday. A good novelist can give us that.

True, historical novels are not history. We don't read
The Scarlet Letter to find out how the Puritans punished
adulterers, but for other quite as important reasons. Although the novelist may work with much of the same material as the historian, he has the advantage, as well as the
drawback, of being able to fill in the gaps in the data. Art
cracks mysteries that facts can't touch. Even a second-rate
novel can tell us a great deal. The stereotypes promoted in
popular fiction alert us to concepts that need examining.
They also remind us of the subjective nature of our own
images. It is no accident that several of the writers of Mormon novels—Whipple, Sorenson, Kennelly, Cannon—
were once little girls in Primary, too. Reading their books,
we see the nineteenth century through a double lens,
magnified through their perceptions as well as our own. It
is useful to see our pioneer grandmother in multiple—as
an Earth Mother, an Amazon, a Pandora, and a Virtuous
Victim. Understanding the imagery of others may help us
become more deeply aware of our own.

I

The Earth Mother is the most affirmative of the fictional stereotypes, the one closest to our own idealized
grandmothers, although she is coarser, less devout. No
matter how forbidding the world outside, she nurtures a
warm circle around a humble hearth. In the Mormon novels she is often Danish, the Jutland cottage in Virginia
Sorenson's *Kingdom Come* being the prototype for little

houses all across Zion smelling of cookies and clean tow-
els. Linnea Ecklund, the bustling heroine of Ardyth Kennelly's books, can set a house or a church to rights in fifteen minutes of earnest effort. Pouring hot coffee to eat
with fresh cake, she insists (with compatriots in any number of other books) that the Word of Wisdom wasn't
meant for the Scandinavians.[3]

Earth Mothers aren't interested in the fine points of
theology. To them religion is primarily a big lap. When
they're not comforting their own children or delivering
someone else's, they are welcoming an orphan. Apostle
Morton, in Jonreed Lauritzen's *The Everlasting Fire*, sur-
veys the six wives of his "first Quorum" and is "thankful
for Coziah, changing diapers on three wailing babies in
the wagon, then feeding two of them from her abundant
breasts—to make up for Letty's lack."[4] Even her name
speaks of comfort. In a later scene she welcomes a gentile
judge who has befriended the Saints, offering him a bowl
of soup from the campfire: "I know you don't deserve it,
Brother Eyring. I can tell you ain't done much, 'cause
you're still breathing." She asks him if he thinks he'll ever
join the Church. When he protests he doesn't know
enough about it, she offers her own freckle-faced creed:

I know people that only know enough about it to yell, "Hallelul-
ya," and they're in. I don't think it's so much what you know as
how you feel about things. Now there's some men that can say
"amen" like a deep belch when one of the authorities says
something, and they think that's going to get them the higher
glory. But they wouldn't give a hungry kid a grain of corn if
they had their wagon box heaped up with it. Now you done a
saintlike thing. . . . If you've done any wickedness you paid it
off with food.[5]

Food—from Danish pancakes to steaming broth—signals
the presence of an Earth Mother.

In *The Giant Joshua* there is a ritual exchange between
another of these women, called the "Yeast Lady," and her
husband: "Oh, vell, Ulia, vhere did I find you!" "Oh,
vell, Lars, what were you doin' there!"[6] Although Julia is

unusual in having been converted in a brothel, all of the Earth Mothers convey a good-natured, open acceptance of human nature, including sex. There is nothing mysterious or seductive about them, and they do not agonize over past sins. Aunt Sophie, in Blanche Cannon's *Nothing Ever Happens Sunday Morning*, welcomes the rain-soaked Matilda on her wedding eve, wrapping her in warm flannel and kind phrases: "Young brides. Always so scared, poor little things. I was like that when I married Will. I didn't know what to expect. I'd lived on a farm all my life, too, but I just hadn't put two and two together. You mustn't be afraid. After a while it all comes natural-like."[7] For the Earth Mother, most things do.

Linnea Ecklund confides to a neighbor that it's not the gospel she finds troublesome: "It's the buttinsky men," but she seldom stays angry at Olaf long.[8] Most Earth Mothers see the men in their lives as wayward but lovable little boys. Linnea has the same attitude toward all officialdom, including Wilford Woodruff. When a solemn presidential visit to an erring home turns out to have been redundant, she refuses to tell him. "All I know is that it would of spoiled everything if he'd of knew. He'd of been disappointed just like anybody. A President's got to be the whole cheese or bust."[9] She's quite willing to let him. Queen of her own domain, she's indifferent to any other.

II

An Earth Mother provides for her family as effortlessly as Raggedy Ann shaking cream puffs from her apron. Not so the Amazon, who is constantly at war with desert and dust and the enemies of the Kingdom. In *The Fancher Train*, a fictionalized account of the Mountain Meadows massacre, two gentiles leave their wagon somewhere in southern Utah in search of fresh milk for an ailing baby. They soon come to a farm where a Mormon woman tends a herd of goats. Sister Wyatt "was tall and her bosom was like a thrusting shelf. She was not fat, but big-boned, powerfully built, her face was like a man's with its set square jaw and grimly thin mouth. Irrigating her vegetable garden was an easy chore compared with her usual work in the fields." She tells the strangers she has nothing to sell. When in desperation they steal a goat, she rides in triumph to their camp with Bishop McKenzie, who is also the Sheriff. Seeing the scrawny baby and the seventeen-year old mother, she momentarily softens—to the Bishop's dismay. "I taken a look at that goat, over there, and I say it ain't my goat," she insists, then fixes her grimly thin mouth against the Bishop himself. "Come on, Isayer, 'for you make a bigger fool of yourself."[10]

An Amazon bends when and how she chooses. Sister Wyatt has been hardened not only by her work in the fields but by persecution. She herself "lost two babies for lack of food—in Missouri."[11] To an Earth Mother that would be reason enough to help a stranger in distress— even one from Clay County. To her it is merely justification for revenge. The milk imagery is significant, though perhaps unconscious on the author's part. Hardship and hatred have symbolically dried up her maternal nature. Elinor Pryor exploits a similar theme in her chronicle of the Missouri persecutions. The novel's heroine, Linsey Allen, watches with horror as her own mother is transformed under the taunts of the mobbers.

Good heavens! Her gentle, ladylike mother, clenching her fists and crying: "If they come here, if they make one move to harm us, they'll have me to reckon with, if nobody else lifts a finger. I can point a gun and shoot it, if I can get close enough—and I know I could use a knife or a hatchet. I've had plenty of practice butchering. Plenty!"[12]

But Mrs. Allen doesn't get her chance. She dies at Haun's Mill with the fixed gaze of a martyr, while her flaxen-haired daughter faints into the arms of the nearest elder and is saved. Strength is seldom an asset to the romantic heroine.

Bathsheba, in *The Giant Joshua*, is "nearly six feet tall, broad of bosom and hip, strong and tireless as a good horse."[13] With black hair standing out on her lip, she clears sagebrush and plasters red rock better than any of her sons. She also makes life miserable for everybody around her, tyrannizing the younger wives and the neighbors, all in the name of righteousness. In the McBride clan in Fisher's *Children of God*, the Amazon is Fanny, a muscular woman with "red hands," "powerful arms" and a "stern mouth" beneath "searching gray eyes." When her husband brings a second wife, she looks her "up and down, quietly, critically, as she might have noted the good and bad points of an ox or a cow."[14] Imagery of livestock is often associated with hard-working women. Martha Corey, in Paul Bailey's *For Time And All Eternity*, moves with "sureness and dispatch—like any well-trained mare to the stall." She is small of stature and capable of sensitivity, yet her daughter thinks of her as a "graying piece of rawhide and sinew."[15] She dies from a bad heart—and perhaps from denying her own nature as well. As any Earth Mother knows, women are meant for gentler work.

If, as Leonard Arrington has said, Utah's women were often successful stockraisers and farmers, there is nothing in the novels to indicate they liked it. When Kennelly's Linnea discovers herself out in the pasture without a corset, she flees Bountiful lest she become as "dumb and heartless and soulless and clompy and manure-heeled as a cow."[16] In most of the books, heroines fight rough hands and straggly locks more zealously than Indians or Feds. Vardis Fisher's women are almost all ugly, but not from lack of primping; Lauritzen's heroines worry about dull hair while fleeing from mobbers; Whipple's swap pages of *Godey's Lady's Book* in a dugout. For the powerful Amazon, winning the west is often secondary to winning a man.

III

As we might imagine, polygamy is central to most of the stories, as it was in nineteenth century fiction about the Mormons. But in the twentieth century, authors are willing to accept idealistic as well as fleshly motives among Mormon males. This approach asks for Pandora. Into the Mormon kingdom of communal concern and spiritual love, she brings the disruption of individualism and desire. What's more, she brings a pretty face. The jacket blurb for Bailey's *For Time And All Eternity* suggests her nature: "With dark, flashing eyes and an exuberant, almost defiant vitality, young Nancy Corey was extremely attractive—and a devout Mormon."[17] What is being exploited here is an apparent conflict between religiosity and sexuality, the notion that under the rim of a covered wagon might sit a flirtatious rebel capable of upsetting Zion. In Bailey's book, Pandora never achieves her full potential. When a pious apostle proposes marriage, she hits him and calls him a "horny old stud," then runs off with a gentile soldier. In a "jokes-on-you" twist of the plot, the gentile turns Mormon and polygamist and Nancy loses her sparkle. A true Pandora would have married the apostle, bringing her irreverence into his household. The spiritual justification for plural marriage is undercut by a character like Clory in *The Giant Joshua*, whose curls won't behave, who can't resist flirting with her husband's son, who bares an ankle just as he launches a solemn lecture. Because she is desirable as well as rebellious, she arouses conflicting emotions in her priesthood lord.

Bishop Eben Benson in Blanche Cannon's *Nothing Ever Happens Sunday Morning* is a perfect set-up for Pandora. He is pompous, self-righteous, ambitious for high Church office. When he encounters beautiful, red-haired May in the lamp-light of Liverpool, he is left in a tangle of confusion. "Until this night he'd had no trouble with his standards, or with his thoughts and feelings, either. But the woman had bewitched him."[18] Unable to leave her, he resolves to convert her, to think only of her soul. But red-haired May has been raised in Florence among musicians and artists, and she knows secrets the tight-lipped women of Utah have forgotten. With perfume and roses and a disarrayed kimono she overcomes his reserve. "You're no better than a light woman," he says. "And you make me no better than your fancy man. We are shameless."[19] But he loves it.

Apostle Morton Baird in *The Everlasting Fire* fears for his faith because of the emotions awakened by his Pandora. He fights the temptation to run away from all the "tugging, pleading, pulling, crowding, crying, quarreling, complaining children" of his plural family and share "the arms and the love of one woman," the beautiful Myra, who can seldom talk about God without mocking.[20] Baird remains true to his higher self—and to Myra. Like the young missionary, Svend Madsen, in Sorenson's *Kingdom Come*, he resolves his conflicts by making passion an Article of Faith. By the mid-twentieth century even popular novelists had discovered the positive value of sex. For most of the authors, Pandora is an affirmative figure.

Not so for Vardis Fisher, who has very little use for women at all. His Brigham Young is not susceptible to perfume. On the trail, he solemnly rebukes a flirtatious wife who wants to be petted and held when graves are being dug on the prairie outside.[21] He dutifully bestows his favors on all the wives but refuses to stay the night with any—until he encounters Amelia Folsom. But by then he's tired of trying to build utopia with petty and rebellious women:

They were so earthy, so much of the flesh and so little of the spirit, so vain and soulless and petulant, that he sometimes wondered if they understood the new gospel in which they lived. If a man kissed and hugged a wife, she dimpled and turned playful like a kitten, and wanted to know if he loved her better than the others; and if he said no, he loved them all equally, then she thought he was a liar or a fool. The benevolently impartial devotion of a man to a score of women, they could not understand or believe in.[22]

The pack of pig-eyed, wasp-waisted women who troop across the pages of Fisher's epic are indeed vain and soulless and petulant—Pandoras letting a box of troubles loose on Zion.

IV

If Earth Mothers live in the kitchen, Amazons in the fields, and Pandoras in the bedroom, the Virtuous Victim must be content to dust the parlor. She is a character from the classic nineteenth century novel of seduction and betrayal, but a much more benign attitude toward polygamy in the twentieth century clothes her in a new gown. The submissive Matilda, blackening her husband's shoes on Sunday morning and obediently handing him his Bible, was once a bride in terror of her own flesh. "For some time she had realized that she loved Eben more than he loved her. She would never have used the word desire, even in her most secret thoughts—love was a nicer word." Kneeling for her bedtime prayer, she had fought "the images of delight from her mind. It was sinful, blasphemous. Shivering on her knees, she'd pray to be forgiven, and she'd feel as guilty before Eben as before God."[23] By the time the novel opens, she has long since buried her passion in overzealous housekeeping and a too-intense concern for her oldest son, leaving Eben to cold sheets and memories of his dead Pandora. Thus, her virtue is a cloak for repression.

Cannon is not the only author to see something pathological in the Virtuous Victim. Illness and betrayal are interlocking themes in Virginia Sorenson's books. Crippled or invalid wives are portrayed with varying degrees of sympathy in *A Little Lower Than the Angels, Many*

Heavens, Kingdom Come, and (though the physical defect
has been displaced to a child) in *The Evening and the
Morning*. If the husband's betrayal intensifies the wife's
illness, the illness makes possible and even justifies the
betrayal. In such a setting, the "other woman" has a
whole new meaning. It is no accident that Cannon, Lauritzen, Sorenson, Whipple, Pryor, Bailey, and Kennelly all
portray second wives in sympathetic terms. Healthy,
practical, willing to share, these women are misunderstood and abused by the glacial Sigurds, the vengeful Ma-
tildas, and the ailing Mercys, who are their husbands'
rightful spouses.

Most twentieth-century novelists are willing to accept idealistic as well as fleshly motives in Mormon men.
They depend on the "unused bodies" as opposed to the
"harem" theory of polygamy. "The great sharing is the
truth I have felt to the marrow of my bones," says Simon
Baker in Sorenson's *A Little Lower Than the Angels*. He
questions whether love alone should be allowed selfishness:

For a man it is even unnatural—did not most men cast their
eyes on many women, suffering under their instincts and the
burden of the other commandment? And did God smile on the
rows of woman-bodies, unused and lonely? Did He smile on
those others sitting by their windows with candles burning before them, and the men passing and looking and presently fur-
tively tapping, and then the doors opened and the candles
snuffed? Did He smile upon the smug wife passing by these
houses with her market basket on her arm and her face averted
with shame for her own kind?[24]

For Simon, logic meets personal need. Mercy's illness has
turned his household upside down. He can see how the
robust Charlot Leavitt might be a blessing to Mercy and
the children as well as to himself. As Brigham Young out-
lines the new order of matrimony, he feels "a weakness,
an excitement that was like something he remembered
from the years when he was very young."[25]

Woman missionaries Lula Roskelly and Mildred Harvey served in the California Mission, c. 1919. #P1834, courtesy of LDS Archives.

Elinor Pryor's *And Never Yield*, a much less sophisticated novel published the same year as Sorenson's, justifies polygamy in similar terms. When her devoted husband explains the new doctrine, Linsey Welles shrinks in horror, yet she recognizes his love for her as well as his fidelity to the Prophet's voice. "How good he was! How infinitely superior to herself, who had neither patience nor faith nor sweetness! Come what might, there was nothing for her to do but to stretch to the utmost in measuring up to him."[26] She very nearly breaks in doing so, but in the melodramatic finale of the book, she understands that for such a man as Nathan one wife is not enough: he needs both "wine and milk."[27]

These novelists see Mormonism as reinforcing two innate male qualities—the capacity for unlimited sexual experience and for devotion to an abstract ideal. They see it as inevitable that the peculiar virtues of women—their fidelity, their devotion to domestic practicalities—become battered in such a system. The plaintive little cry of Mercy Baker, "We women like things we can touch sometimes," speaks for them all.[28] "Polygamy was infinitely harder for a woman," muses Erastus Snow in *The Giant Joshua*, "for a woman was not like a man—a woman since time began craved just one man, all to herself, and the secure possession of one man's love. No gospel could ever mean so much to any woman as her own home, her own mate, and a little sucking mouth at her breast."[29] Or as Ilse puts it in *The Everlasting Fire*: "A man will give his life for something that has meaning to him—as a woman will give her life for man."[30] Thus, polygamist wives are victimized in the novels, not by Demon Lust but by their own nature.

The idea that a Mormon wife might have had more to occupy her mind than sagebrush and the number of favors bestowed next door has not had wide circulation. Achieving women are few in the books. Eliza R. Snow appears in two. In Joseph Furnas', she is a comic figure warmed over from Twain:

Even when she set she looked like she was fixing to jump and run somewhere and work hard to be a Mormon. The neighbor women never knowed when she'd bust in while they was busy and say: "Sister, I want to bless thee," and they'd have to drop whatever it was and kneel down while she blessed them and prayed over them and like as not the biscuit burning in the spider all the time. . . . Or suppose somebody lost a child and was just commencing to chirk up after a month or two, Elizy would turn up some morning and talk about it and cry and sing that hymn she wrote for child funerals: "Your Sweet Little Rosebud Has Left You," and get them feeling terrible all over again.[31]

Although Virginia Sorenson, in *A Little Lower Than the Angels*, takes Eliza's poetry more seriously, she sees it as an extended love lyric for Joseph Smith. Her Zina in *Many Heavens* is a career woman. She attends Dr. Shipp's midwifery school and has fleeting thoughts of going East to become a doctor. But despite the emphasis on her "skilled hands," Zina obviously loves nursing primarily because she loves Dr. Niels. If Niels had been a rustler, it's not hard to imagine her developing a talent for roping cows.

None of this is surprising. At mid-twentieth century, repression rather than oppression was the dominant concern. Even if someone had thought of writing a novel about Ellis Shipp, he would probably have focused on her years as a Virtuous Victim rather than her struggles to obtain an M.D. Each age turns to history for its own uses. We can fault Sorenson for failing to appreciate the Amazon's hoe, but not without revealing our own bias. At the very least, these fictional stereotypes teach us humility. We are not the first generation to find the past more up-to-date than the present.

V

After reading a dozen historical novels, even the most disciplined reader is likely to feel as mindless as Kennelly's Mrs. Orbit.

Mrs. Orbit was the only woman Linnea ever knew who read books. Not only did she buy the paperbacked kind, but she actually went to the library and drew books out, two at a time and read them all through. The beds would not be made, the ironing close to mildew, the cold dishwater not thrown out the back door, the leftovers moldering in the pantry, but Mrs. Orbit had to get through those books to see how they turned out. The stove would not be blacked, the ashes showering down upon the hearth, the house cold, the children as free as birds, herself in a morning sack with an unkempt head of witch's hair, but the books had to be read. For her neighbors Mrs. Orbit was that thing to be mysteriously whispered about, like the drinker or hermaphrodite, the Novel Reader.[32]

Romantic fiction is seldom invigorating. Yet in the Mormon collection, three books are well worth the time. Whipple's *The Giant Joshua*, Sorenson's *The Evening and The Morning*, and Laxness' *Paradise Reclaimed* transcend the stereotypes.

When it appeared in 1941, *The Giant Joshua* was greeted with mixed reviews. The *New York Times* called it "a rich, robust, and oddly exciting novel which brings the Mormons as close home to the reader as they have ever been brought before. Not only in this book are they likeable, but they have a certain magnificence which fully explains their history."[33] The *Nation*, on the other hand, found the book "pretty hard going" and doubted "whether even a first-rate novelist could make much out of the Mormon saga in its internal religious, as opposed to its more conventional external pioneering aspects."[34] While the critics argued the artistic merits of the book, the folks back home were simply shocked. Thirty years later the book seems remarkably true to the faith. Whatever its merits to the outside world, contemporary Mormons will still find it an excellent place to begin in developing an understanding of pioneer life.

In a recent interview, Whipple claimed to have looked up every factual detail as she wrote, "even the botany and all that."[35] She must have, for the reader gets a sense of having been in St. George in the days of the Cotton Mission, almost feeling the ache of hoeing clay, the terror of a bursting dam. More than in any of the other books, there is a sense of the community, with its quiltings and councils, its public and private faces. Whipple does not try to give us the Mormon "epic," but something of the texture of the daily life of ordinary folks. If her feminism shows through, so does her humanity. However critical of Mormon foibles, her book is an insider's portrait. Set against Abijah's pettiness is the loving and homely leadership of Erastus Snow, against Zebedee Trupp's toothless sermons, the salty verses of Lon Tuckett.

True, there is a lot of rhetorical clumsiness in the book. The passages describing Clory's religious experiences are often awkward, especially on a second reading. Whenever things get too bad for her, she turns to a kind of kindergarten mysticism, dwelling on thoughts of "The Unopened Door" and "The Great Smile" (which has a way of turning into Charlie Brown's "Great Pumpkin" once the spell of the book is broken). Yet Clory is one of the very few romantic heroines in all the novels who *has* religious experiences. Whipple is to be commended for that.

The research is sometimes too apparent. Although *Time* found Brigham Young "the most living figure in the book,"[36] anybody familiar with Widtsoe's edition of the *Discourses* recognizes, uncomfortably, the patchwork of aphorism. Yet, this too is forgivable. *The Giant Joshua* makes accessible an important mass of information about the past. And it does something more—it creates an appealing and believable heroine. Clorinda Agatha McIntyre has something of all the stereotypes in her makeup. She is both Pandora and Virtuous Victim in relation to blackbearded Abijah, also known as "Handsome Mac." Yet she is more than the sum of her parts. Despite moments of nobility, she doesn't walk off into the sunset.

Her relationship with Abijah's son, Free, is part "true love" and part pure flirtation. Throughout the book, she is both rebellious *and* faithful, as many real-life pioneer heroines must have been.

Virginia Sorenson is the best known and most prolific of the Mormon novelists. In the twenty years between 1942 and 1963, she published eight books with Utah or Mormon settings. A common theme runs through them all, a celebration of spirit over form, of the future over the past, of freedom over orthodoxy. In the novels set in the nineteenth century, she often extols the virtues of the early Mormons. *Kingdom Come* or *The House Next Door*, a book for young people, might appear on an APYW reading list. *A Little Lower Than The Angels* extols the social vision of Joseph Smith. As long as Mormonism is a persecuted new religion, it is the bigoted gentiles who are the opponents of life and love. In the Utah novels, set after the Manifesto and in the early part of this century, bigoted and narrow Mormons are the villains. In these books she describes the children of Whipple's rugged pioneers, for whom the tougher virtues have softened into comfortable respectability or, even worse, vindictive self-righteousness.

Sorenson sees the sexual experimentation of early Mormons as a potentially healthy reaction to the hypocrisy of Victorian standards. She shows herself open to what our generation calls "alternate life styles." At the same time, she embraces an old-fashioned cult of True Love. As a consequence, many of her novels are curiously adolescent, caught somewhere between the commune and *The Bride's Book*. We can understand, for example, how the romantic Hanne in *Kingdom Come* might choose handsome Svend Madsen over the decaying respectability of her upper-class Danish suitors, but we can only tremble at the happy ending which sends this pampered darling gaily off on an immigrant ship to face persecution, polygamy, and Utah crickets. When *Many Heavens* first appeared, critics praised the curious twist in the plot which made polygamy the savior rather than the destroyer of True Love. It was an interesting concept; a tandem marriage might be preferable to the ugliness of modern divorce. Yet Sorenson's innovation depends on a worshipful admiration of red-bearded Danes, a capacity which few of her readers probably share.

A Little Lower Than The Angels, Sorenson's first novel, is still one of her best. In the story of Simon and Mercy Baker she manages to convey both the polygamist ideal and the grinding psychological toll plural marriage exacted. It is a memorable book. But *The Evening and The Morning,* published in 1949, is better. Its plot centers around an ordinary week near the Twenty-fourth of July in Manti in the 1920s. Kate, a wayward Mormon who has long lived in California, returns home to visit her daughter and grandchildren and to see about getting a small pension due her from her husband's participation in the Black Hawk war. The narrative is an interplay of past and present. Kate's memories of her young married life are woven into an account of the events of the six days. As she observes the lives of her family, she discovers that the crisis which drove her from her home town was both an ending and a beginning, an evening and a morning. The shifting perspective in this book gives Sorenson's theme the complexity it needs. Love is redeeming and glorious; it is also a fantasy. Kate may have been courageous in defying the standards of her little town; she might have been merely foolish. The reader is left not with a moral judgment, but with a sense of life, not with an attitude toward adultery, but with a feeling for particular people and the conflicts they face.

Anyone who has lived in a small Mormon town will recognize Sorenson's Manti, with its irrigation ditches, bubbling fruit kettles, crepe paper floats, lighted front porches, railroad foreigners, Saturday night shampoos, earnest young priests, and too-friendly home teachers.

Now that fewer and fewer members of the Church have ever lived in such a town, her books may have even more historical interest. As we move toward an international Church, they may tell us about a part of our own past even less familiar than the heroic early days. It is interesting to contemplate the decaying Mormondom of Sorenson's youth against the conversion statistics of our own time and to consider how much small-town bigotry remains.

After a glut of romances, Halldor Laxness' *Paradise Reclaimed* is an astringent refresher. Laxness, an Icelander and winner of the Nobel Prize for 1955, became interested in the Mormon story during his first visit to the United States in 1927. As he explained in a letter to Karl Keller, his novel is based on two books written in Icelandic by Mormon authors.[37] One is an account by an immigrant farmer who lived in Spanish Fork for a number of years before returning to his homeland. The other is a tract by a Mormon bishop who filled several missions in Iceland. Some readers may find themselves confused by Laxness' style. It is terse, understated, flat—yet very funny. The motivations of the characters are largely unexplored; the events are presented without analysis as in a folk tale, so that meaning must grow out of plot—and tone. Laxness satirizes the Mormon paradise, with its ox soup, bricks, and sewing machines, but he shows it as successful on its own terms. Poor men have status; abandoned women have homes. The only flaws are for those like Pastor Runolf, who can't measure up; the Josephite woman, who can't believe; the Icelanders, who simply can't be bothered. A majority, no doubt.

Laxness' picture of Mormon women is nothing but our pro-polygamy propaganda given flesh. Bishop Didrik's first wife died crossing the plains, leaving an infant to perish in his arms "farther into the wilderness." His second wife "was called Anna, and wore iron spectacles. . . . She had shared her water-supply with the mother and daughter to the very last drop. She relieved him by lulling the baby to sleep at night after Didrik's beloved had died." In Utah, Iron Anna proves herself capable of baking bricks and managing her husband's kingdom in Spanish Fork, which soon includes a third wife, a "destitute woman" who had been "put in the family way" by the troops of Johnston's army and subsequently held up by redskins and ostracized by fastidious Welsh and Danish Saints. Didrik's fourth wife is "poor old Maria from Ompuhjallur, who was fully seventy years old, crippled with arthritis, and blind. She too had trekked across the wilderness."[38] No doubt but what Didrik had subjected the flesh to the common good. His fifth wife, however, is a young and attractive girl whom he rescues from the arms of a harelipped soldier aboard the immigrant ship. (One more maiden saved from prostitution.) She gratefully takes her place beside her sturdy and saintly sister wives, joining them in protesting the anti-polygamy laws.

The womenfolk of Spanish Fork also met in conference and made preparation to go to Salt Lake City and make their voices heard in the national chorus. First they sang some beautiful Latter-Day Saints hymns, and then attempted to describe their bliss, each in her own way. They thanked the Lord of Hosts for the revelation of being able to see and understand that woman's salvation consists in having a righteous husband, whose virtuous deeds speak for themselves; and there can never be too many women sharing in such a man.[39]

Tone is everything here. Laxness has given us our own Pioneer Grandmother—in human rather than heroic size, in clay rather than bronze.

When the Icelandic convert Steinar and his friend Pastor Runolf go to see the Lion House with its twenty-seven garret windows "all with the same white curtains," they are reminded of the horrible beast their countrymen often talked about, a monster with as "many greedy maws as it was slashed with knives."[40] Laxness seems to be poking gentle fun here at the horrible monster of lust evoked in Mormon defenses of polygamy as well as in the attacks of the gentile reformers. Plural marriage, with its shining windows and productive women, proves that the monster can be conquered and domesticated. In Utah, so the argument goes, life and love are ordered and directed toward the common good. In Iceland, the beast runs rampant and destroys the order of the home. The irony is that for poor Steinar, the beast gets in while he's out discovering this Paradise. He might as well have stayed home repairing the stone walls of his fathers. Because Laxness mistrusts all utopias, his novel is a good one to know about whenever we start taking ourselves *or* our ancestors too seriously. The Universe is vast and Utah arid. An intelligent observer can be forgiven for smiling at the idea of a clump of dusty-bearded outcasts wagging the earth.

Two or three good books out of a score. That's not a bad ratio by anyone's count. For the reader who needs justification, an old comment by Brigham Young will do:

Novel reading—is it profitable? I would rather that persons read novels than read nothing.[41]

Notes

1. These twenty-two novels are listed in the bibliography below. I have excluded fictionalized memoirs, like John Fitzgerald's *Papa Married a Mormon*, as well as books in which Mormons play only a peripheral role—Wallace Stegner's *Big Rock Candy Mountain*, for example, which is set in Utah but virtually ignores the Saints.
2. Kenneth Godfrey tells this story in "Feminine-Flavored Church History," *Improvement Era*, January 1968.
3. Ardyth Kennelly, *Up Home* (Boston: Houghton Mifflin, 1955), p. 32.
4. Jonreed Lauritzen, *The Everlasting Fire* (Garden City, N. Y.: Doubleday, 1962), p. 242.
5. Ibid., p. 307.

6. Maureen Whipple, *The Giant Joshua* (Boston: Houghton Mifflin, 1940), p. 301.
7. Blanche Cannon, *Nothing Ever Happens Sunday Morning* (New York: G. P. Putnam's Sons, 1948), p. 193.
8. Ardyth Kennelly, *The Peaceable Kingdom* (Boston: Houghton Mifflin, 1949), p. 200.
9. Ibid., p. 300.
10. Amelia Bean, *The Fancher Train* (Garden City, N. Y.: Doubleday, 1958), pp. 176, 188.
11. Ibid., p. 178.
12. Elinor Pryor, *And Never Yield* (New York: Macmillan, 1942), p. 104.
13. Whipple, p. 99.
14. Vardis Fisher, *Children of God* (New York: Harper, 1939), p. 622.
15. Paul Bailey, *For Time And All Eternity* (Garden City, N. Y.: Doubleday, 1964), pp. 22, 26.
16. Kennelly, *Peaceable Kingdom*, p. 203.
17. Bailey, jacket.
18. Cannon, p. 29.
19. Ibid., p. 41.
20. Lauritzen, p. 336.
21. Fisher, p. 363.
22. Ibid., p. 465.
23. Cannon, p. 210.
24. Virginia Sorenson, *A Little Lower Than The Angels* (New York: Alfred A. Knopf, 1942), pp. 332–33.
25. Ibid., p. 284.
26. Pryor, p. 355.
27. Ibid., p. 518.
28. Sorenson, *Angels*, p. 403.
29. Whipple, p. 139.
30. Lauritzen, p. 283.

31. Joseph Furnas, *The Devil's Rainbow* (New York: Harper, 1962), pp. 100–1.
32. Kennelly, *Peaceable Kingdom*, p. 12.
33. *New York Times*, 12 January 1941.
34. *Nation*, 8 February 1941, p. 160. The reviewer, Margaret Marshall, says she was "born and raised" a Mormon, which may explain her boredom with the subject matter.
35. "Maurine Whipple's Story of The Giant Joshua," as told to Maryruth Bracy and Linda Lambert, *Dialogue*, 6 (Winter 1971), 49.
36. *Time*, 6 January 1941, pp. 59–60.
37. Karl Keller, "The Witty and Witless Saints of a Nobel Prize Winner," *Dialogue*, 6 (Winter 1971), 48–49.
38. Halldor Laxness, *Paradise Reclaimed*, trans. Magnus Magnusson (New York: Thomas Y. Crowell, 1962), pp. 134–35.
39. Ibid., p. 233.
40. Ibid., pp. 144, 234.
41. *Discourses of Brigham Young*, selected and arranged by John A. Widtsoe (Salt Lake City, Utah: Deseret Book Co., 1954), p. 257.

Bibliography of Mormon Novels

Bailey, Paul. *For Time And All Eternity*. New York: Dou-
    bleday, 1964. Polygamy in central Utah. Although
    Bailey's belles know how to fight and curse, they are
    otherwise indistinguishable from the standard ster-
    eotypes.
Bean, Amelia. *The Fancher Train*. Garden City, N. J.:
    Doubleday, 1958. The Mountain Meadows massacre
    by an author specializing in frontier feuds. Less dra-
    ma than Juanita Brooks' historical account, *The
    Mountain Meadows Massacre*.
Cannon, Blanche. *Nothing Ever Happens Sunday Morning*.
    New York: G. P. Putnam's Sons, 1948. Small town
    Utah, 1900, with flashbacks. An interesting example
    of the sophisticated Mormon's tendency to romanti-
    cize outsiders while debunking the brethren.
Fisher, Vardis. *Children of God*. New York: Harper, 1939.
    From Joseph Smith to the Manifesto. Notable as the
    first of the twentieth century Mormon "epics." Once
    scandalous, now mostly tedious.
Furnas, Joseph. *The Devil's Rainbow*. New York: Harper,
    1962. Joseph Smith as a licker-lovin' con man. Furnas
    cites Linn, Werner, and Bernard DeVoto as his chief
    sources, but he is even more indebted to Mark Twain
    for his characters.

Kennelly, Ardyth. *The Peaceable Kingdom*. Boston: Houghton Mifflin, 1949, and *Up Home*. Boston: Houghton Mifflin, 1955. A two-volume string of bouncy but improbable anecdotes. Said to have been based on the author's Danish grandmother.

Lauritzen, Jonreed. *The Everlasting Fire*. Garden City, N. J.: Doubleday, 1962. A ponderous epic set in Illinois and Iowa. The viewpoint is of a sympathetic outsider whose own life becomes entwined in the Mormon tragedy.

Laxness, Halldor. *Paradise Reclaimed*. Trans. Magnus Magnuson. New York: Thomas Y. Crowell, 1962. An oblique but entertaining novel set in Iceland and early Utah. Some commentators see the hero's quest for the ideal as a parable of the author's own flirtation with communist utopianism.

Pearson, Lorene. *The Harvest Waits*. Indianapolis and New York: Bobbs-Merrill, 1941. Three generations of Utah Danes struggling with polygamy, the United Order, and ultimately the Manifesto. Largely ignored in its own day; almost impossible to find in ours.

Pryor, Elinor. *And Never Yield*. New York: Macmillan, 1942. Missouri and Nauvoo as soap opera. Far inferior to the Sorenson and Whipple novels published the same year.

Sorenson, Virginia. *A Little Lower Than The Angels*. New York: Alfred A. Knopf, 1942. Nauvoo, 1840s. Rhapsodic in its treatment of Joseph Smith; somber in its chronicle of feminine decline.

On This Star. New York: Reynal & Hitchcock, 1946. "Temple City," Utah, 1920s. The tragic love of two half-brothers for the same girl.

The Neighbors. New York: Reynal & Hitchcock, 1947. Indiscretion and guilt in contemporary Colorado.

The Evening and The Morning. New York: Harcourt Brace, 1949. Manti, 1920s, with flashbacks. An apostate grandmother comes home to relive lost passion and pain. A novel of introspection rather than event.

Many Heavens. New York: Harcourt Brace, 1956. Childbirth in and out of wedlock in a small Utah town after the Manifesto. Glimpses of Ellis Shipp and her associates.

Kingdom Come. New York: Harcourt Brace, 1960. Young love in Jutland in the 1850s. Inspired by William Mulder's history of the Danish Mission, *Homeward To Zion*.

In addition to these full length books dealing with Mormonism, Sorenson has published a novel for young people, *The House Next Door* (1954), detailing Gentile-Mormon tension in a Salt Lake neighborhood in the year of Utah's statehood, and a fictionalized memoir, *Where Nothing Is Long Ago* (1955), in which many of the characters familiar from the novels again appear.

Scowcroft, Richard. *Children of the Covenant*. Boston: Houghton Mifflin, 1945. One of the few Mormon novels of this period set in the present. Virginia Sorenson liked it. The *New York Times* called it "no more than a painstaking genre picture of a particularly unlovely small community." The town was Ogden.

Taylor, Samuel W. *Heaven Knows Why*. New York: A. A. Wyn, 1948. An obscure novel by a well-known Mormon writer. Comic and contemporary.

Whipple, Maurine. *The Giant Joshua*. Boston: Houghton Mifflin, 1942. A feminist version of the establishment of the Cotton Mission at St. George. Rich in detail of pioneer life.

Woodman, Jean. *Glory Spent*. New York: Carrick and Evans, Inc., 1940. Presumably about contemporary Utah. Unavailable.

Wormser, Richard. *Battalion of Saints*. New York: D. McKay Company, 1961. Another version of a familiar theme: the love of a Gentile for a young Mormon girl. The author specializes in popular adventures of the Old West.

Reading List

This list includes suggestions for further reading on Mormon women. The books have been chosen for their interest and availability. Some deal with contemporary women. Fiction, most articles and dissertations, and all unpublished diaries, have been eliminated. Readers with specific interests may wish to mine the notes of individual essays.

Allen, James B. and Glen M. Leonard, *The Story of the Latter-day Saints*. Salt Lake City, Utah: Deseret Book, 1976. A recent one-volume survey of the Mormon Church.

Arrington, Leonard J. *Great Basin Kingdom*. Lincoln: University of Nebraska, 1958. An economic history of the Utah settlements.

"The Economic Role of Pioneer Mormon Women," *Western Humanities Review*, 9 (Spring, 1955), 145–64. A classic statement of early economic involvement.

Bailey, Paul. *Polygamy Was Better Than Monotony*. Los Angeles: Westernlore Press, 1972. Story of the author's two grandfathers and their five wives.

Barrett, Ivan J. *Heroines of the Church*. 4th ed. Provo, Utah: Extension Publications, Brigham Young University, 1966.

Beeton, Beverly, "Woman Suffrage in the American West, 1869–1896." Ph.D. dissertation, University of Utah, 1976.

Bennett, Frances Marion Grant. *Glimpses of a Mormon Family*. Salt Lake City: Deseret Book, 1968. The family includes LDS Church President Heber J. Grant.

Bitton, Davis. *Guide To Utah and Mormon Diaries*. Provo, Utah: Brigham Young University Press, forthcoming.

Brooks, Juanita. "A Close-up of Polygamy," *Harper's Magazine*, 168 (December-May, 1933, 34), 307. A warm, but objective comparison of the author's two sets of grandparents.

"Mariah Huntsman Leavitt," *Forms Upon the Frontier; Folklife and Folk Arts in the United States*. Ed. by Austin and Alta Fife and Henry H. Glassie. Logan, Utah: Utah State University, 1969. Another larger-than-life midwife.

Emma Lee. Logan, Utah: Utah State University Press, 1975. The biography of one of the wives of John D. Lee, alleged to be the instigator of the Mountain Meadows Massacre.

Burgess-Olson, Vicky. "Family Structure and Dynamics in Early Utah Mormon Families, 1847–1885." Ph.D. dissertation, Northwestern University, 1975.

Carter, Kate B. *Heart Throbs of the West*. 9 vols. Salt Lake City: Daughters of Utah Pioneers, 1947.

Our Pioneer Heritage. 13 vols. Salt Lake City: Daughters of Utah Pioneers, 1958.

Treasures of Pioneer History. 6 vols. Salt Lake City: Daughters of Utah Pioneers, 1952. Vast collections of pioneer lore compiled by Zion's indefatigable chronicler.

A Century of Sisterhood: Chronological Collage, 1869–1969. Salt Lake City: YWMIA, 1969. An official history of the Young Women's Mutual Improvement Association.

Clark, Waynetta Jean Willis Martin. *Black Mormon Tells Her Story*. Salt Lake City: Hawkes Publication, 1972. The autobiographical account of a black woman's search for religious meaning and her conversion to the Church.

Clayton, Roberta Flake. *Pioneer Women of Arizona*. Mesa, Arizona, 1969.

Corbett, Don Cecil. *Mary Fielding Smith, Daughter of Britain, Portrait of Courage*. Salt Lake City: Deseret Book, 1966. A flattering portrait by an admiring descendant.

Cornaby, Hannah. *Autobiography and Poems*. Salt Lake City: J. C. Graham & Co., 1881. This book gives the flavor of early Utah.

Crocheron, Augusta Joyce. *Representative Women of Deseret; A Book of Biographical Sketches*. Salt Lake City: J. C. Graham & Co., 1884. Interesting reading, but hard to come by.

Croft, Grace Hildy. *With A Song In Her Heart; Biography of Florence Jepperson Madsen*. Nicholas G. Morgan, Sr., 1960. Contemporary account of an accomplished musician.

Crowther, Duane S. and Jean D. Crowther, eds. *The Joy of Being A Woman: Guidance for Meaningful Living by Outstanding LDS Women*. Salt Lake City: Horizon Publishers, 1972. Twenty-three personal articles by Mormon women who have achieved recognition as performers, contest winners, authors, community workers, etc.

Cumming, John and Audrey. *The Pilgrimage of Temperance Mack*. Mt. Pleasant, Michigan, 1967. A series of letters between Temperance Mack and her daughter Almira Covey picturing early religious enthusiasm.

Dialogue, 6 (Summer, 1971), entire issue. This special issue on women was organized by women in the Boston area.

Ellsworth, George. *Dear Ellen: Two Mormon Women and Their Letters*. Salt Lake City: University of Utah, 1974. The nineteenth-century correspondence between Ellen Spencer Clawson in Salt Lake City and her friend Ellen Pratt McGary in San Bernardino is quoted with descriptive essays by George Ellsworth.

Gates, Susa Young. *Heroines of "Mormondom."* Noble Women's Lives Series, Vol. II. Salt Lake City: Juvenile Instructor Office, 1884.

History of the Young Ladies Mutual Improvement Association: Nov. 1869 to 1910. Salt Lake City: The Deseret News, 1911.

Utah Women in Politics. Salt Lake City: n.p., 1913.

Gates, Susa Young and Widstoe, Leah D. *Women of the "Mormon" Church*. Independence, Missouri: Zion's Printing and Publishing, 1928. A few of the very prolific Sister Gates' productions.

General Board of Relief Society. *A Centenary of Relief Society, 1842–1942*. Salt Lake City, 1942.

History of Relief Society, 1842–1966. Salt Lake City, 1966. The two above are official histories.

Gibson, Margaret Wilson. *Emma Smith: The Elect Lady*. Independence, Mo.: Herald Publishing House, 1969. A brief uncritical account.

Hafen, LeRoy R. and Ann W. *The Joyous Journey of LeRoy K. and Ann W. Hafen; An Autobiography*. Glendale, California: Arthur H. Clark, 1973. The story of two contemporary scholars.

Hafen, Mary Ann. *Recollections of a Handcart Pioneer of 1860*. Denver, Colorado: n.p., 1938.

Hartshorn, Leon R., comp. *Remarkable Stories from the Lives of Latter-day Saint Women*. Salt Lake City: Deseret Book, 1973. A mix of current and historical quotations.

Hunter, Rodello. *A Daughter of Zion*. New York: Alfred A. Knopf, 1972. An inside account of the workings of a contemporary Salt Lake ward and the people who populate it. The book intends to make Mormonism conprehensible to the gentile.
A House of Many Rooms. New York: Alfred A. Knopf, 1965. Recollections of a Mormon childhood in rural Utah, ruled over by a memorable patriarch.

Kane, Elizabeth Wood. *Twelve Mormon Homes*. Salt Lake City: University of Utah, 1974. A sensitive and literate account of the journey of Thomas L. Kane and his wife from Salt Lake to St. George in 1873.

Lyman, Amy Brown. *In Retrospect, Autobiography of Amy Brown Lyman*. Salt Lake City: General Board of the Relief Society, 1945. Sister Brown was General President of the Relief Society for several years in the 1940s.

Merrill, Melissa (pseud.). *Polygamist's Wife*. Salt Lake City: Olympus Publishing Company, 1975. The grim and true story of one woman's experiences with modern-day polygamy.

Musser, Ellis Shipp, comp. *The Early Autobiography and Diary of Ellis Reynolds Shipp*. Salt Lake City: Printed by Deseret News Press, 1962. How a permanent day-care arrangement made medical school a possibility for a young mother. A sensitive and fascinating account of the inner workings of a household with several wives.

Noall, Claire. *Guardians of the Hearth*. Bountiful, Utah: Horizon Publishers, 1974. A laudatory account of early Utah's remarkable medical women.

Pearson, Carol Lynn. *Daughters of Light*. Provo, Utah: Trilogy Arts, 1973. Some of the early sisters' accounts of their spiritual experiences have been collected here.

The Flight and the Nest. Salt Lake City: Bookcraft, 1975. A contemporary account of some of Utah's early feminists.

Phillips, Emma. *33 Women of the Restoration*. Independence, Mo.: Herald Publishing House, 1969. This group of women remains in the good graces of the Reorganized LDS Church.

Priest, Ivy Baker. *Green Grows Ivy*. New York: McGraw-Hill Book Co., Inc., 1958. The autobiography of a recent Secretary of the Treasury.

Reid, Agnes Just. *Letters From Long Ago*. Salt Lake City: University of Utah, 1973. Originally published in 1936. A fictionalized account of the true life of the author's mother, shaped as plaintive letters home to her father in England.

Rogers, Aurelia Spencer. *Life Sketches of Orson Spencer and Others, and History of Primary Work*. Salt Lake City: G. Q. Cannon and Sons, 1898. The founder of the Primary reveals herself and others in this memoir.

Sekaquaptewa, Helen. *Me and Mine; the Life Story of Helen Sekaquaptewa as told to Louise Udall*. Tucson, Ariz.: University of Arizona Press, 1969. Includes the story of her conversion to the Mormon Church.

Smith, Lucy Mack. *Biographical Sketches of Joseph Smith The Prophet and His Progenitors for Many Generations*. New York: Arno Press, 1971. Reprint of 1853 edition. The senior female writer of Mormondom tells of her kin.

Sorenson, Virginia. *Where Nothing Is Long Ago; Memories of a Mormon Childhood*. New York: Harcourt, Brace and World, 1963. The author's childhood in Manti, Utah, serves as the basis for a group of short stories.

Spafford, Belle S. *A Woman's Reach*. Salt Lake City, Deseret Book Company, 1974. The collected speeches of a long time president of the Relief Society.

Stenhouse, Mrs. T. B. H. (Fanny). *Tell it All: The Tyranny of Mormonism, or an Englishwoman in Utah*. New York: Praeger Publishers, 1971. Reprint of 1880 edition. A classic critique of Mormonism by an apostate who once bore strong testimony of the Church.

Tanner, Annie Clark. *A Mormon Mother; An Autobiography*. Salt Lake City: University of Utah Press, 1969. A superb memoir with a fascinating account of plural marriage around the time of the Manifesto.

Taylor, Samuel W. *Nightfall at Nauvoo*. New York: Macmillan Company, 1971. The Nauvoo period with fictional additions.

Thayne, Emma Lou. *Never Past the Gate*. Salt Lake City: Peregrine Smith, 1975. A fictionalized memoir of Mormon family life "up the canyon."

Thurston, Katherine Kemp. *The Winds of Doctrine; the Story of the Life of Mary Lockwood Kemp in Mormon Utah During the Last Half of the Nineteenth Century*. New York: Exposition Press, 1952.

Tullidge, Edward W. *The Women of Mormondom*. Salt Lake City: n.p., 1965. Originally published in 1877, this book is the best introduction to nineteenth century Mormon women.

Turner, Rodney. *Woman and the Priesthood*. Salt Lake City: Deseret Book Company, 1972. A conservative scriptural justification for woman's secondary role.

Utah State Historical Quarterly, 38 (Winter, 1970), entire issue. A readable group of articles about early Mormon women in politics and the arts.

Wallace, Irving. *The Twenty-seventh Wife*. New York: Simon Schuster, 1961. The scandalous story of Ann Eliza Young retold with heavy reliance on her own writings.

Widstoe, John A. *In the Gospel Net; The Story of Anne Karine Garrden Widstoe*. 4th ed. Salt Lake City: An Improvement Era Book, 1942. A son's homage to his mother.

Young, Ann Eliza Webb. *Life in Mormon Bondage*. Philadelphia: Aldine Press, Inc., 1908.

Wife No. 19. Hartford, Conn.: Dustin, Gilman & Co., 1875. This vocal young woman married Brigham Young, left him, and told the world about it.

Young, Kimball. *Isn't One Wife Enough?* New York: Henry Holt and Co., 1954. A sociologist looks at Mormon polygamy.

Periodicals

Woman's Exponent (1872–1914)

Young Woman's Journal (1889–1929)

Relief Society Magazine (1914–1970)

Exponent II (1974–   )

Reading List II

Since 1976, when this book first appeared, an impressive number of diaries, histories, collections, institutional histories, and monographs related to Mormon women has been published. We like to think of *Mormon Sisters* as a pioneer itself. Leonard Arrington recently noted that this book "played a key role in the opening of a market for books on women's history. Now they come out in happy numbers."

The following list of the work that followed *Mormon Sisters* is presented as a guide to further reading rather than as a comprehensive bibliography. The list includes a number of compilations consisting of biographies or essays by groups of women. These volumes show, as does this one, the cooperative nature of LDS women, joining together to turn out books. Scholarship has focused particularly on church institutional history and leaders, on polygamy, and on women's political rights. Another area of wide activity has been the publication of diaries, correspondence, and reminiscences, either as the writing of an individual or as part of collected writings on various topics. We are fortunate in having so many of these personal journals, one creative activity available to women with limited resources. The documents listed here can be plumbed for social history purposes; most have been reproduced with complete scholarly apparatus, allowing maximum use.

Excluded from the list are collections of speeches, bibliographies, and books that are particularly difficult to find. Has the nineteenth-century now been exhausted? Certainly not, but much interest now seems to be moving to the turn of the century.

Arrington, Leonard J., and David Bitton. *The Mormon Experience: A History of the Latter-day Saints.* New York: Alfred A. Knopf, 1979. 2nd ed., Urbana: University of Illinois Press, 1992. Two old hands lay out the background.

Arrington, Leonard J., and Susan Arrington Madsen. *Mothers of the Prophets.* Salt Lake City: Deseret Book, 1987. Instructions on raising a church leader.

Sunbonnet Sisters: True Stories of Mormon Women and Frontier Life. Salt Lake City: Bookcraft, 1984. Entertaining accounts of 17 women based on their diaries.

Bahr, Howard M., Spencer J. Condie, and Kristen L. Goodman. *Life in Large Families: Views of Mormon Women.* Washington, D.C.: University Press of America, 1982. Information based on long anonymous interviews with female college graduates, married to college graduates, who have born seven or more children.

Bartholomew, Rebecca. *Audacious Women: Early British Mormon Immigrants.* Salt Lake City: Signature Books, 1995. Lively survey based on records of one hundred women, 1838–1888. She finds confirmation and repudiation of all stereotypes.

Beecher, Maureen Ursenbach. *Eliza and Her Sisters.* Salt Lake City: Aspen Books, 1991. Her essays on the foremothers.

Beecher, Maureen Ursenbach, and Lavina Fielding Anderson, eds. *Sisters in Spirit: Mormon Women in Historical and Cultural Perspective.* Urbana: University of Illinois Press, 1987. Essays on Mormon female theology.

Bradford, Mary, ed., *Mormon Women Speak*. Salt Lake City: Olympus Publishing, 1982. Essays of Mormon experience.

Brooks, Juanita. *Quicksand and Cactus: A Memoir of the Southern Mormon Frontier*. Salt Lake City: Howe Brothers, 1982. Logan: Utah State University Press, 1992. The real life of this modern foremother.

Brunson, L. Madelon. *Bonds of Sisterhood: A History of the RLDS Women's Organization, 1842–1983*. Independence, Mo.: Herald House, 1985. To be compared with the Relief Society headed in Salt Lake City.

Burgess-Olson, Vicky, ed. *Sister Saints*. Provo, Utah: Brigham Young University Press, 1978. Biographies of chosen early Mormon women.

Cannon, Martha Hughes. *Letters From Exile: the Correspondence of Martha Hughes Cannon and Angus M. Cannon, 1886–1889*. Ed. Constance L. Lieber and John Sillito. Salt Lake City: Signature Books, 1989. This fourth wife, twenty-three years her husband's junior, escaped to England during the Underground. She later practiced medicine and was elected to the Utah State Senate.

Compton, Todd. *In Sacred Loneliness: The Plural Wives of Joseph Smith*. Salt Lake City: Signature Press, 1997. He finds thirty-three well-documented wives and eight on the borderline.

Cross, Mary Bywater. *Quilts & Women of the Mormon Migration: Treasures of Transition*. Nashville: Rutledge Hill Press, 1996. A beautiful illustrated social history of Mormon quilts, with many color plates.

Cumming, Elizabeth. *The Genteel Gentile: Letters of Elizabeth Cumming, 1857–1858*. Ed. Ray C. Canning and Beverly Beeton. Salt Lake City: Tanner Trust Fund, University of Utah Library, 1977. The wife of Alfred Cumming, non-Mormon Utah territorial governor during the Utah War, found that Mormon ladies talk about religion, live it, and feel it. "Every act almost of their lives is Mormonized."

Derr, Jill Mulvay, Janath Russell Cannon, and Maureen Ursenbach Beecher. *Women of Covenant: The Story of Relief Society, 1842-1892*. Salt Lake City: Deseret Book, 1992. The fat official history, frank and satisfying.

Embry, Jessie L. *Mormon Polygamous Families: Life in the Principle*. Salt Lake City: University of Utah Press, 1987. Firsthand accounts, based on interviews from the 1930s, 1970s, and 1980s, blast many stereotypes.

Foster, Lawrence. *Women, Family, and Utopia: Communal Experiments of the Shakers, the Oneida Community, and the Mormons*. Syracuse, N.Y.: Syracuse University Press, 1991. An interesting comparison.

Godfrey, Kenneth W., Audrey M. Godfrey, and Jill Mulvay Derr, eds. *Women's Voices: An Untold History of the Latter-day Saints, 1830–1900*. Salt Lake City: Deseret Book, 1982. Illustrated selections from the letters, diaries, and journals of twenty-five Mormon women, with introductions and short biographies.

Hanks, Maxine. *Women and Authority: Re-emerging Mormon Feminism*. Salt Lake City: Signature Books, 1992. Explorations of many voices that legitimize feminist identity within Mormon theology.

Heywood, Martha Spence. *Not By Bread Alone: The Journal of Martha Spence Heywood, 1850–1856*. Ed. Juanita Brooks. Salt Lake City: Utah State Historical Society, 1978. In this vivid account of major events and Salt Lake social life, Heywood marries, as a plural wife, "a good man but not interesting" and finds herself satisfied.

Holzapfel, Richard Neitzel, and Jeni Broberg Holzapfel. *Women of Nauvoo*. Salt Lake City: Bookcraft, 1992. An effort to recover the spiritual heritage of the Nauvoo sisterhood.

Johnson, Sonia. *From Housewife to Heretic.* Garden City, N.Y.: Doubleday & Company, Inc., 1981; Albuquerque: Wildfire Press, 1989. A colorful excommunicant's story.

Larson, Carl V., and Shirley N. Maynes. *The Women of the Mormon Battalion.* Providence, Utah: Watkins Printing, 1996. Information on the thirty-two who made the journey.

Madsen, Carol Cornwall. *In Their Own Words: Women and the Story of Nauvoo.* Salt Lake City: Deseret Book, 1994. A selection of letters and diaries written in Nauvoo along with many later reminiscences, with introductory and biographical information and photographs.

Madsen, Carol Cornwall, ed. *Battle for the Ballot: Essays on Woman Suffrage in Utah, 1870–1896.* Logan: Utah State University Press, 1997. Sixteen essays gathered from publications from 1902 to 1991, along with a suffrage chronology.

Journey to Zion: Voices from the Mormon Trail. Salt Lake City: Deseret Book, 1997. This collection of firsthand accounts of trail life includes pictures of most diarists.

Madsen, Carol Cornwall, and Susan Staker Oman. *Sisters and Little Saints: One Hundred Years of Primary.* Salt Lake City: Deseret Book, 1979. An institutional history.

Newell, Linda King, and Valeen Tippetts Avery. *Mormon Enigma: Emma Hale Smith.* Garden City, N.Y.: Doubleday, 1984; Urbana: University of Illinois Press, 1994. A searching study of the first lady.

Peterson, Janet, and LaRene Gaunt. *The Children's Friends: Primary Presidents and Their Lives of Service; Elect Ladies: Presidents of the Relief Society;* and *Keepers of the Flame: Presidents of the Young Women.* Salt Lake City: Deseret Book, 1996, 1990, 1993. Brief biographies of the leaders of women's organizations.

Richards, Mary Haskin Parker. *Winter Quarters: The 1846–1848 Life Writings of Mary Haskin Parker Richards.* Ed. Maurine Carr Ward. Logan: Utah State University Press, 1996. Charming journals and letters of a delicate English pioneer. A long, biographical introduction is illustrated with old photos, and an impressive glossary identifies all mentioned.

Romney, Catharine Cottam. *Letters of Catharine Cottam Romney, Plural Wife.* Ed. Jennifer Moulton Hansen. Urbana: University of Illinois Press, 1992. Richly detailed correspondence from St. George, Arizona, Mexico, 1873–1917.

Sessions, Patty Bartlett. *Mormon Midwife: The 1846–1888 Diaries of Patty Bartlett Sessions.* Ed. Donna Toland Smart. Logan: Utah State University Press, 1997. The extended personal accounts of Utah's premiere midwife.

Smith, Barbara B. *Women of Devotion: Profiles of Fifteen Remarkable Mothers of Today.* With Shirley W. Thomas. Salt Lake City: Bookcraft, 1990. Wives of General Authorities.

Snow, Eliza Roxcy. *The Personal Writings of Eliza Roxcy Snow.* Ed. Maureen Ursenbach Beecher. Salt Lake City: University of Utah Press, 1995. A careful edition of her few private texts.

Solomon, Dorthy Allred. *In My Father's House.* New York: Franklin Watts, 1984. Account of twentieth century polygamous family of Dr. Rulon Clark Allred written by his twenty-eighth child.

Tanner, Mary Jane Mount. *A Fragment: The Autobiography of Mary Jane Mount Tanner.* Ed. Margery W. Ward. Salt Lake City: Tanner Trust Fund, University of Utah Library, 1980. A circumspect autobiography and frank letters of an aspiring poet and writer with a long introduction quoting diaries from 1872–1885. Her book *Fugitive Poems* includes the verse: "Farewell, hopes of fame and fortune,/I must bid you all good bye;/While I go to boil potatoes,/And prepare the chicken pie."

Udall, Ida Hunt. *Mormon Odyssey: The Story of Ida Hunt Udall, Plural Wife.* Ed. Maria S. Ellsworth. Urbana: University of Illinois Press, 1992. Includes her Underground journal, 1882–1886.

Warenski, Marilyn. *Patriarchs and Politics: The Plight of the Mormon Woman.* New York: McGraw-Hill, 1978. Explores the "astonishing anti-female bias" she finds "deeply rooted in and perpetuated by patriarchal religion."

Whitley, Colleen, ed. *Worth Their Salt: Notable but Often Unnoted Women of Utah.* Logan: Utah State University Press, 1996. Biographies of eighteen Mormon and non-Mormon women who contributed to Utah history.

Contributors

The authors have furnished the following updates.

Christine Rigby Arrington graduated from Utah State University with a B.A. in English. She also holds an M.F.A. in writing from Columbia University and an M.B.A. from Stanford University. For the past fifteen years, she has worked in magazine publishing, first as a journalist and editor at *Time* and *Savvy* magazines, and then on the business side. She spent seven years with the giant German publisher Gruner & Jahr in London and New York as director of strategic planning and creator of a profitable custom publishing business. For the past two years, she has been the Publisher of *Fine Cooking* magazine at the Taunton Press in Connecticut. She is the proud mother of daughters Alexis and Olivia.

Maureen Ursenbach Beecher has made the study of Mormon women her career, with Eliza R. Snow almost always in the picture. Her explorations, some with colleagues, have produced such works as *Sisters in Spirit*, edited with Lavina Fielding Anderson; *New Views of Mormon History*, edited with Davis Bitton; an issue of *Dialogue* devoted to Mormon letters; a collection of her essays on Snow, *Eliza and Her Sisters*; and *Women of Covenant: The Story of Relief Society, 1842–1892*, authored with Jill Mulvay Derr and Janath Russell Cannon. With *The Personal Writings of Eliza Roxcy Snow*, she has shifted her focus to editing and publishing women's texts as literary as well as historical works. As general editor for Utah State University Press of the series "Life Writings of Frontier Women," she assists others in the discovery and publication of the autobiographical narratives of nineteenth-century women. She teaches from such texts in the English Department of Brigham Young University. After she retires from her current employment with the Joseph Fielding Smith Institute for Church History, she looks forward to working with a series of Canadian women's life writings. As her two children, Daniel and Bronwen, now university students, move into adulthood, she anticipates new moves in unimagined directions.

Claudia Lauper Bushman worked on *Mormon Sisters* while editing *Exponent II* and pursuing a Ph.D. at Boston University, having married into the history business. The family moved to Delaware where she founded the Newark Historical Society and was the director of the Delaware Heritage Commission, which celebrated significant happenings, a perfect job for someone who likes projects. The Bushmans moved to New York City in 1989, where Claudia teaches American Studies at Columbia University and revels in the city's cultural riches. She holds steady at six children, all of whom have finished college and married, though she hopes to produce more than the present six books and expects more than the current fourteen grandchildren. She is currently exploring the world of John Walker, an antebellum Virginia farmer who called himself, "a poor illiterate worm."

Heather Symmes Cannon was a full-time mom, president of the League of Women Voters, and town meeting member at first publication. A few years later, she became a single parent and earned an M.B.A. from Boston University to support her family. She returned to her hometown, Chicago, and did marketing research for Quaker Oats and later Kraft. In 1993, she moved to Philadelphia to work for Campbell Soup, where she is group marketing research

manager. Her favorite assignments have been Philadelphia Cream Cheese, Kraft Macaroni and Cheese, and
V8. She stopped saving copies of the research reports
she'd issued when the stack reached waist high, so she has
no idea how many hundreds of her reports reside in the
files of the three Fortune 500 companies where she has
worked. Meanwhile, her three children grew up beauti-
fully, graduated from college, went on missions, married
in the temple, and produced four grandchildren.

Jill Mulvay Derr earned degrees from the University of
Utah and the Harvard Graduate School of Education
(M.A.T., 1971). She taught two years in the Boston public
schools before returning to Utah, where she launched a
career in researching and writing the history of Mormon
women, in affiliation with the History Division of the LDS
Church Historical Department. In 1977 she married C.
Brooklyn Derr and they moved to Alpine, Utah, where
they still reside, though for three years they and their four
children lived abroad in France and Switzerland. She has
published numerous articles and two books, *Women's
Voices: An Untold History of the Latter-day Saints, 1830–1900*,
compiled and edited with Kenneth and Audrey Godfrey,
and *Women of Covenant: The Story of Relief Society,
1842–1892*, co-authored with Janath Russell Cannon and
Maureen Ursenbach Beecher. She is currently a research
historian with the Joseph Fielding Smith Institute for
Church History at Brigham Young University.

Nancy Tate Dredge served as editor of *Exponent II* from
1975 to 1981 and has continued on its board since that
time. She has spent most of the past twenty years raising
her five children—Elisabeth, David, Margaret, Anne Lara,
and Jonathan—and serving on a variety of PTA boards
and sundry other volunteer activities. Professionally, she
has been a free-lance editor in the field of educational
publishing, working for, among others, Houghton Mifflin,
D. C. Heath, Silver-Burdett-Ginn, and Ligature. Nancy is

currently grandmother to Jackson, Mason, and Eryn; care-
taker to Rutabaga (Rudi), the dog; and wife/companion to
Paul, the consultant, in an ongoing adventure of life discovery.

Judith Rasmussen Dushku teaches political science at
Suffolk University in Boston, with particular interests in
international women's rights, group politics, political
advocacy, minority issues, and effective political action.
She has traveled the world attending conferences and will
teach in Romania and adjacent countries in 1997. She separated from her husband in 1980 and was divorced later,
spending ten years in the world of single mothers. Her
children are Aaron, now in Ecuador with the Peace Corps;
Ben, who snowboards in Colorado; Nate, an actor at NYU;
and Eliza, the movie star who has kept them all active in
"The Business." Judy married Jim Coleman, a retired
writer with four grown daughters, in 1991. She leads the
choir in the Belmont Ward.

Stephanie Smith Goodson has lived in Pittsburgh,
Houston, and Idaho Falls since leaving Boston. She has
been involved with the Girl Scouts; volunteered in the
school libraries, as PTA vice-president, and as a birth
mother counselor; managed a hair salon; been an emer-
gency medical technician; taught and supervised early
morning seminary; taught the home bound and worked
as a substitute teacher; and tutored in English as a second
language. Two of her five children will graduate from BYU
in 1997. Another will be serving as the fourth missionary
in the group and plans to pursue a master's degree in
social work when she returns.

Cheryll Lynn May has served for the last eight years as
public information officer for the Utah State Court
System. She is also an adjunct associate professor in the
University of Utah Political Science Department. In the
last two decades, while raising three children with her

husband Dean, she has done consulting work with many levels of government and published articles on state court activities, Utah and Mormon history, and on various political topics. She served for fifteen years as dining-out editor for *Utah Holiday Magazine* and is now teacher training coordinator in her local Mormon ward.

Carolyn W. D. Person divorced, remarried, and divorced; had six children and now has four grandchildren; and removed to the Wasatch Front. Her professional enterprises include an M.F.A. from the University of Utah, after which she toiled at the Utah Arts Council and local galleries, typing. She created and exhibited a variety of art work and sold some. She sang, danced, and played music in two professional performing companies, one specializing in Balkan music, the other in that of Central Asia. She has been excommunicated from the LDS church, which she continues to perceive as a huge burden lifted from her psyche. She invested five years in a New Thought metaphysical program and as many in study and meditation on "older thought," speculations which suggest a male-female cooperative society with Mother Goddess influence. She enjoyed one decade attending Elko's Cowboy Poetry Gatherings and perfecting her western swing dance style at local cowboy bars and another riding pillion behind motorcycling companions. She looks forward to experiencing "the sixties" all over again as an arts dilettante, generalist, and grandmother. She continues her personal resistance to male authority and institutions and wonders if anything matters anyway in a universe of billions of galaxies spiraling furiously apart. Her consciousness was freshened in the Cambridge time of feminist sisterhood and she has kept the faith, trudging on relentlessly despite the cosmic chill, illumined by Hubble, blasting in from eternity.

Carrel Hilton Sheldon was a young mother with a two-year-old and a nursing infant when she researched and wrote "Mormon Haters" in 1972 for an LDS Institute class presentation. She was one of the "founding mothers" of *Exponent II* and served as *Exponent II*'s first business manager. In 1975, when *Mormon Sisters* was deemed "too hot to handle" by the Mormon press, she published the book, arranging a $3,000 bank loan, supervising the layout, contracting for the printing and binding, providing storage (in what otherwise could have been her dining room), and advertising and distributing the 5,000 copies. Her third child was born before publication, and she has raised four fabulous, handsome, brilliant, and talented sons. For the past ten years, she has been the business manager and part owner of The Potomac Group, an IT consulting firm. She continues to work on the board of *Exponent II*, and at age fifty, she is back in college, finishing her degree in business management. She loves school, tolerates work, and greatly enjoys reading good books and exploring new ideas. She is nourished by walks on the beach, watching birds and sunsets, and learning about nature. She adores her husband, delights in her children, and is gaga over her new granddaughter. For her, fifty feels young and life looks good.

Laurel Thatcher Ulrich is James Duncan Phillips Professor of Early American History and Professor of Women's Studies at Harvard University. She is the author of two scholarly books, *Good Wives: Image and Reality in the Lives of Women in Northern New England, 1650–1750* (New York, 1982) and *A Midwife's Tale: The Life of Martha Ballard Based on Her Diary, 1785–1812* (New York, 1990), and the co-author with Emma Lou Thayne of a collection of personal essays, *All God's Critters Got A Place in the Choir* (Salt Lake City 1995). She has degrees in English from the University of Utah (1960) and Simmons College (1971) and a Ph.D. in history from the University of New Hampshire (1980). She received the Pulitzer Prize in History in 1991 for *A Midwife's Tale*.

Index